Story of an Accusation

Terence Reese

Better Bridge Now

CHESS & BRIDGE LTD

First published in Great Britain in 2004
by Chess & Bridge Limited
369 Euston Road, London NW1 3AR

Distribution:

USA and Canada: Master Point Press
331 Douglas Avenue, Toronto, Ontario, Canada M5M 1H2;
tel: (416) 781 0351; web: www.masterpointpress.com

For all other enquiries, please contact the publishers,
Chess & Bridge Limited, 369 Euston Road, London NW1 3AR;
tel: 020 7388 2404; fax: 020 7388 2407;
email: chesscentre@easynet.co.uk; web: bridgemagazine.co.uk

British Library Cataloguing in Publication Data.
A CIP record of this book is available on request from the British Library.

ISBN 0-9530218-8-2

Typeset by
Wakewing Ltd, 73 Totteridge Lane, High Wycombe, Bucks HP13 7QA

Printed in Great Britain by
The Cromwell Press, Trowbridge

Contents

Foreword

Following the death of Boris Schapiro in 2002, Masterpoint Press decided to publish a revised edition of *The Great Bridge Scandal*, which presents the case against Reese and Schapiro. To balance the scales of justice we offer this new edition of Reese's own account, with some important additional material.

Story of an Accusation was written as the 'trial' progressed. Early chapters describe the intense rivalries in competitive bridge, events at Buenos Aires and reaction in London. The proceedings at the inquiry contain some extraordinary twists and turns, not previously made public. Was it all just an American 'scare'? What induced the British officials to testify against their countrymen? Exactly where did the truth lie? These are some of ther fascinating questions which you will seek to answer for yourself.

Acknowledgements

The Bridge World (a registered trademark of Bridge World Magazine Inc) for permission to use portions of the article by Alphonse Moyse Jr in the July 1956 *Bridge World* citing exhibits from the 1965 World Bridge Championship (Copyright © 1965 McCall Corporation)

Ron Tacchi and Marc van Beijsterveldt for proof-reading.

Mark Horton
Editor, Better Bridge Now

Preface

This is a personal story, not a legal document. It has been written from the standpoint of innocence, because Boris Schapiro and I were innocent. But I have not set out to prove a case or to play down the evidence that was given against us. Whatever the verdict of the Inquiry, no reader will mistake the force with which the case was presented.

I say 'whatever the verdict', because one quality this book must necessarily possess is suspense. I began to write it soon after the Inquiry started, and from then on the narrative has kept pace with the 'trial'. This preface was written long before its close.

Non-players will see that the technical evidence, apart from a few hands that are an integral part of the story, is reserved for an Appendix. There I assume that the reader has some knowledge of the tournament game.

No doubt the British Bridge League, which arranged for the Inquiry, will express the thanks of all players to the members of the court who served such an unexpectedly long stint. As for Boris and myself, how could we ever have imagined that we would receive such wonderful support from Mr Tim Holland and the directors of Crockford's., or that we would be defended by so fine an advocate as Mr Leonard Caplan, QC? Even so, we could not have carried on throughout this long year without the encouragement and goodwill of our expert witnesses and of a host of friends, both known and unknown.

My secretary, Marjorie Hiron, made a number of good suggestions for the book and surprisingly injected a certain amount of 'acid'; as though it were needed.

Terence Reese

Reese and Schapiro playing in the open room against Belladonna and Avarelli of Italy. Swimer is in the 'captain's chair' on Reese's right.

Reese about to lead aganist Avarelli and Belladonna. Butler (wearing glasses) is behind Avarelli. Dimmie Fleming is taking notes for BRIDGE Magazine, but Kempson decided not to publish any deals.

Obiter Dicta
(L.f. *obiter* by the way + *dictum* a thing said)

It is an unfortunate fact that the most frequent way in which bridge reaches the headlines of the daily press is through scandalous behaviour of one sort or another.

Of all such cases, one stands head and shoulders above the rest, the accusations made against Terence Reese & Boris Schapiro at the 1965 World Bridge Championships.

Story of an Accusation is Reese's account of events before, during and after the event.

* * *

Writing in the May 1965 issue of BRIDGE MAGAZINE, Ewart Kempson reported as follows:

> Our World Championship team of Mr M J Flint, Mr M Harrison-Gray, Mr Kenneth Konstam, Mr T Reese, Mr A Rose and Mr B Schapiro will have no difficulty in finishing second and may well win the world title in Buenos Aires this month. The South American team is likely to finish at the foot once again, but have a fair chance of entrusting the wooden spoon to North America. Italy will naturally start favourites, but my money goes on the British team. If they can all be induced to play CAB or Acol, my book would make them five to four on.'

I don't know if Kempson was taking a sly dig at the Little Major, but there were no dramatic system changes and Great Britain was heading for second place when the 1965 Championships became a cause célèbre that has intrigued the bridge world ever since.

One month later Kempson's Editorial ran as follows:

> Heartiest congratulations to Italy on her seventh successive victory in the World Championship, a magnificent achievement which is unlikely ever to be equalled.
>
> The Italians had already won the title when incidents – which have been reported on radio and in newspapers throughout the world – led to an unhappy ending to the 1965 championship in Buenos Aires.
>
> The two British players accused of cheating returned to England under this horrible, black cloud ... and alone. All the other players who took part in the championship went on to Rio de Janeiro for a holiday tournament.

I cannot believe that Mr Reese and Mr Schapiro were guilty of using private finger signals in Buenos Aires, and I hope an appeal will be lodged and that they will be exonerated.

Mrs A L Fleming's daily reports from Buenos Aires were to have been published in this issue; in the circumstances I shall not publish anything on the 1965 World Championship. The sooner this contest is abandoned, the better it will be for the game.

Fortunately, the World Championships were not abandoned, and it was soon announced that a formal enquiry would be held into the accusations.

Meanwhile, *The Bridge World*, in its July 1965 issue, went into print.

* * *

The scandal in Buenos Aires

ITALY'S seventh successive victory in the World Championships at Buenos Aires – a triumph of no little magnitude – was overshadowed, hence to some degree spoiled, by the unprecedented, shocking 'cheating' charges against Britain's Reese and Schapiro. Not since the Culbertson–Lenz match of the early 1930s did news media throughout the world give such extraordinary coverage to contract bridge, and it was sad indeed that the reason for this splurge was what it was.

On my return from Argentina in New York I found a folder crammed with requests – often demands – from readers for a complete airing of the charges and evidence against the British pair. Evidently, the world's bridge-playing community gave priority to the shocking news rather than to the Italian performance – however magnificent and unblemished that performance was.

So, bowing to demands, I will defer my own technical coverage of the matches in order to present all the details of the scandal.

Chronology of events

The first encounter between Great Britain and the United States took place on Monday, May 17. Almost immediately, B Jay Becker of the US noticed something that surprised and disturbed him: Reese and Schapiro, his opponents in that session, were holding their cards in strange and ever-changing ways. It was the changes that were so arresting – and, later, so significant. Almost all bridge players, and especially experts, are creatures of habit. If they hold a hand of 13 cards in a certain way, that is the way they hold all hands. They do not project two fingers around one hand and three or four fingers around another.

Vaguely suspicious, but by no means convinced, that 'something was going on', Becker simply observed the changing finger patterns during the rest of the session. Conviction grew, and when the session was over he confided his suspicions to partner Dorothy Hayden (and to her alone), under a pledge of absolute secrecy. It was one thing to harbour suspicions and quite a different thing to broadcast them – and Becker is a cautious man, not one to 'run off at the mouth'.

On Tuesday, May 18, Becker and Mrs Hayden, who had time off in the US match against Argentina, sat in the pit and watched Reese and Schapiro play against an Italian pair. There was nothing unusual in such a visit; members of one team frequently watched – 'cased' – the performance of pairs, especially outstanding pairs, they would come up against later.

After this period of observation Dorothy Hayden was in full agreement with Becker that something was going on between Reese and Schapiro.

The matter had now entered an extremely serious phase – but a phase that was equally delicate and difficult. Suspicion, even conviction, about a 'code' was not enough; proof had to be adduced. And the only way to gather proof was by deciphering the code, assuming that it existed. Becker and Mrs Hayden had no idea what the changing finger-patterns might mean.

After secret discussion they decided to enlist another observer who would then also become an adviser. They chose their close mutual friend Alan Truscott for this twin role, exacting a pledge of secrecy from him too. Aside from friendship and trustworthiness, Truscott, bridge editor of The New York Times, was a sound choice because until recently he had been a British citizen, and, further, Secretary of the British Bridge League. Truscott, shocked and incredulous, nevertheless agreed to become a bridge detective. He watched Reese and Schapiro in their next session. Yes, he confided to Becker and Mrs Hayden, he was convinced that something very bad was in progress.

Thus reinforced, Becker and Mrs Hayden saw that continuance of secrecy and discretion could amount to treason. They went to their team captain, John Gerber, and gave him their findings.

On Friday afternoon, May 21, Gerber, Truscott, Becker and Mrs Hayden, the latter two having another session off, sat in the pit and watched Reese and Schapiro in a match against Argentina. They also watched switches of British partnerships in the day's other sessions, and thereby collected damning evidence of both a positive and a negative nature. When the suspected partnership was in operation, the strange and ever-changing finger patterns persisted. When Reese played with Flint, and Schapiro with Konstam, there was nothing strange in the manner of card-holding – no changes from board to board. This, all agreed, was of the highest significance. It was perfectly obvious that the other members of the British team (Harrison-Gray, Rose, Konstam and Flint) were beyond reproach.

Still, with all the 'observation' in the world, positive and negative, there could be no proof of cheating by Schapiro and Reese unless their code – now an established fact in the minds of the four observers – could be broken. At that point a blank wall was still standing.

A note is necessary here. It will be asked: 'Why, since Britain was over 100 IMPs ahead of Argentina, would any British partnership risk the use of a code of signals?'

It must be borne in mind that rules had been laid down by the World Bridge Federation to apply to a possible three-way tie. In that event the team with the lowest quotient would be dropped, and the other two teams would engage in a play-off. It had become clear that Argentina would be beaten all around, but the margins of victory could be vital.

After the last session on Friday, or, to be more exact, at about three o'clock Saturday morning, Becker, Mrs Hayden and Truscott, carrying hand records of Friday's British–Argentina boards, held a bull session in a restaurant. Each had an inidividual list of the number of fingers exposed by Reese or Schapiro throughout a session. What was or could be the references of fingers to card-holdings?

On examination of the records, no correlation could be found as to the distribution of the hands nor to high cards or point-count. These were dead ends. The inquiry was getting nowhere.

Then came the break, the light. A memory gnawed at Dorothy Hayden's consciousness. In a deal she had played earlier – in the session when she had been alerted by Becker – she recalled the odd sight of one finger of Reese's hand across his cards, and she recalled also that he had turned up with the singleton ace of hearts. She racked her brain further. Yes, there had been another one-finger display, and that time too the hand had contained a singleton heart. Could that possibly be the code?

Electrified, the trio applied their 'lists of fingers' to the specific heart holdings of each hand. On board so-and-so Schapiro had shown three fingers. How many hearts did the record show? Three. On board such-and-such, Reese had exposed four fingers. How many hearts had he held? Four. And so forth and so on right down the line of boards.* Coincidence became a practical impossibility; the precise correlation became proof to within all but an unimaginable degree of error.

---

*A 'complication' will have struck all readers: how could six, seven or even eight hearts be indicated? Simple. At times fingers were held in touching positions; at other times they were spread apart. Thus, two, three or four touching fingers meant two, three or four hearts; for a greater number of hearts add the digit three to the number of spread fingers, so that two became five, three became six, and so on. Suits of nine or more cards could reasonably be expected to take care of themselves.

Before noon on Saturday, Gerber was informed that the code had been broken. He did some independent cross-checking and hand analysis, and action could no longer be delayed: the World Championship was nearing its conclusion. Gerber could do little on his own.

He conferred privately with Robin MacNab, President of the American Contract Bridge League, and with Waldemar von Zedtwitz, both members of the Executive Committee of the World Bridge Federation, under the auspices of which the championships was being conducted. The evidence supplied by Truscott, Becker and Mrs Hayden and by Gerber's own notes was meticulously sifted, not only as to the correlation of fingers to hearts but by analysis of unusual bidding or defensive play on certain boards.

It was decided that the British captain, Ralph Swimer, had to be informed. His sense of shock was indescribable, pitiable. He was also incredulous – at first. But he listened, and he looked at the evidence, and he then called in Sir Geoffrey Butler, President of the British Bridge League, a member of the WBF's Executive Committee, and Chairman of its Appeals Committee.

Before I go further, I must pay due homage to the conduct of these British gentlemen, Swimer and Butler. Shocked, dismayed, perhaps even feeling besmirched, they carried on with dignity and honour. They offered to become observers themselves. And did so later that day. First they watched Reese and Schapiro with other partners. There were no irregularities, none whatsoever. Then in a following session Swimer deliberately put Reese and Schapiro back together. Swimer and Butler took their own notes, later did their own cross-checking of fingers to hearts. Von Zedtwitz acted as an independent observer.

Butler called a meeting of his Appeals Committee and invited Swimer, Gerber and Truscott to be present. The evidence was again gone over and discussed at length. Reese and Schapiro were sent for, informed of the charges and the evidence, and were given the chance to speak for themselves. Both denied the accusations – but not, according to all accounts, with vehemence. Schapiro said almost nothing; Reese spoke generally of the impossibility of 'proving innocence'.

Now a meeting of the Executive Committee of the WBF was called. President Charles J Solomon, Honorary President General Alfred M Gruenther, Robin MacNab, Waldemar von Zedtwitz (all of the United States), Carlo O Perroux of Italy, Johannes Hammerich of Venezuela, and Alfredo M Lahougio of Argentina were present at this meeting, which lasted for many hours on Sunday. Either at this meeting or at the earlier meeting of the Appeals Committee British captain Swimer expressed himself as '110 percent sure' of Reese and Schapiro's guilt. I cannot give a direct quotation as to Butler's views, but he was widely quoted in American newspapers and news magazines as having said that the case was 'well documented'.

Swimer announced that he was conceding (his word, I believe, though 'forfeiting' would seem to have been more appropriate) all of his team's matches. Britain had already lost by a huge score to Italy, had beaten Argentina decisively, and was leading in the match against the United States.

A wrap-up

My subtitle, wrap-up, is not apt to be definitive – this case, I imagine, will not be wrapped up for a long, long time.

However, at the moment there are other facets that I believe will interest readers.

One of the points that has, I imagine, perplexed the bridge-playing public is the special importance of the heart suit in a code of signalling. Life, in its extraordinary spread on this scandal, observed (not too knowledgeably): 'There is nothing special about the heart suit; exact knowledge about any of the four suits would be equally invaluable to an expert. This, of course, is not quite true. Granting the high value of knowledge concerning any suit, the fact remains that knowledge concerning hearts lends extra advantage. This, of course, stems from the fact that it is normally, usually most expensive to 'lose' the major suit, which can so easily occur if weakish hearts must be shown or indicated in the face of an opposing bid. There is considerably less danger in losing a minor suit.

Suppose, for example, that East bids One Spade and South holds:

♠ x x
♡ A Q x x
♢ A x x
♣ K x x x

Suppose further that the vulnerability is unfavourable for South. A double of the One Spade is obviously fraught with risk, but on the other hand a pass can be equally costly. Irrespective of the high cards that may or may not be present in North's hand, a double by South patently becomes very much safer if he knows just one thing: that his partner has five cards or even four in the heart suit himself. Complete safety is of course out of the question, but far smaller 'edges' than this can be of inestimable value in any card game.

On defence, knowledge of partner's length in any suit conveys an advantage that is equally obvious. As a hypothetical case, take this bidding:

West	North	East	South
–	–	–	1♠
Pass	2♠	Pass	4♠
All Pass			

Suppose West holds this sort of hand:

♠ A 2
♡ A 8 5 3
♢ Q 6 4
♣ Q 7 3 2

Normally West has a highly unenviable guess as to the opening lead. Most experts would, I imagine, choose a low club, possibly a low diamond. However, if West knows that his partner has a doubleton heart, the underlead of West's ace stands out like a beacon. There is no chance of running up against a singleton king in South or North – the other adversary would have to hold an unbid six cards in the suit. Thus the chance of being able to give East a heart ruff would be excellent, and myriad other 'situations' would stem from such knowledge.

The question will naturally – very naturally – be asked. What formal disposition was made of this case by the World Bridge Federation?

The answer is short and simple. No disposition. It was merely announced that the record would be turned over to the British Bridge League for its deliberations – in my view, a fantastic decision.

* * *

The same July 1965 issue of *The Bridge World* also contained the following article:

The case against Reese and Schapiro

THE Bridge World presents, without prejudice, some of the hands being considered by the British Bridge League as collateral, not principal, evidence in conjunction with the charges against Reese and Schapiro.

The Bridge World makes no specific representations or comments concerning these hands – all judgements are left to the reader. We offer only one generality: a single deal, or two or three, can never be conclusive. The crucial question is whether or not there is a 'pattern'.

Great Britain vs United States
Deal 30. Love All; Dealer East

East passes, South bids One Club and West holds:

♠ 10 9 5 3
♡ K J 10 8 6
♢ 9 4
♣ 6 5

Reese bid 1NT, which was explained as a two-way bid introduced by the English expert Nico Gardener. In this style One No-trump can be either a natural, strong, balanced hand, or a weak hand which offers some distributional salvation when doubled.

The complete deal was:

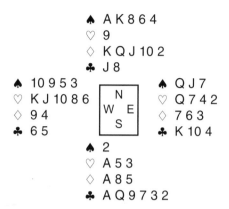

The full auction was:

West	North	East	South
Reese	*Becker*	*Schapiro*	*Hayden*
–	–	Pass	1♣
1NT	Double	Pass	Pass
2♦	2♠	Pass	3♣
Pass	3♦	Pass	3♡
Pass	4♦	Pass	5♣
Pass	6♣	All Pass	

In the other room the British North/South bid Six Diamonds and made Seven. In this room South made Six Clubs.

Deal 50. North/South Game; Dealer East

East opened Three Spades. South held:

♠ K 5
♡ K 10 6 2
♦ K
♣ A Q 8 7 6 2

Reese, South, doubled, and Schapiro bid Four Hearts. The entire deal was:

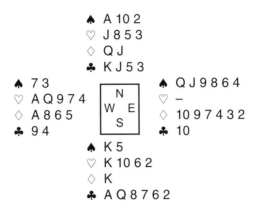

West doubled Four Hearts and beat it one trick.

The contract and result were the same in the other room after a slightly different auction. Erdos, South, passed Three Spades, and bid Four Hearts when his partner made a balancing double.

Great Britain vs Italy
Deal 25. East/West Game; Dealer North

North passed and the bidding by East/West went:

West	East
	1♣
1♠	1NT
2NT	

What should East bid now with:

    ♠ 9 7 6
    ♡ A 8 6 5
    ◇ A J 9
    ♣ A 9 7

Schapiro, East, bid Three Hearts, and the complete deal was:

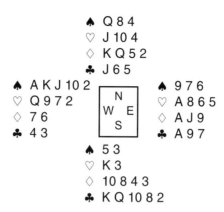

♠ Q 8 4
♥ J 10 4
♦ K Q 5 2
♣ J 6 5

♠ A K J 10 2   ♠ 9 7 6
♥ Q 9 7 2   ♥ A 8 6 5
♦ 7 6   ♦ A J 9
♣ 4 3   ♣ A 9 7

♠ 5 3
♥ K 3
♦ 10 8 4 3
♣ K Q 10 8 2

Three Hearts was raised to Four Hearts, and the contract failed after a club lead. Declarer won the opening lead and attacked trumps. When South won the second round of trumps he cashed a club trick and shifted to a diamond, after which the defence was sure to make one trick in each suit.

The Italians reached Four Hearts from the other side of the table after the following Little Roman Club auction:

West	East
–	1♣
1♥	2♥
2♠	2NT
3♥	4♣
4♥	Pass

South had doubled Four Clubs, but North led the diamond king, and Pabis-Ticci, sitting East, established the diamond jack for a club discard from dummy and made his contract. 12 IMPs to Italy.

East/West were vulnerable and did not bid. North opened with One Spade in third seat and South responded 1NT. What should North bid, holding:

♠ A K 8 4 2
♥ A
♦ Q J 10 4
♣ A Q 9

Schapiro's bid was 3NT. The complete deal was:

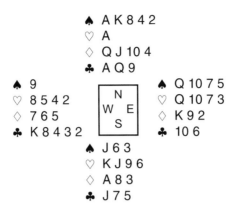

```
                    ♠ A K 8 4 2
                    ♡ A
                    ◇ Q J 10 4
                    ♣ A Q 9
    ♠ 9                          ♠ Q 10 7 5
    ♡ 8 5 4 2          N         ♡ Q 10 7 3
    ◇ 7 6 5        W     E       ◇ K 9 2
    ♣ K 8 4 3 2        S         ♣ 10 6
                    ♠ J 6 3
                    ♡ K J 9 6
                    ◇ A 8 3
                    ♣ J 7 5
```

West led a club and eleven tricks were made. The Italian North/South got to Six Spades, down one against a heart lead. (Six Spades could have been made had declarer known the location of a few cards.)

Deal 54. East/West Game; Dealer East

The Neapolitan bidding went:

North	South
Forquet	Garozzo
–	1♣
1♡	1NT
2♣	2◇
3NT	Pass

The One Heart response showed at least 6 points and not more than one ace or two kings in top cards. The no-trump rebid showed 18–20 points and Two Clubs was Stayman.

With no natural suit bid, West had a wide choice of leads from:

```
                    ♠ A 9 7 5
                    ♡ 10 8 6
                    ◇ 8 7 3
                    ♣ Q 9 8
```

Reese led the heart six and the complete deal was:

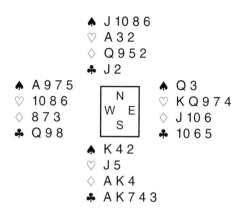

Garozzo, declarer, ducked hearts twice, and won the third round with dummy's ace. He ran the spade jack, which was permitted to hold. Next he made the unusual play of running the club jack, judging that the hearts were on his right and that East must be kept out of the lead. West won the queen of clubs and returned a club. South made nine tricks when both minor suits broke.

When the British played in 3NT, Avarelli, West, led the spade five, and declarer had no difficulty in making the contract with an overtrick via the normal lead of a low club toward the J-2 in dummy.

Deal 127. North/South Game

The bidding proceeded:

West	North	East	South
Reese	*Forquet*	*Schapiro*	*Garozzo*
–	–	–	Pass
1♣	Double	1♡	2◇
2NT	Pass	3♣	All Pass

Three Clubs was down one, and Italy gained 5 IMPs when the Italian East/West bid and made Two Spades.

The complete deal was:

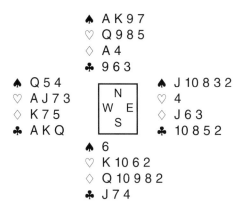

Great Britain vs Argentina
Deal 30. Love All; Dealer East

West opens One Spade in third position, is raised to Three Spades and continues to Four Spades. North has to lead from:

♠ 9 5 4
♡ A 8 6 5
♢ A 5 4
♣ Q 10 2

Schapiro led the heart five, and the complete deal was:

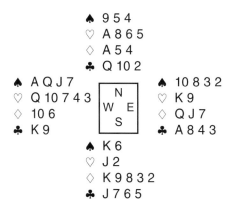

West took the jack with the queen and returned a heart. North put up the ace and played a third heart. Dummy's spade deuce was overruffed by the six, and South put North in with a diamond for a fourth heart lead. South got another overruff, followed by the diamond king, for down two.

The British bidding was the same, but the Argentine North led a trump. Ten tricks were made and Britain gained 11 IMPs.

Deal 68. *Love All; Dealer West*

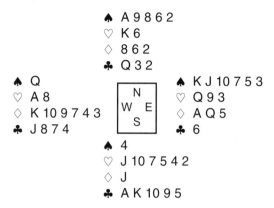

♠ A 9 8 6 2
♡ K 6
♢ 8 6 2
♣ Q 3 2

♠ Q
♡ A 8
♢ K 10 9 7 4 3
♣ J 8 7 4

♠ K J 10 7 5 3
♡ Q 9 3
♢ A Q 5
♣ 6

♠ 4
♡ J 10 7 5 4 2
♢ J
♣ A K 10 9 5

The bidding went as follows in one room:

West	North	East	South
	Reese		*Schapiro*
Pass	Pass	1♠	2♡
3♢	3♡	3♠	4♣
Double	4♡	Double	All Pass

The spade opening lead was won with the ace and a low trump was led from dummy. East played low and the ten forced the ace. A diamond was returned to the ace, and East led the spade king. South ruffed with the heart jack and led to the heart king. He entered his hand with a club and ran the club nine successfully, thus making the doubled contract for a score of 790 points.

The British West was permitted to play in Three Diamonds and made eleven tricks after the lead of the heart king. Britain gained 14 IMPs on the board.

* * *

THE appearance of these articles was like a red rag to a bull to Kempson, and this was part of his Editorial of September 1965:

> Most of the world's magazines have followed the example set in *BRIDGE Magazine* – the oldest of them all – of delaying comment on the Buenos Aires affair until a verdict is reached and announced.
>
> That, I would have thought, was the only fair thing to do, for the World Bridge Federation went into the case and then came out of it by a side door, perhaps rightly, without making an announcement.
>
> *The Bridge World*, alone as far as I know among the bridge magazines of the world, saw fit to publish in its July issue two articles on the affair. The first, entitled The Scandal in Buenos Aires, was written By Mr A Moyse, Jr, the Editor.
>
> Referring to the passing of the alleged incidents to Mr Swimer, the British captain, and to Mr Butler, the chairman of the BBL, Mr Moyse had this to say: 'Before I go further I must pay due homage to the conduct of these British gentlemen, Swimer and Butler. Shocked, dismayed, perhaps even feeling besmirched, they carried on with dignity and honour.'
>
> We make a soft woollen cloth in Yorkshire. It is known as flannel.
>
> The second article, presented by *The Bridge World*, was entitled 'The Case Against Reese and Schapiro'.
>
> Although I have no intention of making any comment on the affair until a verdict is announced, I am strongly opposed to presenting a case against anybody without giving him the opportunity to defend himself. I was, therefore, more than willing to publish the article by Mr Reese which appears in this issue. It is his answer to *The Bridge World*'s case against him.

* * *

For or against

ONE of the minor amusements of the 1930s was to read the chauvinistic writings of one C G Grey, editor of the Aeroplane. 'I have always held,' he wrote once, 'that in the Spanish conflict we should be strictly neutral, with a natural bias in favour of General Franco.' I sent the cutting to 'This England' in the New Statesman and won the weekly prize. The incident came back to me when I read A Moyse, Jr in the American Bridge World on the subject of the 'affair'. He headed his piece, frankly enough, 'The Case against Reese and Schapiro', but went on to say: 'The Bridge World presents, without prejudice, some of the hands being considered by the British Bridge League as collateral, not principal, evidence in connection with the charges against Reese and Schapiro.'

'Without prejudice' is good, for the selection is of course entirely one way. At least, it is meant to be. Whether it would have that effect on an intelligent reader is another question.

The inquiry is still in progress and unlikely to be concluded for several months. What takes place at the inquiry is private and I can make no comment on the general issues. But I think I can, without impropriety, reproduce one or two comments of my own on the selection of hands given by Moyse. These hands are not necessarily the same as those that will be adduced at the inquiry, nor of course is there any mention of the deals that we shall bring forward in a contrary sense.

The Test

The basis of the charge, as everyone knows, is that Schapiro and I communicated length in hearts to one another by means of illegal signals. If you want to support that charge by reference to the hands played, what you have to show is that a number of illogical, uncharacteristic, and implausible bids or plays were made that can be explained only on the basis that the players had improper knowledge of one another's hands. Obviously it is useless to quote hands where a normal, or at least easily understandable, action is taken which happens to turn out well in the existing circumstances. The starting point must be: Assuming that the players had no illicit knowledge, is their bidding and play understandable? With that in mind, let us proceed to the hands.

The examples
US, deal 30. Love All; Dealer East

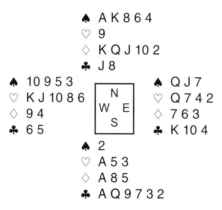

West	North	East	South
Reese	*Becker*	*Schapiro*	*Hayden*
–	–	Pass	1♣
1NT	Double	Pass	Pass
2◊	2♠	Pass	3♣
Pass	3◊	Pass	3♡
Pass	4◊	Pass	5♣
Pass	6♣	All Pass	

As Moyse is kind enough to explain, we were playing the Gardener 1NT overcall. 'In this style,' he goes on, '1NT can be either a natural, strong balanced hand, or a weak hand which offers some distributional salvation when doubled.'

So, what is the complaint? This was the second hand Schapiro and I had played against the Americans and it was natural that we should take an early opportunity to introduce a diversion. The bid of Two Diamonds can cost nothing, for it is understood in any experienced partnership that when a player has started 'fooling around' he must be left to find his own way out. Six Clubs was just made. At the other table the British North/South bid Six Diamonds and made Seven.

US, deal 50. North/South Game; Dealer East

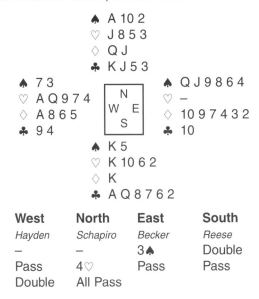

```
                    ♠ A 10 2
                    ♡ J 8 5 3
                    ◊ Q J
                    ♣ K J 5 3
  ♠ 7 3                          ♠ Q J 9 8 6 4
  ♡ A Q 9 7 4      ┌───────┐     ♡ –
  ◊ A 8 6 5        │  N    │     ◊ 10 9 7 4 3 2
  ♣ 9 4            │ W   E │     ♣ 10
                   │   S   │
                   └───────┘
                    ♠ K 5
                    ♡ K 10 6 2
                    ◊ K
                    ♣ A Q 8 7 6 2
```

West	North	East	South
Hayden	*Schapiro*	*Becker*	*Reese*
–	–	3♠	Double
Pass	4♡	Pass	Pass
Double	All Pass		

We were playing optional doubles, in the American style, and had agreed to follow the Roman principle that doubles of a weak Two- or Three-bid should promise defence in two, but not necessarily three, suits.

The objection to a double, of course, is that partner may respond Four Diamonds. If that happens South must either pass, or bid Four Hearts and see if this is doubled, or go to Five Clubs. Not ideal, but one cannot have it all ways when opponents open Three Spades. The double, as compared with Four Clubs, has these advantages: (1) It gives you a much better chance of reaching game in hearts; (2) It will suit you well if partner passes; and (3) Partner may well be able to bid 3NT (in my opinion he should have done so here).

Four Hearts doubled was one down. It is interesting to note the bidding at the other table. The opening Three Spades was passed up to the American, North, who doubled, and South then bid Four Hearts. Imagine the howls if this had been our auction! How can North double, why did South bid hearts, etc? (It is an amusing exercise to build a case against other pairs by making this kind of selection. Thrusters such as Walter Avarelli and Giorgio Belladonna offer great scope.)

Italy, deal 25. East/West Game; Dealer North

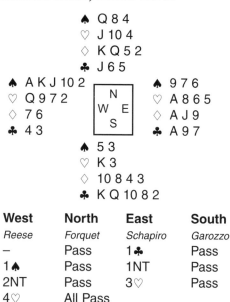

	♠ Q 8 4	
	♡ J 10 4	
	◇ K Q 5 2	
	♣ J 6 5	

♠ A K J 10 2   ♠ 9 7 6
♡ Q 9 7 2   N   ♡ A 8 6 5
◇ 7 6   W   E   ◇ A J 9
♣ 4 3   S   ♣ A 9 7

	♠ 5 3
	♡ K 3
	◇ 10 8 4 3
	♣ K Q 10 8 2

West	North	East	South
Reese	*Forquet*	*Schapiro*	*Garozzo*
–	Pass	1♣	Pass
1♠	Pass	1NT	Pass
2NT	Pass	3♡	Pass
4♡	All Pass		

To judge from the publicity given to this deal in the New York papers, you might think it was the most remarkable auction of the year. Note, to begin with, that there is nothing clever in reaching Four Hearts, and that we didn't make it; that the Italians reached the same contract; and that if East knew his partner held four hearts he could open One Heart without exciting any comment. As it was, there was an obvious risk, from his point of view, that the heart suit would be shut out.

At rubber bridge East would probably pass 2NT, but at IMP scoring one must take any reasonable chance of a vulnerable game rather than hang at 2NT. Surely it is plain that when East bids Three Hearts his main object is to coax a rebid of partner's spades? East's hand is much better suited for a trump contract than for no-trumps. Transfer, for example, West's king of spades and make it the king of diamonds or clubs: then Four Spades becomes a playable contract.

Italy, deal 35. East/West Game; Dealer South

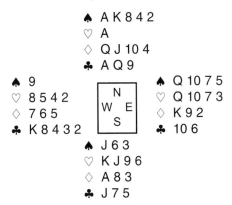

```
                  ♠ A K 8 4 2
                  ♡ A
                  ◇ Q J 10 4
                  ♣ A Q 9
  ♠ 9                          ♠ Q 10 7 5
  ♡ 8 5 4 2        ┌─────┐     ♡ Q 10 7 3
  ◇ 7 6 5          │  N  │     ◇ K 9 2
  ♣ K 8 4 3 2      │W   E│     ♣ 10 6
                   │  S  │
                   └─────┘
                  ♠ J 6 3
                  ♡ K J 9 6
                  ◇ A 8 3
                  ♣ J 7 5
```

Schapiro opened One Spade after two passes and raised my response of 1NT to 3NT. The Italians reached Six Spades and were one down.

The implication here is presumably that North would not have bid 3NT had he not known that South held four hearts. As to that, possession of four hearts will not necessarily save the partnership from danger in hearts; J-x-x-x is someway inferior to K-J-x. However, let us examine the alternative, Three Diamonds. If that produces 3NT, all that North has done is increase the likelihood of a heart lead. If it produces Three Spades, it will still be doubtful whether you should bid game in spades or no-trumps. And if partner raises to Four Diamonds, what do you do? Plod on foolishly to Five, I suppose.

As I see it, 3NT is a perfectly good bid. And anyway, their argument is nonsensical, for if North knows that South holds four hearts he can bid Three Diamonds, knowing that partner will take satisfactory action.

Italy, deal 127. North/South Game; Dealer South

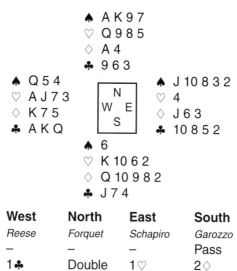

	♠ A K 9 7
	♡ Q 9 8 5
	◇ A 4
	♣ 9 6 3

♠ Q 5 4		♠ J 10 8 3 2
♡ A J 7 3		♡ 4
◇ K 7 5	N W E S	◇ J 6 3
♣ A K Q		♣ 10 8 5 2

	♠ 6
	♡ K 10 6 2
	◇ Q 10 9 8 2
	♣ J 7 4

West	North	East	South
Reese	*Forquet*	*Schapiro*	*Garozzo*
–	–	–	Pass
1♣	Double	1♡	2◇
2NT	Pass	3♣	All Pass

Here you have a baby psych by East, easily recognised by West. What do they expect me to do, with 19 points, a vulnerable double on my left, and a free bid on my right? The upshot of the manoeuvre was that we were down in Three Clubs, while the Italians made Two Spades on our cards.

Italy, deal 43. East/West Game; Dealer East

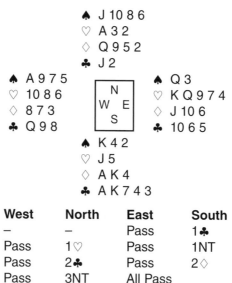

	♠ J 10 8 6
	♡ A 3 2
	◇ Q 9 5 2
	♣ J 2

♠ A 9 7 5		♠ Q 3
♡ 10 8 6		♡ K Q 9 7 4
◇ 8 7 3	N W E S	◇ J 10 6
♣ Q 9 8		♣ 10 6 5

	♠ K 4 2
	♡ J 5
	◇ A K 4
	♣ A K 7 4 3

West	North	East	South
–	–	Pass	1♣
Pass	1♡	Pass	1NT
Pass	2♣	Pass	2◇
Pass	3NT	All Pass	

'With no natural suit bid, West had a wide choice of leads,' says Moyse, and adds pregnantly: 'He led the six of hearts.' We held them to the contract, while at the other table South made an overtrick.

Let us examine the 'wide choice'. South's One Club is conventional and the response shows a minimum of 6 points. Two Clubs is Stayman. The inferences to be drawn from the bidding are that South has length in the minors, North in at least one major, and that the opponents have something in hand (as North jumped to 3NT).

Obviously you don't want to lead away from the queen of clubs, and a diamond would not be dynamic. As between spades and hearts, a spade will be disastrous if dummy's long suit is spades, while a heart will not necessarily be bad. The best chance, surely, is to find partner with Q-J-x-x or better in hearts. If he has strength in spades you may be able to run those later. I stand by the six of hearts.

In any event, if there is a wide choice, surely one is permitted to make the best choice on occasions? (There are plenty of examples where we did not.) This was the other 'lead' hand:

Argentina, deal 30. Love All; Dealer East

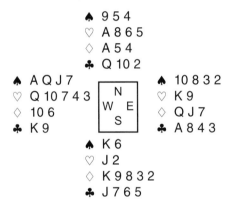

```
              ♠ 9 5 4
              ♡ A 8 6 5
              ◇ A 5 4
              ♣ Q 10 2
  ♠ A Q J 7              ♠ 10 8 3 2
  ♡ Q 10 7 4 3    N      ♡ K 9
  ◇ 10 6       W   E     ◇ Q J 7
  ♣ K 9           S      ♣ A 8 4 3
              ♠ K 6
              ♡ J 2
              ◇ K 9 8 3 2
              ♣ J 7 6 5
```

After 1♠ – 3♠ – 4♠, Schapiro led the five of hearts. Declarer won with the queen and returned a heart. He ruffed a third heart with a low trump and finished two down.

If West had drawn trumps, as did the declarer at the other table after a trump lead, I don't suppose we should have heard about the hand. The implication, I presume, is that North was directed to the heart lead by the knowledge that South held a doubleton.

Tell me a better lead, on the bidding, than a low heart. With his balanced distribution and unpromising defence, North must look for a lead that may achieve something. A trump is too negative. As between the others, there is no reason to risk a club, as no side suit has been bid. A heart stands the chance of gaining a trick if partner has something like K-x or Q-x, and in any event the underlead may be deceptive.

Argentina, deal 68. Game All; Dealer West

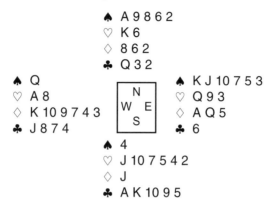

```
                    ♠ A 9 8 6 2
                    ♡ K 6
                    ◇ 8 6 2
                    ♣ Q 3 2
    ♠ Q                              ♠ K J 10 7 5 3
    ♡ A 8              N             ♡ Q 9 3
    ◇ K 10 9 7 4 3   W   E           ◇ A Q 5
    ♣ J 8 7 4          S             ♣ 6
                    ♠ 4
                    ♡ J 10 7 5 4 2
                    ◇ J
                    ♣ A K 10 9 5
```

West	North	East	South
Rocchi	*Schapiro*	*Attaguile*	*Reese*
Pass	Pass	1♠	2♡
3◇	3♡	3♠	4♣
Double	4♡	Double	All Pass

I won the spade lead in dummy and led a low heart from the table. East played low and the knave fetched the ace. A diamond was won by the ace, and I ruffed a spade with the ten of hearts. Later finessing the nine of clubs, I made the contract. At the other table West was allowed to play in Three Diamonds.

The criticism here, I imagine, is directed at North's Four Hearts, when he might have passed over the double of Four Clubs. But my Four Clubs, in this sequence, is not necessarily a long suit: it can be something like A-J-x-x or A-K-x-x, bid with the intention of helping partner to decide the best action should opponents go to Four Spades over Four Hearts. North would not consider passing the double of Four Clubs on three trumps.

Apart from that, if North is supposed to know that South holds six hearts, he can assume that South knows it as well and can transfer to Four Hearts after he has been raised in the suit.

Well, there you have it – eight deals out of the 198 that we played together. Readers of a full-column advertisement in the *ACBL Bulletin* were promised 'Ten Significant Deals from the Case against Reese and Schapiro'. They may feel they haven't got their money's worth.

* * *

REESE & Schapiro retired from Championship play. When Reese was chosen to captain the British Open team for the World Championships in Rye, New York, 1981, the WBF credentials committee refused to sanction his appointment. In Lille, in 1998, Boris Schapiro, partnered by Irving Gordon, won the World Senior Pairs Championship. Reese died in 1996, Schapiro in 2002.

Reese (right) and Schapiro in play against Becker and Mrs Hayden in the bridgerama room.

The only photograph extant, taken during the bidding stage. Schapiro in fact held a void heart on this deal, Reese three hearts.

Reese and Flint playing in the open room against Rocchi and Attaguile of Argentina. Konstam is on Flint's left.

1 The Green Sickness

BRIDGE IS A STRANGE GAME. It engages certain emotions more powerfully than any other activity in life.

At most games players find their own level and are roughly content with it. At bridge there is no reliable method of individual comparison. Every player is free to think he plays as well as the next one; and for some unexplainable reason most players are extremely anxious to convince themselves and others that they play better than they do. It touches their amour-propre.

Because of this, bridge reveals character. A man who in ordinary life gets by as a sound and well-adjusted citizen may show himself at the bridge table to be stupid, vain, obstinate, greedy and dishonest. A couple who bill and coo at one another from dawn to dusk will storm and sulk when they play cards.

According to an article in the *New York Times*, bridge has led to hundreds of divorces and four murders. The most famous of these was the Bennett case, at Kansas City in 1929. In the course of a friendly game against two neighbours some disharmony arose, culminating in a hand where Mr Bennett went down in a contract of Four Spades. Mrs Bennett made a remark about bum bridge players and Mr Bennett slapped her face. Mrs Bennett rushed upstairs to get a gun and a few seconds later shot her spouse dead through the bathroom door. She was tried for murder and acquitted. The line of play suggested by Mrs Bennett was actually no better than that adopted by her husband. I have often wondered whether, if the jury had been bridge players and had fully understood that, they would have taken so lenient a view.

If people for whom bridge is just a pastime can be so dramatic about it, imagine the jealousy and competitiveness at the top, where international honours are at stake. Except in the Olympic years there is a European championship, to which Britain sends an open and a women's team. If during this championship one of the players left at home telephones another and says excitedly, 'Have you heard the news?' it doesn't mean that Britain has beaten Italy, the champions; more likely, they have lost to Finland. Such is the green sickness that overlays the tournament world.

For readers who are not familiar with this form of the game, I must say a word about the procedure in tournament bridge. It rests on the duplicate principle, the same hand being played twice. Suppose that Britain is playing a team-of-four match against Italy. Two British players, occupying positions known as North and South, face two Italians sitting East-West.

The four deal and play, but the cards are not thrown into the middle as in ordinary rubber bridge. Each player keeps his own cards in front of him and puts them back in the appropriate slot of a 'duplicate board', which is a form of container. This board is later taken to the other room, where the same hand is replayed, but now Italy is North-South and Britain East-West. The effect is that a pair's real opponents are not so much the players at their own table as the pair holding the same cards at the corresponding table. The results are compared and so the score is determined. The luck of the deal, in the form of holding good or bad cards, is eliminated.

The story of this book begins with the British trials for the European Championship at Baden Baden in 1963. The players entered in pairs and after a preliminary round were formed into teams. The winning team consisted of Boris Schapiro, Jeremy Flint, Terence Reese and Ralph Swimer. All four play an important part in this book.

The late Guy Ramsey, in his book *Aces All*, called his chapter on Schapiro 'The Joker' and wrote:

> The only word for Boris is 'irrepressible'. The bridge world is full of stories about him – many of them quite true; many of them, surprisingly, emanating from himself. The volatility of his temperament, occasionally a technical weakness, is by the same token a source of psychological strength, both at the bridge table and away from it.
>
> The central core of his personality is aggressive self-confidence, The prominent eyes are balanced by heavy jowls which give pugnacity to his whole expression.

Boris is shrewd but tactless. His epitaph might be: 'Unlike King Charles II, Boris never did a foolish thing and never spoke a wise one.'

Jeremy Flint was no more than a bright light on the horizon of bridge when Guy wrote his book in 1955. Now in his middle thirties, he is young as bridge champions go, but very experienced. With long, fair hair and a high, thin nose, he could put on a top hat and look like an Edwardian man-about-town. In certain ways I can see a reflection of myself. Jeremy has the same dislike of regular toil. He follows the horses professionally and is prepared for any kind of speculative venture on which he can bring his intelligence to bear. His qualities of mind, and approach to bridge, are similar to my own.

As I have been personal about the others I ought to say something about myself. Guy called me 'The Stylist' and described me as 'tall and slim, with a thin face dominated by a sharp-cut nose. His manner is marked by a superciliousness which is sometimes humorous, sometimes mordant'. Not so slim nowadays, alas. I learned to play bridge when I was seven and can remember dismounting from my chair to sort my cards behind a cushion. My mother was a great organiser in the early days of contract. At Oxford I played in the first university match; the outstanding player among our opponents was Iain Macleod.

After a not very serious year in business I became assistant editor of the pre-war *British Bridge World* and in the same year wrote my first book and played in my first international match. This was about 1937 and in those easy-going days it seemed natural enough, if one had a hobby and was not ambitious outside it, to indulge that hobby, making a little money from rubber bridge and playing in all the tournaments. After the war, while the official bodies were heaving themselves slowly to their feet, I formed the Tournament Bridge Association. Through this I obtained regular broadcasts and about the same time wrote the first of my books on advanced play. By 1950 I was well launched as a bridge journalist. Fairly able in all these fields, I have made a successful career but I do not conceal from myself that I might have employed my talents in a more worthwhile way. Realising that, I have no complex about it.

Ralph Swimer, the fourth in our team for the Baden Baden trials, is a businessman and moves in a different set from ours. He is dark and saturnine.

Boris and I had been close friends and a successful partnership, reckoned among the world's best, for 20 years, but in these trials I played mostly with Flint. This was because he and I were in the process of developing a highly complicated bidding system called the Little Major and we wanted to practise the system together. Boris struck up a not very fluent partnership with Swimer.

The team we beat in the final of the trials consisted of M Harrison Gray, Alan Hiron, Kenneth Konstam and Joel Tarlo. A team of six is allowed in the European championship and it was generally expected that the selectors would take the four winners plus a pair from the runners-up. In practice they chose three players from each team – Gray, Konstam and Tarlo, together with Schapiro, Flint and myself. In the closing stages of the trials Boris had been highly critical of his partner's play. There was nothing unusual in that, but it may have had some bearing on the selectors' decision to omit Swimer. I certainly thought so at the time.

We won the championship at Baden Baden and the same team of six played in the Bridge Olympiad at New York the following year. About 30 countries took part and we headed the field in the qualifying round. In the semi-final we lost a close match to Italy, who easily beat the US in the final. During these two events I played about an equal amount with Flint and with Schapiro.

There was no European championship in the Olympic year, so Britain, as European title-holders, qualified for the World Championship at Buenos Aires in 1965. This was to be a four-cornered event, the other teams being Italy, holders of the Bermuda Bowl, North America, and Argentina, representing South America.

The British Bridge League selection committee was prepared to invite the same six players for Buenos Aires if they were all agreeable. However, bridge teams, even when successful, seldom develop into mutual admiration societies and I for one thought the team could be improved for this special task. There were no individual weaknesses but there were problems of partnership. Among them, both my partnership and my friendship with Boris were wearing thin. The happiest of couples can have a rough patch after 20 years and in our case the Little Major was playing the part of the 'other woman'. Boris, an intuitive rather than an analytical player, had tried to play the system, but it didn't suit his talents and I tended to become impatient. I liked playing with Jeremy and I liked playing the system with him. We arranged to play together in the trials, which were on a pairs basis.

It was a delicate situation and I managed it badly. My decision to play with Flint hurt and offended Boris in a way I had not foreseen. He fixed up to play with Kenneth Konstam, a fine player whose record included six wins in the European championship. 'Konnie' is another who has made bridge an important part of his life. At the table he worries his lower lip and has an intimidating air. Away from it he has considerable charm of voice and manner. Most bridge players are willing to let the social world go by, but Konnie likes to observe correct forms. If there are prizes to present at a club a hundred miles away, an overseas visitor to be entertained, a personage to be greeted, he is there.

The trials were played over two week-ends at the Hamilton Club, with ten invited pairs in contention. Boris had worries apart from his strained relations with me and throughout the play he was in a highly nervous and aggressive mood. He was desperately keen to do better than Flint and myself, but as it turned out we played in good luck and won by a clear margin. Boris and Konstam finished second, and Swimer and Albert Rose were third. By the terms of the trial the selectors were committed to the first two pairs. The problem was the third pair. Swimer and Rose had not been entirely happy about some of their results and there was a general feeling that Harrison Gray should be in the team. Gray and Rose were an experienced partnership and the upshot was that the selectors chose these two, leaving out Swimer. Somewhat foolishly, the British Bridge League announced the team to the press without waiting for the players to accept the invitation.

Rose and Swimer were neighbours in Hampstead and their wives were friendly. Peggy and Minnie, it was said, had already made their plans for shopping expeditions in South America. As this was the second time that Swimer had been the odd man out, nothing was more certain than that Rose would feel called upon to make a demonstration. Thus it was no surprise to anyone except, presumably, the selectors, when he declined the invitation, giving no reason. The League promptly announced that it would send a team of five, with a captain who could play if required. One virtue of this plan was that it would save money. The financial structure of tournament bridge in Britain and America rests on what is known as the 'master points' system. In all tournaments above a certain level players are charged a small additional entry fee and compete for certificates that entitle them to the rank of Club Master, Local Master, County Master, One Star Master, and so on up to Life Master. Although even the highest ranks testify to prolonged endeavour rather than outstanding skill, the system works.

Boris and Konnie thought that a team of five would be no handicap, but I had my doubts and Gray was dissatisfied as he would have no regular partner. Someone soon had the idea that if Swimer were made non-playing captain Rose might withdraw his refusal to play. Rumours of this plan quickly circulated. 'The selectors won't wear it,' said Harold Franklin, who was one of them. There were dark suggestions that the tail was trying to wag the dog. Nevertheless, Konstam wrote on behalf of the team that (a) our majority recommendation for captain was Swimer, and (b) we all hoped that Rose would be asked to reconsider. By keeping the two propositions independent we hoped to save the selectorial face. At the same time Rose wrote to withdraw his refusal, making no conditions.

It was obviously a compromise, not to say a 'deal'. Of the four selectors who arbitrated on the matter, Geoffrey Butler, the Chairman of the British Bridge League, and Jack Marx were in favour, Harold Franklin and Reg Corwen, who had captained many British teams in the past, were against. They disapproved of the machinations that were going on and may also have thought there were better and more experienced candidates for the job of captain. Finally Butler, not at a formal meeting, but on the plea that time was getting short, used his casting vote. That is how Ralph Swimer became captain of the British team.

It would be wrong to suppose that the pangs attending the birth of this team were anything unusual. It happens all the time at all levels. At that, selecting the men's international team is an armchair ride compared with selecting the team for the European ladies championship. There the selectors have to contend not merely with the warring females but with husbands and attachments. In the end six players are selected, the rest, inevitably, are not. The attachments, more partisan even than the spouses, at once allege favouritism and intrigue and in some cases pass on to protests, petitions and resignations.

Before Swimer's appointment I had written to Butler about the captaincy, as we were all asked to do, and had gone on to refer to the atmosphere at the trials. I said that the position between Boris and myself was impossible and that I did not wish to be subjected to any pressure to play with him in Buenos Aires. Unwontedly, I kept a copy of this letter.

This interlude in my relationship with Boris makes an unedifying story, I know, but I have to relate it because it is relevant to what happened later. In the weeks before we left for Buenos Aires tempers cooled and we became friends again. I still hoped to play the Little Major with Flint, especially in the critical match against Italy, but it was plain that the others, including Flint himself, wanted Boris and myself to resume our partnership.

We flew to Buenos Aires on Wednesday, May 12, with reasonably high hopes. I felt we had just about the strongest team available. To complete the description of the players, M Harrison Gray is a veteran of the tournament world. He is heavy in build, with a high colour. The small moustache and bald head gave him some resemblance to Clement Attlee when both were younger.

Albert Rose has a silk-importing business. He is dark, fairly short, with a trim moustache and dapper looks. He likes to be friendly. When he sees me after an interval it is always, 'Terence, my dear chap, how are you keeping?' with a handshake and an arm on my shoulder. At the table he is something of a fidget, constantly riffling his cards and transferring his cigarette from mouth to ashtray and back. Though as experienced as any of us, Rose was the only non-professional of the six players. There is no formal distinction between amateur and professional in bridge, but we describe as professional anyone who derives a substantial part of his income from writing, teaching or playing.

Rose and Swimer both took their wives. The tenth in our party was Geoffrey Butler. At a later stage Counsel was to use the phrase '... and what might be called the British Official, Butler'. I cannot improve on that.

With Jeremy Flint the only member of the team under 50, we were somewhat advanced in years ('average age seventy-five, if you count Gray,' Boris told a reporter). However, it was unlikely that the schedule, less arduous than in the European championship, would bother us. In bridge, long experience and assured technique preserve the stamina better than young legs.

We reckoned to beat Argentina and in the past we had generally managed to defeat the Americans, who had not won the world championship since 1954. The present American team, chosen by the bad method of pairs trials, appeared to contain weaknesses. If only we could play our normal game against Italy, six times world champions! Much would depend, I thought, on our line-up.

We flew in at midday on Thursday and admired the handsome boulevards on our way into the town. The Plaza Hotel, where the championship was to be played and where we were all staying, was large but old-fashioned. My bedroom held a secretaire in place of a wardrobe. After unpacking I went down to inspect the playing rooms and in particular the 'bridgerama'.

However experienced a player may be, the big thrill in any championship comes when his captain says, 'Dinner jacket tonight. You're on bridgerama.' Say that the session is due to begin at 9.00pm. The other pair in your team is despatched about half an hour earlier to another room, where they start play so that some boards will be ready when bridgerama begins. As nine o'clock approaches, you and your partner sit in the lounge outside the bridgerama hall, studying the opponents 'bidding sheet'. That means, the system and conventions they will be using. An official comes over to check that you will be ready when summoned. People wish you good luck; you know that in a few minutes they will be watching the play and enjoying your mistakes. The official appears again and beckons you over.

With the opposing pair you walk down the long hall, which is beginning to fill up. The four of you are introduced in turn and step onto the platform to bow to the applause. Behind you is the big electrically operated board known as bridgerama. It is in the form of a Maltese cross, with four compartments for the hands of North, South, East and West. At the moment the board is unlit and empty, but as soon as you are out of sight, slides containing the four hands of the first deal will be slipped into the appropriate spaces. A bulb will light up behind each card so that the spectators in the darkened auditorium will have a clear view of the whole deal. On another board the bidding will be shown. After the introductions the players are led away to a room behind the scenes where there is a commentator with a microphone. He relays the bidding and play to an operator in the bridgerama hall who sits behind a contrivance that looks like a cross between a piano and a typewriter. As the play develops, he touches the appropriate keys; when a card is played the light behind it goes out. An expert commentator, or in some cases a team of commentators, analyses the bidding and play. He will also tell the audience what happened when the hand was played half an hour before at the other table.

The peril of playing on bridgerama lies in the fact that the audience can see all four hands and therefore can 'play' much better than you can. It takes a first-class observer to judge fairly in such circumstances. You know, as you sit in your little room, that if you make a bad, or simply unlucky, bid or play there will be a roar from 500 spectators. You have to put that out of your mind. Quite fatal, of course, is to try something clever, playing to the gallery. In a world championship any obvious 'boob' is on everyone's lips within an hour and remains in black and white for ever. It is much worse than missing an open goal. There was a fine hall for bridgerama at the Plaza Hotel, presumably a ballroom in the normal way. The two matches taking place each day would be shown on bridgerama in turn. Two players from each team would sit in the bridgerama room and the remaining four would be in one of the 'closed rooms', where spectators are not allowed.

For the second match, the one not on bridgerama, there would be one table in another closed room and one table in the 'open' room. There the spectators can watch 'live'. The scene is like a boxing ring with the card table in the centre and tiered seats. At the corners of the table there are four special chairs, two for the scorers and one for each team captain. Throughout the week the open room at the Plaza Hotel had a slightly sad, carpentered air, with poor lighting. Both the open room and the bridgerama hall led off from a big central lounge. On the whole it was an excellent setting for the championship.

So far we had met only the home players. The Italian and American teams arrived the next day. Italy had her famous 'Blue Team', Forquet and Garozzo, Avarelli and Belladonna, D'Alelio and Pabis Ticci. We had always been on friendly terms with the Italians, who bore their successes lightly and played a very correct game.

We also knew most of the American team. Their star player was Howard Schenken, a relaxed but somewhat morose New Yorker who sighed deeply before taking any decision at the card table. His partner was Peter Leventritt, a more cheerful and extrovert character. In moments of animation he would prance around with his left arm bent at the elbow, the hand drooping loosely from the wrist.

Their second pair was B J Becker and Dorothy Hayden. Becker, a bland little man with sandy hair and a perpetual smile, had formed his partnership with Hayden after the 1960 Olympiad. It was said that they fell into conversation on the plane coming back from Turin and discovered that bridgewise they were soul-mates. Hayden had not previously been regarded as an outstanding woman player but the two had been steadily successful in pairs events. The third pair, Ivan Erdos and Kelsey Petterson, had been the surprise qualifiers from the American trials. Erdos, a confident young man of Hungarian origin, had played his early bridge in Britain. There was a suggestion of pro-amateur in this partnership. In slight mockery of the American style we always referred to Petterson as 'the West Coast lawyer'.

The American captain, John Gerber, from Texas, had a trenchant way of speaking and picked a quarrel with Boris on the first Saturday. We did not start with any feeling of hostility against the Americans, but the two teams did not fraternise. Come to think of it, they were seldom on view before the afternoon session began. The surprise, for us, was the Argentine team and its captain. In the European championship the host country, more than any other, bursts itself to be charming to everyone, but the Argentines started right away with complaints that they had not had time to study the Little Major. We had despatched a full and clear summary several weeks before, but they said they had only just received it. A special session was arranged on Friday, at which Jeremy and I were subjected to a barrage of questions. The summary was later translated into Spanish; doubling its length, I noticed.

While Flint and I were defending ourselves against the Spanish sharp-shooters, Konstam chartered a taxi and carted off Swimer to sign the Visitors' Book at the British Embassy, far away on the outskirts of the town. This important task concluded, we were ready for battle.

The draw was not what we would have chosen. We were due to play Italy in the first round on Saturday, Argentina on Sunday, North America on Monday. This sequence would be twice repeated, the championship lasting over nine days. The schedule was 48 boards (i.e. hands) a day, divided into sessions of 14, 14, and 20. A session of 14 boards would normally take about an hour and three-quarters. The Italians soon outgeneralled us in one important particular. We were guests of the home country so far as the hotel was concerned and we were directed towards a special players' dining room, where the service at first was poor and the choice limited. Italy's resourceful captain, Perroux, arranged for his team to have their meals in a private room, where no doubt they fared better. Apart from that, it was Perroux's way to keep close control of his players and to conduct a searching inquiry into any set of boards where they had dropped points.

The question was, how would we line up for the opening session against Italy? Flint is an expert on the Italian systems and he and I had prepared together a number of skilful counter-measures. I hoped we would start, but Swimer put me in with Boris, and Gray with Rose. These matches are decided by what are known as international match points and at the end of 14 boards we were 18 points down, which was disappointing but not so far serious. At this stage Rose complained of a slight headache and was not keen to continue. Swimer left Boris and me together and played Gray with Konstam. In this session we lost a further 21 points.

Now Swimer had his worst inspiration of the day. For the evening session I continued with Boris, and Gray was given a third partner, Flint. Jeremy is a front runner rather than a puller-back of points, and if he was going to play at all at this critical juncture he should have played the Little Major with me. As it was, he started uncertainly, making two doubtful bidding decisions at the slam level in the first four boards he played. He and Gray played well afterwards, but Boris and I brought nothing in and we finished the day 63 points down. With only a third of the match gone this was not necessarily fatal, but it was like being two goals down to Inter Milan after half an hour's play. You could lay heavy odds.

What I found so surprising was that Swimer had not sought anyone's advice about his dispositions. At any rate, he did not consult either Gray or myself. Captains vary in this respect and it is true that, like selectors, they always get the blame. Louis Tarlo was criticised at Baden Baden for taking too little advice, and Sidney Lee in New York for taking too much. As we did well in both tournaments, they may both have been right. On

Sunday we were due to play Argentina, and Flint and I started in the closed room. It was in some ways the most extraordinary session I have ever played in a championship. The Argentine players had got hold of the mistaken idea that we intended to play the Little Major only against their team. Perhaps they thought we were treating them lightly. It soon became clear, at any rate, that they were under special instructions how to comport themselves against the system.

In principle, a player is entitled to know the meaning of his opponent's bids. The normal course, when one wants such information, is to ask the player's partner, beginning with the formula, 'What do you understand by that bid?' If you think that in giving the explanation the partner may convey information to the first player you have the right to ask the first player to leave the table. It is something I have never done, but when Boris and I played the Little Major against the Americans in the qualifying round of the 1964 Olympiad we were in and out of the room about ten times in 18 boards.

Our Argentine opponents asked no questions at all. Instead, one of them, whenever it was his turn to bid, leafed through all five pages of his summary before announcing 'Passo'. Jeremy and I kept our tempers and gave no sign of impatience.

After the session we told Swimer that on no account would we play against this pair again. It was now our turn to 'place round', so we could choose our opponents. Some misunderstanding must have occurred, for when we arrived in the closed room for the next session the same pair was awaiting us. We could have referred back to our captain, but we decided to let it pass.

In this session our opponents made a formal claim against us in rather unusual circumstances. Departing from custom, one of them asked Flint the meaning of two bids in hearts which I had made. There had been a misunderstanding, as can easily happen in a system like ours, and Flint told them that he placed me with first-round control in hearts, possibly a void, whereas in fact I was looking at K-Q-x-x. We reached an inferior contract of Five Clubs, which I was allowed to make. The opponents contended that their line of defence had been affected by the wrong information they had been given. Their protest was upheld by the Appeals Committee and we were deprived of 6 IMPs. It did not matter very much, as we had established a fair lead.

On Monday we met the Americans and I played the first session with Flint on bridgerama. This was a highly critical moment, for Boris was sitting out and would be watching the Little Major in action. It was not to be expected that he would be indulgent to any shortcomings.

As it happened, we had one major calamity. The details, if non-bridge players will bear with me for this one example, were not unamusing. These were the cards we held:

```
        Reese                          Flint
        ♠ 10 3                         ♠ A
        ♡ A K 10 8 4    ┌──────┐       ♡ Q J 7 6 5 2
        ◊ 10 3          │  N   │       ◊ Q J 9 8 7
        ♣ A K 6 2       │W   E │       ♣ Q
                        │  S   │
                        └──────┘
```

I was the dealer and opened Two Hearts, which in our system showed a fair major-minor two-suiter. I was actually minimum for the bid. Flint responded 2NT, which is conventional and simply asks about my distribution. At this point various rebids on my part would have an artificial meaning, and the bid I made, Three Diamonds, in fact told him that I did not have a singleton or void spade and that my second suit was clubs (don't ask why, it would take too long to explain).

In view of his own high cards East could be sure that I held two aces and the only question was whether I held one or two losing diamonds. Jeremy could have enquired about my holding in the suit by a jump to Five Diamonds. This would have been an 'Asking Bid' and my response of Five Hearts (in accordance with a schedule for which the mnemonic is OKAIO) would have denoted two losers and ended the bidding.

Instead of employing this glorious sequence on which we had laboured for months, Jeremy went straight to Six Hearts, which, of course, had to go one down. Whether he thought I was too addled to recognise Five Diamonds as an Asking Bid, or whether he was just impatient, I never discovered.

The American pair at the other table also reached an impossible slam, so we did not lose on the board, or indeed on the session, but Jeremy and I were subjected to much barracking when we compared scores later. We expected this, but we were nevertheless annoyed. In the evening I played with Boris against Becker and Hayden. As a small diversion, I made a formal complaint to the American deputy captain about the chewing of gum by his players. We finished the day 22 points ahead.

Aware, presumably, that things were not going too smoothly, Swimer called a team meeting the next morning. Swimer himself said very little. Jeremy and I were still peevish about the events of the previous afternoon and I had angry words with Boris. He protested, fairly enough, that his criticisms had been sincere, not malicious, he simply wanted to win the match. Boris was also in trouble with Gray. In an early session Gray had had one of his brainstorms, making a particularly unsafe safety play, and Boris had been unbearable about it. For the next 24 hours, whenever he saw a journalist or a player from another team, he would call across to him and as they walked away could be heard saying, 'I've got a rather interesting safety play on which I would like your opinion...' We all complained about the lack of consultation between captain and players, but nothing was settled. Konstam confided to Flint that he had never played in a team where there was so little sociability. Later in the day we dropped more points to Italy and on Wednesday we went further ahead against Argentina.

On Thursday Boris and I played the first two sessions against Becker and Mrs Hayden. In the first session especially they played rather poorly, and with Gray and Rose in good form at the other table we outpointed the Americans by 63 to 2. Some ground was lost back in the third session, but we finished the day 48 in front. On Friday we completed the match against Italy, losing by 121 IMPs. Boris and I had played in six of the nine sessions; it was the biggest reverse of our career.

We still had a small theoretical chance of winning the championship. The match between America and Italy was still undecided; if America beat Italy we could be the winners, on total IMPs, of a three-way tie. Thus we had an interest in increasing our lead against Argentina on Saturday. I played the first session with Flint and sat out for the next 14 boards. We gained heavily on both occasions. Swimer made a point of Boris and myself playing together for the final session. On our way to the open room we learned that America had fallen well behind Italy and had no chance of winning. This meant that our match against the Argentine no longer had any significance. To finish second, we had to avoid losing points to America on the final day. The only enlivenment of this last session against Argentina was the appearance of Geoffrey Butler in the 'captain's chair' at my elbow, making notes on a pad. Butler with his notebook is a familiar figure when youthful trialists are in contention, but this was the first time we had noticed him anywhere near the table during this championship. I drew Boris's attention to the phenomenon with a quizzical glance, which he returned. One gets to bed late at these tournaments and at about half past ten the following morning I was struggling to life when the phone rang in my room. I recognised Albert Rose's high voice. 'Terence, it's Albert.' 'Yes, Albert?' 'Terence, there's something going on. Ralph has been closeted with the committee for nearly an hour. They want you and Boris. Can you come down?'

2 A Day to Remember

WHEN A PLAYER is asked to attend a committee meeting, the presumption is that some sort of claim or protest has been made against him. It may be on a technical point, without any imputation of unethical play; or an opponent may claim, in the vernacular, that he has been hotted. These are the commonest grounds of protest in tournament play:

(1) Some failing in deportment, such as making a bid or playing a card with undue emphasis, or taking advantage of partner's hesitation. It is not improper to take time over a bid or play, but it is incorrect to draw inferences from the tempo of partner's play.
(2) Use of a convention that has not been announced. (A convention is an agreement between partners to use a bid in a special sense, not obvious on the surface.) In principle, players have a duty to announce their conventions in advance. If some rare convention is used, the partner of the player who has made the bid must say to his opponent, 'That bid has a special meaning. Would you like me to explain it?'
(3) More serious, a private understanding which the players have deliberately concealed. For example, a pair may make frequent use of a particular kind of psychic (i.e. bluff) bid. Once they begin to expect this, so that they deceive opponents without the risk of deceiving one another, they are on the borders of a private convention.

No-one had ever made a complaint of this sort against Boris and myself. It took me about 20 minutes to shave and dress after Albert's mysterious phone call. When I got downstairs I went along the passage towards the committee room and saw Swimer coming out. He looked white and strained, as he had since the beginning of the week. 'Oh, there you are,' he said. 'Will you come with me?' As I followed him I saw Boris in one of the public rooms nearby, puffing furiously at his pipe.

This was a meeting of the Appeals Committee. Geoffrey Butler, chairman of this committee, sat in the centre of the room. Mostly standing around at the back were Charles Solomon, President of the World Bridge Federation, R MacNab, President of the American Contract Bridge League, W von Zedtwitz, described as Vice-President Emeritus, and John Gerber, captain of the American team, not actually a member of this committee. 'This is Mr MacNab, president of the ACBL,' said Solomon in his gravelly voice. 'I think you know all the others. Will you take this chair?' Butler spoke first, to the following effect:

'I have the very unpleasant task of telling you that you and Boris Schapiro, whom we have already interviewed, have been under observation for several days. Mr Becker and other witnesses will say that you have been using finger signals to show how many cards you held in the heart suit. When you held a singleton heart you had one finger showing on the back of the cards, with two hearts two fingers, and so on. What have you to say?' My head whirled. This was something of a completely different order from the technical offences described above. 'I don't know what you are talking about,' I said abruptly. 'There's not a word of truth in it. I am tired of hearing this sort of accusation every time one plays against the Americans. It happened at Como, again at Turin, and now the same thing here. It is absolute nonsense.' These were quite different incidents, concerning different players. At Lake Como in 1958 Italy played the United States in a straight match for the World Championship and I was there as a journalist. Italy took an early lead and soon the Americans, particularly one very contentious player, were saying that the Italians were using illegal signals. Exactly how matters developed behind the scenes I cannot say, but the upshot was that all the players were required to hold their cards below the table during the bidding.

When the next session began in the open room, only neutral journalists were admitted and they were required to sit at a prescribed distance away from the table (lest they, too, were in the plot!). As may be imagined, play began in a highly charged atmosphere. Halfway through the bidding of the first hand the swarthy Giorgio Belladonna suddenly pushed back his chair, jumped to his feet (I thought he had cramp) and exclaimed in mock horror, 'Je peux voir les pieds de mon partenaire!' (I can see my partner's feet!)

I described this incident later on the television programme Tonight. The match came to an uneasy conclusion and some hostile articles appeared in the American press. The charge was not maintained officially, however. The player principally concerned in making the accusation was suspended and the Italians received an apology.

There had been a number of similar cases in championship play. An accusation made at Vienna in 1957 against two famous Austrian players, inadvisedly repeated in a book, led to a long legal process. The publishers eventually withdrew. Had the case come to court I would have been a witness for the plaintiffs – that is, for the players who had been accused and were suing for libel.

There had been two celebrated affairs in France. The first concerned a pair who had been notably successful in pairs events carrying money prizes, as they sometimes do on the continent. No-one professed to have observed anything, but suspicion arose because their record in partnership exceeded the world's estimate of their abilities. Their performance in the European championship was analysed and a pattern emerged which led experts to conclude that something was wrong. On this internal evidence alone the players were suspended. The other French case had an almost opposite history. Three observers maintained that they had intercepted signals, and after a long inquiry there was an equivocal verdict. Further study of the hands the pair had played on an earlier occasion strengthened the view that they were innocent, and in the end they were completely rehabilitated in public esteem.

British players also have been the target of such accusations. One or two members of an American team that played some unofficial matches in Britain in 1950 raised an outcry against a well-known pair. The 'evidence' was internal, such as a surprise lead from K-x against no-trumps which happened to find partner well at home. In the European Championship at Palermo in 1959 a question was raised against a British pair for no better reason than that one of the players had a habit of stroking his chin and making other gestures when in deep thought. The episode at Turin which I mentioned in reply to Butler was trivial in itself but of some importance now because it concerned Boris and me. It occurred in the 1960 Olympiad, won by France, with Britain second. Apparently an American kibitzer (spectator) professed to have observed that when we held up our cards to show them to spectators before the bidding began we held them in the right hand when we were strong, in the left hand when we were weak. A more obvious or naive way of signalling could scarcely be imagined. The American officials reported the allegation to the British tournament director, Harold Franklin. He promised to keep his eyes open when we got back to Britain and later wrote to the Americans to say there was nothing in it. Boris and I did not hear of the matter till Franklin told me about it several months afterwards.

Bea Tarlo, wife of the British captain at Turin, reminded me later of another incident at this tournament. I have the inelegant habit, in reflective moments, of chewing the lower strand of my tie. Bea, who throughout the fortnight sat beside me whenever we played in the open room, could bear it no longer: 'Darling,' she said, using the form of address she employs to all her friends, 'do put that tie away. You know what the bastards are like: they will say you are giving signals. They are watching you like hawks, I can sense it.' As soon as I mentioned Turin, Solomon intervened: 'This has nothing to do with anything that happened at Turin. I dismissed that from my mind a long time ago. It was the first thing I asked Mr Becker and he said he had never heard of it.'

Becker had played at Turin and his team had been heavily defeated by Britain in both the qualifying and final rounds. He had also played at Como and I dimly remembered that an article of his in the American Bridge World had suggested unfair play by the Italians. As to the present tournament, the only significant thing I had noticed was that he often turned full face to look at his opponents during the bidding. This is normally done, not for reasons of suspicion, but in order to gather any minute indication from an opponent's demeanour. Some people admire this quality, which they call 'table presence'.

Butler chimed in to say that he too had never heard of the incident at Turin. Then Gerber took up the tale:

'I first heard of the present affair on Friday morning,' he said. 'Mr Becker reported to me that early in the week he had observed what he described as suspicious hand movements by Mr Schapiro and yourself. He noted that you both held your cards in different ways at different times and concluded that signals were being exchanged. Observation was kept when you played against Italy on Friday afternoon and the same thing was noticed. Yesterday morning Mr Truscott reported to me that he and Mr Becker had broken the code. They had found a connection between the hand signals and the heart suit. I consulted with my deputy captain, Mr Kehela, and other officials, and we decided to inform your captain, Mr Swimer.

'Mr Swimer reported the matter to me,' said Butler. 'It was arranged that you should play against Argentina in the open room last night. I watched the second half of that session and what I saw confirmed what I had been told. Except for two hands where you held a void, and one or two occasions when my vision was obstructed, the signals throughout corresponded with the code as I had been told it.'

'I watched the first ten boards of the same session,' said Swimer, speaking for the first time. 'On every deal the number of fingers shown by both of you corresponded with the heart holding.'

The clichés about not believing one's ears are unequal to that moment. Was it possible? Was the British captain here not, as I had mistakenly supposed, to defend his players, but to support the accusation?

Had I been wise I would have reserved my defence, as the lawyers say. There were many common-sense arguments that would come better from a third person. Signalling at bridge is easy enough and anyone who gave his mind to it could evolve a simple and effective code which no-one would ever detect. They were making us out to be fools as well as cheats.

If I was going to say anything I ought to have asked what happened when we held no hearts or five hearts or six hearts, etc. Later all these gaps were plugged. And for some reason it did not occur to me to ask Butler and Swimer how, sitting behind me, they could judge with any certainty how many fingers I was showing on the other side of my cards. What I did say was:

(1) It might well be true that I held my cards in different ways at different times. I might also vary during the bidding of a single hand.
(2) What value was there in evidence produced by someone sitting at my elbow who could see what cards I held and could also see, when the hand was played, what my partner held? He would have every opportunity to correct any uncertain impressions.

(3) The only true evidence lay in the match records. 'Go through the records,' I told them, 'and see if there is any indication of collusive play. I don't recall any clever psychic bids or brilliant leads. I know we made a lot of mistakes, particularly against Italy. Do you think we couldn't have done better in that match if we had had a cheating system?'

This speech was the cue for the entry of a new witness. 'Mr Truscott has examined the match records,' said Butler. 'I think we ought to hear what he has to say.'

Alan Truscott now took the chair next to me. Had he been in the room all the time (as he said later)? I hadn't noticed him. But of course he would be there. He had been a prospective witness in the affair at Vienna when the Austrians were accused. He had emigrated to the States three years ago and now wrote for the *New York Times*. He pulled out of his pocket some scraps of paper on which he had written down a number of hands.

'I have not had time to examine all the records,' he said, addressing himself to me rather than to the meeting. None of the hands means anything by itself, but you reached every good contract in hearts and no bad ones, with one curious exception. That was a hand you played in One Heart with J-x opposite 10-x-x-x.'

He produced eight hands where it was contended that our bidding or opening lead had been influenced by improper knowledge of the heart distribution. In my opinion the hands were quite valueless in the sense attributed to them, especially as many relevant circumstances were not mentioned. To appraise a bid or lead one must know the state of the match, the exact inferences to be drawn from the opponents' bidding, and other such details. I answered him sharply but made little impression, for the committee members were not following these exchanges at all closely.

When Truscott had finished, Solomon brought the interview to a close, saying that the committee would ask to see us again later.

I found Boris in the room where I had seen him on my way in. 'What's all this bloody nonsense about?' he asked as I came up. 'God knows. I didn't know what to say, did you?'

'I just said it was balderdash,' he answered; or thereabouts. His interview had only lasted a few minutes.

As we were walking away, Swimer left the committee room and overtook us.

'I am going to put in the other four for the first session,' he said. 'I don't want you two to play until this business has been cleared up.'

None of the British team was in our dining room at lunchtime. Boris, beyond food, had a drink at the bar with Jeremy Flint. 'He was in a state of shock,' said Jeremy afterwards. 'He kept on repeating, "This is a nice state of affairs."'

I found a worried group in the hotel lounge before the afternoon session was due to begin. 'Nobody has told us what's happening,' said Konstam. 'All we know is that there has been some protest and that you and Boris are not playing.'

There were people standing around and I was not disposed to go into details. I told him not to worry and wished him luck. Jeremy Flint gave a description of what went on that morning and afternoon.

'Swimer simply told us we were going to play as a team of four throughout the day,' he said at the subsequent inquiry. 'He would not give any reason. At one point he said to the team, "I don't want you to have anything to do with Reese and Schapiro." I didn't realise it was so serious, or I would have insisted on a team meeting. As it was, I felt we were jockeyed out of any discussion and more or less steam-rollered into playing on.'

Many people who were sympathetic to Boris and myself said afterwards that they could not understand why the rest of the team did not back us up and refuse to play on; but as Jeremy said, for all he knew it was only a temporary storm and there seemed no sense in giving up the match to America. Win that and argue later. He had no idea, of course, that Butler and Swimer were intending to concede that match.

Later in the afternoon Boris and I were summoned to another meeting. This time it was the Executive Committee of the World Bridge Federation. Everyone who had been present in the morning was there, except for von Zedtwitz, who had left on other business. In addition, there was Dr Labougle of Argentina, C A Perroux, the Italian captain, T Hammerich from Venezuela, and General A Gruenther, Honorary President. The General, who had been Eisenhower's Chief of Staff during the war, opened the proceedings.

'I want you two gentlemen to feel that you have all the protection and advantages you would get under your own British system,' he began. It seemed unlikely.

Swimer and Butler now gave their evidence in more detail. Swimer said he had watched the first ten hands of the evening session against Argentina and had taken notes of the number of fingers showing on the back of the cards of both players. A pantomime followed in which he read from his notes and Hammerich, holding the match records, turned over the pages and echoed the numbers called out by Swimer. ('Reese three fingers' – 'Reese three hearts'; 'Schapiro two fingers' – 'Schapiro two hearts', and so on.) I call it a pantomime because (a) this supposed checking had already been tested out before we came in, and (b) as Swimer had been sitting at my side he already knew, without needing to see the match records, exactly what we both held on every deal. On one hand, according to his notes, we had both shown two fingers but held five hearts. He explained that according to his information two fingers on the back of the cards might show either two hearts or five.

Butler had watched the second half of the same session, taking Swimer's chair beside the table. He likewise read from his notes and Hammerich chanted the counterpoint. Butler's record was less complete. When the first hand was being played he was climbing through the ropes and had not observed the signals. On some occasions the holding had not corresponded to the code as he had been told it. Once he had omitted to make a note. Once his view had been obstructed by a spectator. ('That's right,' Boris said afterwards of this unlikely happening. 'A spectator jumped on to the table and got in Butler's way. I remember it distinctly.')

Twice I had shown four fingers but held a void (no hearts). Butler had noted that on the second occasion I 'lowered my left hand'. This he interpreted as possibly the gesture to show a void. He stressed that on several occasions he had not known even after the play of the hand whether Boris's holding had coincided with the alleged signal. Neither he nor Swimer had seen the match records until now.

Sitting near the table, it is very easy to see during the play how many cards any player has of any suit. Butler was saying that on most occasions he had not discovered at the time what Boris held. Despite the gaps in his story, the combined evidence was strong. I did not think this was the moment to challenge the witnesses directly. All I could do was repeat the arguments I had used in the morning.

'What strikes me, as a layman,' said General Gruenther at one point, 'is that you don't seem to make any violent rebuttal of these charges.'

'Well, you tell me, General,' I replied. 'How does one rebut this sort of accusation?' Indeed, that was the difficulty. If somebody says you made certain movements and there was a pattern to it, what can you answer? You can deny it, but you cannot disprove it. To take a comparable situation, suppose that when you come in after a game of golf you learn that someone has reported to the club secretary that on three occasions you improved your lie in the rough. How can you defend yourself? However much you deny it, the moment is past and the damage is irreparably done. Writers in the American magazines later drew unfavourable conclusions from the fact that I treated the accusation coolly. What did they expect me to do – wave my arms about like a Spaniard? I have too keen a sense of the ridiculous to perform the motions of conventional indignation. One might have expected Boris to be more demonstrative, but in moments of stress he relapses into paralysed silence.

I reminded the committee of our moderate performance against Italy. Turning to Perroux, I asked if the Italian players had any suspicion that we were not playing fairly. My question was repeated to him in French by the Argentine delegate. 'Absolutement non,' he replied.

On the subject of the internal evidence the committee seemed to have shifted its position. The hands were no longer put in as makeweight. 'You are not accused of winning illegally but of signalling illegally' was the argument.

Butler made one remark that was widely quoted:
'You have an ingenious mind,' he said to me. 'You invented the Little Major. Perhaps that was not as successful as you hoped, and so you invented the Little Heart.'

I report this remark as Boris and I recall it. When it was put to Butler at the Inquiry he did not agree that he had spoken the sentence about the Little Major not being successful.

According to the official report of this meeting, a lengthy discussion took place after we left. In the course of this, General Gruenther said he had been greatly impressed by the checking of the heart suit from the notes produced by Swimer and Butler. Three or four examples could well have been coincidence, but when in 19 successive hands the signals coincided his mind was convinced. This had not been the evidence by any means, but one can understand how he gained that impression.

Though the tournament was buzzing with rumours by this time, the general public, who were there in large numbers for the final day, had no reason to suspect that anything was amiss. Many of them, carrying programmes or copies of my books, asked for my autograph. May be more valuable than you think one day, I reflected.

During the afternoon's play the British team had dropped a few points to America, but with only 20 boards remaining the match was virtually won. Or so we thought; for in the press room, at least, everyone seemed to know that the British captain was going to concede the match a few boards from the end. It was being continued meanwhile for the benefit of the paying public. I was watching on bridgerama later in the evening when I was called out by Solomon and Butler.

Solomon and I went to a quiet corner and had an urbane discussion about the terms of the public statement that the committee proposed to make. In the draft he read to me, no finding was announced and the matter was referred to the British Bridge League. 'We can't sweep it under the carpet, you realise that,' he said, repeating a remark he had made earlier. I asked whether it was necessary to mention Boris and myself by name. Solomon said the committee had considered this but felt that the rest of the team might be compromised.

'Perhaps you could put it to them?' I suggested. 'I hardly think they would object.' Solomon undertook to consider this.

It was now past midnight and everyone was waiting for the announcement. I had some messages to write for my newspapers, so I decided to grasp the tiger by the tail and go along to the press room.

This was quite small, with space for about four people to sit and type on either side of a centre table. The committee was in session next door, When the typewriters were silent one could hear conversations from the adjoining room very clearly. Perhaps this, more than indiscretion on the part of some committee members, accounted for the frequent leakage of information. After a while a secretary came in, holding a sheet of paper on which the committee's statement was written. She hesitated when she saw me but I gave her no assistance. Then she read out the statement:

> Certain irregularities having been reported, the Appeals Committee fully investigated the matter and later convened a meeting of the Executive Committee of the World Bridge Federation. The Captain of the British team was present.
>
> As a result of this meeting the Captain of the British squad decided to play only K Konstam, M Harrison Gray, A Rose and J Flint in the remaining sessions and very sportingly conceded the matches against North America and Argentina. A report of the proceedings will be sent to the British Bridge League.

I made a note of the contents and went on with the article I was typing. Nobody said anything. Then Dick Frey, editor of the American Contract Bridge League Bulletin, went to a telephone three feet away from me and dictated to a news agency a full account of the affair, describing in detail the allegations made against us.

The committee had made a tiny compromise, it will be noted, in naming the other four players, not Boris and myself directly. Had the statement gone forth to the world in that form, with no adornment, the case would not have aroused so much interest and would not have been prejudged. 'Certain irregularities' covers a wide field. Perhaps Solomon and his colleagues thought they had found a formula to avert a worldwide scandal. If so, their illusions were soon to be dispelled. The local correspondents had already written their stories and were simply waiting for the 'off'. It is a curious fact, in the field of evidence, that when people read that someone has been charged with an offence they may take it or leave it; but once they are supplied with details of time, place and method, they attach themselves much more firmly to the accusation. When 'finger signals' were mentioned in the news agency messages, papers all over the world felt free to embroider on the official statement and from that moment we were 'dead ducks'.

Other correspondents who had been in the press room when the statement was read melted away so that they could transmit their messages more discreetly. When I looked up after finishing my daily piece for the *San Francisco Chronicle*, I was alone. Returning to the playing rooms I ran into Flint, in a state of mingled amusement and agitation. He and Konstam had made an excellent start against their American opponents in the closed room, but about half-way through the session on Bridgerama it had become evident that owing to a rare error in organisation the players had been wrongly seated. Konstam and Flint had been playing the same cards as Rose and Gray, so no comparison was possible between the two teams. Obviously they would not be asked to start again at this hour. A few minutes later the committee's statement was read out and the bridgerama audience learned of the British captain's 'very sporting' concession. As a result, Britain was placed fourth and last in the championship, behind Italy, North America and Argentina.

It required some nerve to stay around in the public rooms throughout this day and into the early hours. My friends thought it courageous, my enemies shameless.

3 A Change of Climate

LONDON TIME IS ABOUT five hours behind Buenos Aires time, so the story was too late for the morning papers. My first telephone call, at about 8.30am local time, was from the foreign editor of the Evening News. Almost every national paper followed. At the same time, local representatives of papers that had not printed a word about the bridge championship as such were clamouring for interviews. They spoke to Schapiro downstairs, then came up to me for five minutes that turned into 20 because of the long-distance calls.

I told them all substantially the same thing: that accusations of this kind were not uncommon; that we completely denied all the charges; and that I could not comment on the action of the British officials. They all wanted to know what plans Boris and I had for the future. Boris had already said that it was a miserable tournament anyway and he never wanted to play championship bridge again. I said I had not made up my mind about this.

At about midday I had to tell the telephone operator, 'No more calls.' Soon after, there was a knock at the door.

'Who is it?'

'Dick Frey. They told me you weren't taking any calls, Terence, but I have a proposition to pass on, which I think it might be to your advantage to hear.'

Looking heavy and owlish in his red dressing-gown, he sat on a fragile bedroom chair and with a we're-all-professionals-in-this together air related the proposition. The American magazine Sports Illustrated was doing a big coverage and was prepared to commission an article from me, giving my side of the story. The fee was generous. It was evident that Frey too had had a busy morning, turning over the wheels of professional journalism. Albert Dormer, a British colleague, told me of Frey's concern for publicity during the 1964 Olympiad in New York. The main excitement on that occasion was the refusal of the Lebanese and United Arab Republic teams to play matches against Israel. Bridge players are not interested in politics, but the teams were obliged to obey the instructions of their governments. Assisted by the fact that Omar Sharif, the film star, was captain of the UAR team, Frey got the dispute into all the newspapers. When Dormer remonstrated with him for pushing it so hard, Frey answered, 'But this is the first time bridge has been front-page news since Culbertson's day!'

Dormer told me of another amusing incident when he was Frey's assistant on the Bulletin. A customer wanted to advertise 'Bridge Jackets', which would carry chevrons and shoulder flashes denoting past achievements and master point status. They would also contain a sort of poacher's pocket for bridge accessories, from pencils to periscopes, from handbags to hand grenades. 'I don't think we can accept the advertisement until the merchandise is actually in production,' said Frey solemnly. The whole project, Bert insisted, was only just across the border of fantasy.

Reverting to Buenos Aires, Boris and I had a late lunch at the golf club with members of the Italian team and their friends, who were extremely sympathetic and succeeded in raising Boris's spirits. Back in the hotel, I wrote the piece for Sports Illustrated. I knew we would never be able to turn back the tide of American opinion, but I took the opportunity to express some of my feelings in a paragraph like this:

> What of the future? Schapiro says he will never play tournament bridge again. I haven't made up my mind about that. Certainly, in most ways there wouldn't be much to regret. I say nothing personal about the people involved in this case, but the world of tournament bridge is full of envious and evil-minded maggots that no self-respecting stone would shelter.

One compensating feature of this Monday evening was that Boris and I did not feel called upon to attend the official banquet, always an exceedingly boring function which starts late and proceeds interminably. We had dinner at the hotel and went for a long stroll. When we got back at eleven o'clock, dinner-jacketed stragglers from the cocktail party were still on their way to the banqueting room.

'You certainly cast a pall over the proceedings,' Jeremy told us the next morning. 'Even under the stimulus of alcohol nobody had much to say.'

The American papers reported with satisfaction that the British players and captain had received as great an ovation as the Italian winners. This was interpreted as a demonstration of sympathy for their misfortune in being associated with such villains. As individuals, the players were reacting predictably to the situation. Flint was loyal to us, and Konstam was obviously much distressed by the whole affair. Gray, who had won many championships in teams with Boris and myself, was being carefully neutral. He was asked by the Americans to write a piece about the internal evidence (i.e. the hands we had played) and did so, but not in a sufficiently one-sided way to satisfy them; his contribution was spurned. Rose, from the midst of the enemy camp, greeted me with mute sympathy, like a distant cousin at a funeral. No doubt the applause for the British team, from which the Italian party abstained, was a sign that the public was on the side of the accusers. Most of the local people were psychologically quite willing to accept the charges against us.

'It's your fault,' Boris informed me. 'You annoy them all with your aloof manner. It's the same at the European, you don't make any effort to mix with the other teams.' 'I can't talk their blasted lingo like you,' I replied childishly. 'Besides, I've got something better to do in the mornings than run round telling everyone how well I played the night before.' Boris speaks fluent German, French and Russian, and can carry on his style of amorous banter in Spanish, Italian and Danish. As to my alleged aloofness, this proceeds simply from the fact that I am not a naturally good mixer.

Later in the day the British team was due to fly to Rio de Janeiro to play two friendly matches against Brazilian teams. There was some talk of abandoning the fixture, but the general feeling seemed to be that as all the arrangements had been made, and the present troubles were no affair of the Brazilians, the team should go. This decision was much criticised later, on various grounds. Officials in Britain thought that Butler and Swimer should have shown a greater sense of urgency and returned straight home to make their report. Friends of Boris and myself could not understand the team going off on a holiday jaunt and leaving us to return alone. I must say it all seemed rather different at the time. Certainly we did not request any change of plan. Still crowded by the press, we had made arrangements to leave for London the following day.

Before the team departed, Swimer made one remark to Boris of a conciliatory nature. 'If you have any difficulty at Quents [a gaming club],' he said, 'let me know and I will do something about it.' We wondered what.

Some time in the morning the Italians bade us ceremoniously farewell. Last to shake hands was Walter Avarelli, a judge: 'Je suis toujours votre ami. Vous le savez.' By Wednesday there were only some Americans (from the bridge party) left in the hotel. They were civil enough. Solomon told me he was issuing to the press a denial of a remark attributed to him. The players, apart from those who had brought the accusation, maintained a 'we know nothing about it' attitude. Sammy Kehela told me he did not believe the accusation and was going to write to that effect in the Canadian papers. The Argentine players and officials avoided us during these last three days. Their attitude (as expressed later in a letter to the Bridge World by Arturo Jacques) seemed to be that their tournament had been spoiled and it was our fault.

The journey home took about 20 hours, with four stops and two changes of crew. Three times we listened to 'Miss Pennyweather, your stewardess', or one of her sisters, instructing us what measures to take should the aeroplane fall incapably into the ocean. The first English papers we saw were comparatively restrained, but that soon changed. As we left Lisbon, a kind friend in the seat behind us said in a smooth English voice, 'Perhaps you two gentlemen would be interested to read this?' It was a full-page spread of the 'Bridge Aces Say, "We are Not Cheats"' variety. I thanked him gravely.

Just what we expected at the airport I hardly know; certainly not what happened. We came off the plane to meet a battery of 30 cameramen, plus radio and television reporters. That we expected, but before we reached the Customs, in a passage-way far beyond the limits allowed to non-passengers, we saw Rixi Markus and Joan Durran (famous women internationals) advancing to throw their arms around us. A dozen more friends from the bridge world, and our closest friends outside bridge, were not far behind. Honor Rye, now married to Jeremy Flint, and another friend, Jack Ip, drove to London Airport instead of Gatwick. Ah well, the thought was there.

Before we left the airport we gave interviews on BBC and ITV. On the following day I was asked to appear in Tonight. The interviewer said he did not want to refer directly to the 'case', but it would interest viewers if I could give a general idea of how it was possible to cheat in tournament bridge. As there was a caption saying that we completely denied the allegations made at Buenos Aires, I saw no harm in obliging him. It is actually very easy to cheat at bridge without being detected. A simple gesture, a positioning of the hands or cards or head, can be used to tell partner whether one is weak, medium or strong in relation to the last bid made. A system of spacing between the cards held in the hand can convey any number of messages about strength or distribution. After writing down the contract at the end of the bidding a player can leave his pencil at an angle that will ask for a particular lead. Apparently it was somewhat naive of me to illustrate these possibilities. I learned later that simple-minded members of the public had gathered the impression that I was demonstrating our own cunning devices.

In general, the climate of opinion was completely different from Buenos Aires. In the next few weeks Boris and I had friendly calls and letters from every part of the world, including America. We had a hilarious welcome at Stamford Bridge, where the bookmakers know us well. The papers for which I write supported us without question. We learned that the committee of Crockford's had sent us a cable in Buenos Aires, which in fact never reached us. An article in a Liverpool paper by Gerald Abrahams, headed 'This Accusation Is Absurd', was posted on the club notice board. Abrahams, who is a chess expert, remarked that he would as soon believe that Botvinnik had surreptitiously nudged a pawn when nobody was looking.

Despite these encouraging signs I never made the mistake of thinking that players in Britain would reject the charges out of hand. For one thing, there were plenty who would be happy to see 'Reese and Schapiro' brought down from their eminence. For another, there were professional rivals who would calculate the possible opportunities for themselves should I be disgraced and lose my writing jobs.

In the lower ranks of the bridge community support was strong. People who had read my books and, perhaps, watched me play during the last 20 years were not disposed to accept that I had suddenly gone mad. And of course there were many who had strong opinions about the way in which the affair had been handled. Louis Tarlo made this point in a broadcast as soon as the news broke.

Official action would rest with the British Bridge League. The League is the respondent body to the European Bridge League, which treats Britain as a single unit. It has an executive council composed of delegates from the English, Scottish, Welsh and Northern Ireland Bridge Unions. An emergency meeting of the Council was called for May 30, the day after Butler and Swimer were due back from Rio. Butler went to the meeting with a copy of the BBL constitution under his arm and took his accustomed place in the Chair. He had his notes of the proceedings at Buenos Aires and was ready to give the meeting his version of what had occurred.

The Council members were not prepared to treat the matter in this way. It was pointed out to Butler that his status was that of a witness, and a new chairman was appointed for the business in hand. As no official report from the World Bridge Federation was available, the Council decided not to hear any unofficial report of the WBF meetings. Butler gave an external account of the sequence of events, the meetings that had taken place and the statement that had been issued. The press was told that no decision had been taken as no official report had been received. Another meeting was called for a fortnight later. Meanwhile Butler wrote up his notes into an official Report and sent it to Solomon for confirmation.

There were, I suppose, three ways in which the BBL might have tackled the affair:

(1) They could have accepted the Report, saying that if the evidence was good enough for the British captain and delegate, they were satisfied.
(2) They could have pointed to unsatisfactory features of the procedure, such as Butler's appearance as the principal witness in front of his own committee, and the fact that Boris and I had not had an opportunity to marshal our defence. Instead of trying to disentangle the conflicting evidence about who had seen what, they could have appointed a jury of international experts to examine the true and lasting evidence of the match records.
(3) They could institute a further investigation into all aspects of the affair. This could be done in two ways – either by appointing a committee themselves or by arranging for an independent inquiry.

The more legalistic members of the Council favoured the idea of an independent inquiry in which British forms would be observed. At the second meeting Louis Tarlo, a solicitor who had been captain of the team at Baden Baden, was able to report that Sir John Foster, QC, MP, had provisionally expressed willingness to act as chairman of such an inquiry. The League accepted this offer with gratitude and the press was so informed. Of the ten Council members who arrived at this decision, four told me in strict confidence that but for their own resolute intervention the Council would have settled for the first of the alternatives mentioned above, that of accepting the Report. I suppose they thought I would be grateful. We were expected to welcome the Inquiry as an opportunity to prove our innocence in open court, and so forth; nor could we demur to that proposition without seeming to lack confidence. But in fact the scheme contained certain hazards for us. An independent chairman could not know about the bridge world and the strange passions it evokes; and the technical evidence, so important for our case, would be, for him, second-hand evidence.

We had already chartered as our solicitor Eric Leigh Howard, a golfing friend of mine who is also a bridge expert. We now learned of a most generous offer by Tim Holland, of Crockford's, to support our defence in every way. This enabled us to instruct Counsel and we were delighted to find that Mr Leonard Caplan, QC, was able to take the case. I had met him before when he was acting for Crockford's in another matter.

Newspaper and magazine articles arriving from America gave us a clearer idea of the case we had to meet. The source for most of them appeared to be an article by Becker in the Journal-American. The heading was 'How J-A Expert Tripped Bridge "Cheats"'. Leaving out the trimmings such as 'shocking disregard for the honor code', this was his story:

In the very first match against Britain he became aware that there was 'something wrong' in our bidding. He watched each player closely, looking for a clue. He found himself unable to escape the conclusion that illegal messages were being transmitted.

Then he found the key. It was the way we held our cards. Most players have a consistent way of holding their cards but we varied our method with each hand. He knew there was a code involved but was unable immediately to figure it out. After the session he told his partner, Mrs. Hayden, of his suspicions and asked her to watch the 'finger movements' next time they played us. What she saw made her share Becker's suspicions.

When Britain played Italy in the open room the next day, the two of them recorded the number of fingers shown on each hand. Late that night they went with Truscott to a restaurant and went over the code carefully. At 4.00am they cracked it, discovering that the number of fingers shown outside the cards corresponded to the holding in the heart suit. Two, three or four fingers held wide apart, instead of close together, showed five, six or seven hearts respectively.

Becker went on to comment on the 'tremendous advantage' conferred by such a code. He ended by saying that the changing finger positions did not occur when we played with other partners. There were several discrepancies between this account and that of the Report. It was the first time we had heard of the 'separated fingers' theory, which had not been mentioned when we were in Buenos Aires. Substantially the same story appeared in *Life*, *Time* and other publications. The double-page spread in *Life* contained posed illustrations purporting to show how the signals were transmitted. Among them was the signal for a void, derived from Butler's interpretation of a perfectly normal movement on a single hand. Striking a new note, *Il Giorno* had a picture of Boris and a heading, 'Inglese Segnalava Con Pipa' (The Englishman Signalled With His Pipe).

The cartoonists had fun. One showed two Red Indians exchanging smoke signals between mountain tops with the caption, 'Four hearts … Double'. The American humorist, Art Buchwald, had a brilliant piece in the New York Herald Tribune. A home game is in progress and at one point George says to Fred:

'Why did you do that?'

'Do what?' Fred wanted to know.

'Scratch your head.'

'Because it itched,' Fred said heatedly. 'What do you want me to do when my head itches?'

'Why didn't you scratch your head before I dealt?'

'Because it didn't itch before you dealt. What are you trying to say anyway?'

'Never mind. It just seemed strange that I never saw you scratch your head before.'

'Well it so happens I scratch my head a lot. Do you want me to tell you before I scratch my head?'

'Why can't you scratch your head after the bidding?'

'I will if it itches after the bidding. But what's the sense of scratching if it doesn't itch?'

There was more trouble later when George picked up a glass with four fingers and bid 'Two Hearts'.

At our first consultation with Counsel we did not underplay the case that would be made out against us. Copies of the Report were available and from this we learned for the first time that the Executive Committee at Buenos Aires had taken a vote and found us guilty, except for Perroux, who had abstained. This was not generally known, even in America.

We understood that the British Bridge League proposed to instruct Counsel and, if possible, secure the attendance of Becker, Truscott and Mrs. Hayden to give their evidence.

'These three are very closely associated,' I told Caplan. 'For the purpose of evidence they are more like one person than three. Can't we make something of that?' Caplan is tall and dark, with a long, narrow face. You might put him down as an art connoisseur.

'Not really,' he answered. 'They are still three minds and three pairs of eyes.'

Boris mentioned various circumstances that might account for hostility on the part of some of the witnesses. 'Malice is a weak defence,' said Caplan flatly.

No doubt, but I didn't see how we were going to avoid it in the end. How otherwise could we challenge the evidence of people who would say they had intercepted signals which we knew we had never given? I tried again:

'You realise,' I said, 'that this is not like an ordinary case? The good name of the witnesses on the other side is as much at stake as ours. They will stick to their stories.'

'I have that very much in mind,' Caplan answered. Many people were asking, and continued to ask, why we did not promptly issue libel writs. Counsel advised against this for two reasons. At that time we thought the Inquiry would be concluded in two or three months, and it seemed better to wait until then. Secondly, if we began litigation it might be impossible to proceed with the Inquiry at all, as the whole matter would be subjudice.

Before we left, Caplan asked us to demonstrate how we normally held the cards. He also asked us to find as many photographs of ourselves as we could, taken during the bidding. This proved to be a far-sighted request.

A meeting of all the parties was held at Sir John's chambers to discuss the form of the Inquiry and make some progress with a time-table. The solicitor for the British Bridge League was John Pugh, a friendly rival in the bridge world for many years. He took me aside to say that he was open-minded about the case and had taken the job only because, if he did not, somebody else would. The BBL Counsel was Mr Simon Goldblatt, a comparatively youthful advocate with a knowledge of bridge that was to embolden him, with the aid of his advisers, to plunge deeply into the waters of analysis.

The BBL had already offered to provide an Assessor to assist the Chairman when technical bridge matters were discussed. We proposed a candidate also, and eventually Tony Priday and Alan Hiron undertook this role. Priday is a member of the BBL Council, a bridge correspondent and a British international. Hiron is also an international player and conducts the bidding competitions each month in Bridge Magazine.

There was some discussion as to whether the hearings should be private or public. There was no thought of admitting the general public, but it would have been possible to allow one or two pressmen to take notes of the proceedings. Alternatively, an agreed statement could be issued after each hearing. We (that is, the defence) retired to consider this. There were arguments both ways, but the most important seemed to be that Boris and I did not want to be continuously in the news. It was decided, therefore, that the hearings should be private and no statements issued, except of a very general nature.

Another point discussed was that of privilege. Since it was not, in the legal sense, a judicial inquiry, privilege was not automatic. Caplan at first said he would not advise his clients to grant immunity from slander actions to the witnesses on the other side. He later withdrew from that position, as I think he had always intended to do. It was understood that qualified privilege would attach to anything said at the Inquiry but not, of course, to any repetition outside.

Sir John Foster is tall and shaggy, with a slight suggestion of a scholarly gipsy, resonant of voice, most courteous in manner. He said he would like to sit with a colleague who would have the same status as himself and proposed General Lord Bourne. 'He is a man of the world with plenty of common sense. I sat with him on another case recently. I know his wife plays bridge. He's away at the moment, I haven't said anything to him, I thought I should put it to you gentlemen first.'

Slightly to my surprise, Caplan deferred acceptance of this suggestion. When we left he said:

'I thought it my duty to remind you that a distinguished General was on the committee that found you guilty. A significant remark of his is quoted in the Report, which will be part of the evidence in this case.'

It seemed to me impolitic to frustrate the Chairman's obvious wish, especially for a reason that would not be flattering to his judgment. I remarked that if their published memoirs were anything to go by, Generals were not inhibited from disagreeing with one another.

4 'Is that a Question?'

IT SOON BECAME EVIDENT that the pace of the Inquiry was going to be slow. Sir John Foster and General Lord Bourne both had their parliamentary duties, and Counsel are always busy people, so it was not easy to arrange times to suit everyone. Some weeks before the date arranged for the first hearing I had a telephone call from Rixi Markus, always in the centre of things.

'I think we have got a witness for you,' she said. 'Sammy Kehela is over here, seeing his family, and I told him about the Inquiry. He watched some of the play and he doesn't think you were guilty of anything.' Kehela had been a promising young player in Britain ten years ago. He was now the leading authority and player in Canada and had been appointed coach to the American team because of his expert knowledge of European bidding. Popular with everyone, he has the precise phrasing of a university lecturer.

I asked Rixi to put Kehela in touch with Eric Leigh Howard. An appointment was made for the following Monday. Eric phoned me that afternoon and said:

'This could be very important. Apparently Kehela watched on the last evening, the same session as Swimer and Butler. He had been told the "code" by Becker and when he began watching he was convinced that the charges were true. He observed, however, that on a number of occasions the heart holding did not correspond with the "signals". Later he looked through the match records and found nothing to support the idea that you had any sort of improper knowledge.' This was manna from heaven! Our great difficulty lay in countering the evidence on observation.

'We had only an informal talk,' Eric went on, 'and I shall have to get a full statement from him later. He is flying back to Canada at the end of the week, so we must arrange an emergency hearing. I have been on to the main parties and everyone except the General can manage Friday. We won't try to get the Assessors at this short notice.

This defence evidence would be out of turn, of course. The normal procedure is for prosecuting Counsel to make his opening speech and produce his witnesses before the defence begins. It was an anxious week. First, Kehela showed signs of witness's nerves. He had expected to give his evidence privately to Sir John, not at a formal hearing with solicitors and Counsel. At the last moment he nonplussed our legal department by declaring that he would not give his evidence in the presence of Boris and myself. He would not say why. 'Caplan is very worried about this,' said

Eric gravely. 'He says it's not safe to go into court unless we know the reason.' The mystery was cleared up a few hours before the hearing. Kehela did not want to say in our presence that at one period he believed the charges were true. Such delicacy of feeling was something new in the case.

'We're meeting at ten o'clock,' Eric informed me. 'As Kehela is being a bit temperamental it might be wise for you and Boris to keep out of sight to begin with. We will call you to the meeting when Kehela has finished.' We were assuming at this point that Kehela's evidence and cross-examination would take only an hour or two and that Mr Goldblatt would then begin his opening speech.

Boris and I paced the Temple gardens till about 11.20 the next morning. When we presented ourselves at 2 Hare Court we were much relieved to hear that our witness had arrived and the meeting was in progress upstairs.

Kehela's evidence-in-chief

No shorthand writer was present on this occasion, so my account of what was said is based on the notes taken by Counsel and solicitor. This is a summary of Kehela's evidence-in-chief:

'I was deputy captain and coach of the North American team and attended the championship in that capacity. I first heard of the allegations from Gerber after lunch on Saturday, May 22. Later in the afternoon Becker and Mrs Hayden gave me a fuller account of the code which Reese and Schapiro were supposed to be using. They told me that whenever they held one, two, three or four fingers on the back of their cards this meant that their holding in the heart suit was one, two, three or four cards respectively, but when two fingers were spread apart this meant a holding of five hearts, and three fingers spread apart meant a holding of six hearts. It was not known how a void of seven or eight cards were signalled.' We had read this part of Kehela's statement with some surprise. Up till then we had supposed that the 'spread fingers' theory was something they had thought of retrospectively. Swimer and Butler knew nothing of it, and it was not mentioned at either of the meetings in Buenos Aires. However, as Caplan pointed out, if we had lost one defensive point we had gained another: Kehela knew more about the alleged code than Butler or Swimer, so his conclusions were the more significant. Resuming the evidence:

'After dinner on Saturday I watched Italy and the US for a while on bridgerama and then went to the open room to watch the final session between Britain and Argentina. The boards I saw were numbers 125–134. When I entered the room Swimer was in the captain's chair, at Reese's side. Soon after, he surrendered his place to Butler.

'Of the nine or ten deals I watched, during which Reese and Schapiro held between them 18 to 20 separate hands, I found that in three or four deals there was complete coincidence between the fingers on the back of the cards and the number of hearts held by the players. In one deal, or perhaps two deals, there was coincidence in the fingers of either Reese or Schapiro. 'In all the other deals there was a conflict between the number of fingers on the back of the cards and the number of hearts held.

'The average holding per hand of any suit, including of course the heart suit, is three or four.

Both Counsel checked the records and found that one of us held three or four hearts on eleven occasions between boards 125 and 134. Kehela then commented on his subjective impressions: 'At the start of my observations I was completely convinced that Reese and Schapiro had been signalling to one another. I watched, not to find out if they had cheated, but how they had done so.

'I met Becker and Mrs Hayden after the session and at that point I was still assuming that the allegations were true. So far I had not analysed what I had observed.

'My doubts arose on the Sunday afternoon in the following way. Forquet, a member of the Italian team, asked me whether I had heard about Reese and Schapiro cheating and then the whole story came up. Forquet did not think they had been exchanging signals. He knew Reese and Schapiro well from having played matches against them and he felt that in the course of this championship they had played rather below their usual form against Italy.

Testimony of this sort – 'what somebody said to me' – is inadmissible according to the rules of evidence unless the remark was made in the hearing of someone on the other side of the case. As the Inquiry proceeded, a good deal of hearsay evidence was allowed. Unless there was a protest by Counsel, Sir John was generally willing to hear any evidence that would help fill in the picture.

'Towards the evening,' Kehela went on, 'I began to have serious doubts. I reflected that Britain had lost to Italy by a staggering margin and Reese and Schapiro had not produced their ordinary form. The signals, if any, did not appear to have done them any good. I reflected also that the last session against Argentina had been completely unimportant for the British team, who already led by 150 points.

'I began then to study the hands Reese and Schapiro had played together. The analysis did not show any indication of their having cheated.' The witness described one hand from the Italian match, one from the American, and one from the session he had watched against Argentina, which strongly suggested that we did not know how many hearts one another held.

'Another point that struck me,' he continued, 'was that Reese could not have failed to observe that Butler, sitting immediately behind him, was taking notes.' Kehela then described the manner in which he had conducted his observations:

'I was about three yards from the table. My view was completely unimpeded and Butler could not have seen more than I did. My method was to look at the hand of Reese or Schapiro and then walk round to the other side to make a cross-check.'

When Butler gave his evidence he maintained that Kehela could not have walked round in this way because of the 'dense throng' of spectators crowding the benches. There, as we shall see later, Butler was in error.

Kehela concluded his evidence-in-chief with a reference to the affair at Como which I have already described. On that occasion all the US players thought the Italians had been cheating. In general, he said, US players thought the standard of ethics was lower among European players. They thought players over here were more prone to give illicit signals and take advantage of hesitations.

Kehela cross-examined

Mr Goldblatt said early on that he intended, without disrespect, to refer to the main characters in the case by their surnames alone, so I feel free to do likewise.

Goldblatt, then, began his cross-examination with some questions about the hands that Kehela had brought up. The first was Italy 55, where as West I held at Game All:

$\spadesuit$ 10
$\heartsuit$ A 8 2
$\diamondsuit$ A Q 9 7
$\clubsuit$ J 8 7 6 4

South opened One Spade in front of me and I passed. It is close whether the hand is worth a take-out double, vulnerable. The sequel was calamitous. North raised to Two Spades, Boris held a useful hand but was unable to come in, and South bid Four Spades. They made this, while Six Diamonds was on for us. At the other table the Italians doubled on my hand and eventually, after competitive bidding, reached Six Diamonds. As it happened, they failed to make it, but we still lost heavily on the board as their other pair had made a vulnerable game at our table. For the purpose of the present case, the significant thing was that East held a doubleton heart. The main danger of doubling on the West hand is that in a competitive sequence partner may bid high in hearts on a four-card suit. If West knows that his partner has only two hearts (as according to the prosecution he did know) then this particular danger ceases to exist.

Furthermore, East is likely to hold some length in the minor suits, so there should be a playable contract somewhere. On this basis it is quite safe, and may be essential, for West to double. I don't say it was a particularly strong hand for us, but because of the result it would naturally catch the eye of anyone looking through the records. We could make a slam, yet we never entered the auction.

With a view to establishing that I would not double in any event, Goldblatt invited the witness to agree that I had the reputation of being a cautious bidder. Caplan intervened to say that if remarks were going to be made about our bidding tendencies, Schapiro and I ought to be present to hear them. We were accordingly summoned from downstairs and remained during this part of the cross-examination.

When Kehela stressed that the double would be quite safe if partner were known to be short in hearts, Goldblatt suggested that East might hold his main length in spades, not the minor suits. It was all a little unrealistic because the point was a simple one: in the absence of improper knowledge, the double is borderline; possessing knowledge of the doubleton heart, the double is sound tactics.

The next example quoted by Kehela was US 74, the deal previously acknowledged by Truscott. Sitting East/West, Schapiro and I held:

♠ A 7 4		♠ K 5 3
♡ J 9	N	♡ 10 6 5 2
◇ K J 10	W E	◇ A 9 8 4
♣ K 10 7 6 3	S	♣ 5 2

After East and South had passed I opened One Club as West. Boris responded One Heart, which I passed, and we were two down vulnerable. This was not a brilliant performance by a pair supposed to know how many hearts each other held. Obviously I could have rebid 1NT, which shows no extra values. Also, East could have responded One Diamond instead of One Heart.

The third hand, Argentina 130, concerned an opening lead. Our opponents were in 3NT and Schapiro, on lead, held:

♠ J 9 3
♡ J 10 7 6
◇ 7 5 3
♣ A Q 8

The player on his left, the dummy, had opened One Heart, and spades had been bid and supported. Boris chose to lead the seven of hearts through dummy's suit. As I had a doubleton, actually 5-2, the lead did not seem 'inspired'.

To every point that Kehela made about these hands Goldblatt produced a counter-argument. There were many crossed lines and Kehela began to show signs of impatience. Goldblatt, speaking very quietly and not looking at the witness, had a way of dropping remarks into the middle air that were interrogatory neither in tone nor grammar. He might say, for example, 'The partner could hold five spades, or even six' or 'Reese was not obliged to make another call on his hand.'

'Is that a question?' Kehela kept asking.

'They are all questions,' said Sir John helpfully.

While Kehela was giving his answers Goldblatt often conferred with his instructing solicitor, a more experienced bridge player. Kehela was annoyed.

'Do you want to hear my answer to your question or not?' he asked.

'Counsel are like that,' intervened Sir John quickly. 'They are quite accustomed to holding a conversation, taking notes, and listening to an answer all at the same time. It does not imply any disrespect.'

Goldblatt next invited the witness to consider the bidding on a different hand, Argentina 68. I suggested quietly to Caplan that this was not a proper course to take in respect of hands that the prosecution wanted to bring forward: the point was not what another expert would think of the bidding but whether, having heard our explanation, he would accept that what we did seemed reasonable to us at the time. Caplan interrupted to make this point. 'I am seeking to test the validity of this witness's evidence,' said Goldblatt, and no further objection was made.

This was Argentina 68, with the bidding at our table:

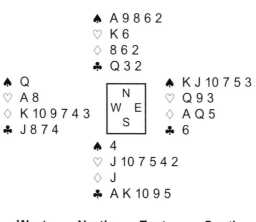

	♠ A 9 8 6 2	
	♡ K 6	
	◇ 8 6 2	
	♣ Q 3 2	
♠ Q		♠ K J 10 7 5 3
♡ A 8	N	♡ Q 9 3
◇ K 10 9 7 4 3	W E	◇ A Q 5
♣ J 8 7 4	S	♣ 6
	♠ 4	
	♡ J 10 7 5 4 2	
	◇ J	
	♣ A K 10 9 5	

West	North	East	South
Rocchi	*Schapiro*	*Attaguile*	*Reese*
Pass	Pass	1♠	2♡
3◇	3♡	3♠	4♣
Double	4♡	Double	All Pass

West led the queen of spades and with the assistance of the bidding, plus imperfect defence, I made the contract. At the other table West played in Three Diamonds, just making.

Goldblatt first made a tentative suggestion about North's Three Hearts. 'The normal expert bid,' said Kehela shortly.

'Then what about Four Hearts?' Goldblatt asked.

On the surface it might seem odd, for North has Q-x-x of his partner's second suit and only K-x of hearts, which he has already supported. The implied suggestion was that North would have passed the double of Four Clubs had he not known (illicitly) that South held six cards in hearts.

Here was an example of the very point I had asked Caplan to make. By a reference to my learned book, *Develop Your Bidding Judgment*, I could have established that in our partnership the bid of Four Clubs did not necessarily show a long suit at all and that North would have been quite wrong to pass with fewer than four trumps. Kehela answered adroitly enough that he would have passed the double of Four Clubs himself, but it was a matter of style and partnership understanding, there was nothing remarkable in the bid of Four Hearts. After the discussion of this hand Goldblatt indicated that he had finished his questions on technical matters, and Boris and I were asked to withdraw. It had been an entertaining session.

Turning to the matter of observation, Counsel asked Kehela whether the number of fingers on the back of the cards tended to vary. Kehela agreed that they did vary but were mostly three or four. In the majority of cases where he observed coincidence between fingers and hearts held, there were three or four hearts. 'As to whether I also observed absence of coincidence, the answer is "yes". What happened for instance was that I looked at the back of Schapiro's cards, where he held three fingers, and I found that his heart holding was different. I said to myself, "Not this time." I was not greatly surprised, because the match was not crucial.'

Kehela's next answer crossed one of our intended lines of defence:

'When I did see what I thought to be signals the fingers tended to remain the same. During the bidding the fingers remained static.' Part of our case was that we might hold the cards in different ways at different times during the bidding. We were going to suggest that the witnesses, particularly Butler and Swimer, might have been affected by seeing the number of hearts we actually held. Asked why he did not intervene on the day of the committee meetings at Buenos Aires, Kehela explained that his doubts arose only later in the course of that day.

'At the time when I was watching I did not think the result of my observation was critical,' he said. 'I studied the records later and thought there had been a miscarriage of justice.

'I was not casual in watching, though my recollection may be casual.'

In other words, what he saw, he saw, though he did not analyse it at the time.

'I was well able to recognise the absence of coincidence,' he continued, gathering strength. 'I knew the alleged signal for five and six cards. I saw fingers spread when three or four cards were held. 'At least six hands did not correspond with the signals. This is a snap recollection. I had no difficulty in observing at any time. I was there throughout the second half of the final session. Whilst still in Buenos Aires I told Gerber, Solomon and others that I was not convinced. Garozzo (another Italian player) told me the same. I told Truscott my doubts. Later in Toronto I communicated with a number of people from the press and also wrote to various magazines expressing my doubts. In my mind there is a strong doubt.

'I want to make it clear that though my evidence is favourable to Reese and Schapiro I came here of my own volition simply as a friend of the court.'

That was the end of the cross-examination. Caplan asked only one question in re-examination and obtained this answer:

'I am satisfied that Reese and Schapiro were not using signals throughout the session I watched.'

That was rather more than the witness had said at any time during his evidence-in-chief.

There had been a break for lunch earlier on and it was too late in the afternoon now for any further proceedings. Boris and I had already left. Later in the day we phoned Kehela and thanked him for everything he had done. He left for Canada the following day.

Legally minded friends, knowing in general what Kehela's evidence had been, assured us that we could not lose the case after this. I realised that was putting it too high. His early evidence especially had been somewhat vague; it was not as though he had been able to say that on a specific hand he saw such and such a position of fingers, not coinciding with the heart holding. It was also unfortunate that his period of observation covered that of Butler only and not Swimer. We could certainly argue, however, that the different impressions received by Kehela and Butler proved that this sort of observation was open to error. If Kehela had watched the same hands as Swimer there might have been a similar conflict.

We did not know that later witnesses were going to suggest to the court that Kehela's evidence had been false from beginning to end.

5 Observation and Inference

IN THE MIDDLE of July I went to Deauville for the bridge and golf tournaments, as I do every year. The leading continental players were all friendly. Sessions of the Inquiry had been fixed for July 20 and 21 and it was expected that the American party would be coming over to give their evidence at the end of the month.

While in Deauville I learned from a *Sunday Telegraph* reporter that the Americans would not, after all, be appearing at the end of July and for one reason or another would not be giving their evidence before the last week of September, at the earliest. In August they wanted to play in their 'Summer Nationals' and in September there were difficulties at our end. I described the delay as 'insufferable and iniquitous'. Schapiro, interviewed in London, said he felt like consigning the whole lot, Americans and British Bridge League, to another place. It was true, one tended to forget that this was not a criminal case; no-one could force us to attend this or any other inquiry.

When the prosecution opened its case on July 20 we were a full complement. It was the first time we had met General Lord Bourne, one-armed, rugged and genial. He had been GOC Berlin at the time of the airlift and later C-in-C Middle East Land Forces. Sir John Foster was Conservative MP for Northwich and in the previous Government had been Under-Secretary of State for Commonwealth Affairs. After an outstanding career at the Bar he had specialised in arbitration.

We had to move the furniture around to make room for everyone in the cluttered lawyer's room. Sir John and the General sat on one side of a large table, faced by Goldblatt and the two solicitors. Caplan sat at the left of the table, with Schapiro and myself behind him. The shorthand writer sat at the opposite end, later yielding place to the various witnesses. Tony Priday, smiling enigmatically behind his copy of the match records, occupied an armchair on the right of Sir John, and Alan Hiron, painfully deprived of his Sherlock Holmes pipe, sat on the left of the General. The proceedings were a mixture of formal and informal. Counsel did not stand to make their speeches, but nobody smoked.

Opening speech for the British Bridge League

Goldblatt began by defining the charge and reading various Passages from the Laws of Contract Bridge to establish that the accusation was one of deliberate cheating and not simply an infringement of a rule of the game. Finger signals, he pointed out, were of a different order from the offence known in the Laws as 'the giving of unauthorised information'. This preamble seemed hardly necessary to me, but I suppose it is a habit with lawyers, when formulating a charge, to relate it to some ancient statute.

After describing the order of play in the championship and giving some account of the scoring, Counsel came to the central part of his Case, making a distinction between the case on observation and the case on inference.

'The prosecution contends', he said, 'that cheating was taking place throughout each session at which Reese and Schapiro were playing together. For the purpose of proof one must divide the case into two parts. One part is observation and the second part is inference. There are a number of hands where the finger movements of Reese and Schapiro were directly observed by witnesses whom it is intended to call. They will be able to tell you what the signals were which were given. But this direct evidence of observation covers a small percentage only of the 198 hands that Reese and Schapiro played together. If that evidence satisfies you, of course, it is enough by itself to establish the case of cheating.'

Yes, we expected him to say that. But suppose the evidence of our witnesses, based on the match records, established that we could not have been operating any code? Where would that leave everybody?

'The case on inference,' Goldblatt continued, 'is that we say only, working through the 198 hands that these two played together, certain bids and certain plays – mainly bids but occasionally plays – were suggested by knowledge between these two players of the division between them of the heart suit. I make no secret of the fact that the case on inference is necessarily a much weaker case than that under the heading of observation.'

Counsel described the events leading up to the observation:

'It was not until the third day, the Monday, that any suspicion arose. It was aroused in the mind of the American player Becker, who is one of the players invited over here to give evidence of what he saw. Beyond consulting his partner, Mrs Hayden, at the end of this session, US 29–48, there was no further action taken about it until the next time these two Americans played together against Reese and Schapiro, which was, in fact, on Thursday, May 20. We shall be hearing evidence from Mrs Hayden of how she changed from scepticism to conviction as a result of what she observed during that session.

'Having consulted together after the end of play on that day, Becker and Hayden decided to bring someone else into the picture. The person they chose was Alan Truscott, a former British international, now living in America and bridge correspondent of the *New York Times*. They also informed the American captain, Gerber. On the next day, Friday, when Britain was playing Italy, Becker, Hayden, Truscott and Gerber all watched part of the session, but as it turns out the only person who took any notes from that session was Hayden. I do not have any copies of the notes that she took, but it is hoped she will in fact be bringing them over with her when she comes.

'After the end of play on the Friday Becker and Hayden, plus Truscott, got together to try and work out the meanings of the signals they had been observing, the signals being a use of either one, two, three or four fingers held by each of these players behind their cards during the course of the auction. It was in the early hours of Saturday morning that Hayden came up with the beginnings of an answer. She remembered two hands on which one finger had been shown by one or other player. The one-finger signal was much the rarest of the signals which had been observed. On both occasions, US 51 and Italy 120, the player who had given a one-finger signal was holding a singleton heart. They went on to consider the two-finger hands. They discovered two hearts or five hearts held in every hand where the notes recorded a two-finger signal by the player concerned. Following on from there, it was found that three fingers corresponded with the holding of three hearts and four fingers corresponded with the holding of four hearts. Either then or later, but probably then, it was also worked out that the difference between a two-heart and a five-heart holding would be signalled by keeping the two fingers together for two hearts and spreading them apart for five hearts.'

Sir John asked about the signal for six hearts, and Caplan wanted more precise information about the spread fingers and the time when this was worked out. 'I think one should know at this stage,' he said, 'what is the prosecution's case as to when this alleged code was completely broken, so that one may know when people were told "here is the whole code" as distinct from "here is part of what we think is the code".'

'I cannot give the exactitude of this,' replied Goldblatt carefully. 'The witnesses will be able to give us that.'

What puzzled Boris and myself, as the story unfolded, was why we had heard nothing at Buenos Aires of these notes allegedly made by Mrs Hayden. She had not given evidence before the committee and the Report made no mention of any notes.

Goldblatt then moved on to the session against Argentina on the Saturday evening:

'The reason why I am dealing with the matter in this way is that there were observations made by other people during the final session where Reese and Schapiro played together, that is, Argentina 125-144. The British players [he meant the captain and delegate] were brought into it for the first time then. It will appear from their evidence that at that stage they did not know the code for a void, or for a six-card holding or above.'

Lord Bourne: 'About this code which you have described, it is all a matter of conjecture so far. Was this entirely confidential among the three Americans?'

Mr Goldblatt: 'The cracking of the code was done by the three Americans together and at the time when they worked on the code the only other person to know about the allegations was the American captain, Gerber. By the middle of the next day the British players had been brought into it. The British captain, Swimer, and what one might call the British Official, Butler, both made direct observations during the final Argentina session, boards 125-144. So what I have been giving you is a tale of the gradual building up of suspicion, evidence, inference, and of course the gradual expansion in the number of people who knew about it.'

Counsel thought that seven or eight, perhaps ten, people knew of the allegations by the time of the session against Argentina. Lord Bourne sought confirmation that there was only one session at which the suggested code could have been tested out.

Mr Goldblatt: 'That is right. But depending on the evidence of Hayden and the notes she took, there will be other hands and other sessions for which records of finger signals existed.'

Caplan was interested in the fact that Hayden had actually been playing at the time when she noted the first of the one-finger signals, US 51.

Mr Goldblatt: 'Yes, she was playing during US 49–62 on Thursday and she was playing again during the following session, US 63–76.'

Lord Bourne: 'The next day she was fully occupied playing?'

Mr Goldblatt: 'The next day she and Becker were at leisure for the first two sessions.'

Lord Bourne: 'They had time to think about things.'

The General had a gift for making significant remarks that could be taken in more than one way.

Caplan enquired whether, at the time when Swimer and Butler made their observations, they had been told what was the suggested code for five hearts. Goldblatt was unable to give the exactitude of that either. 'They will have to tell us about that,' he said.

Counsel then turned to a new subject, that of probabilities. He wanted to establish that a random coincidence between fingers and hearts, repeated over a series of deals, was virtually impossible. According to Alan Hiron, a mathematician, the method of calculation was incorrect; it was not important, for we had no intention of pleading coincidence.

Reverting to matters of observation, Goldblatt stated that one of the witnesses would say he had watched Schapiro playing with a different partner from myself. During that session Schapiro had held his cards in the same way for every hand, in each case with four fingers behind the cards.

Counsel's next point was that the 'movement of fingers' must have been something different from the ordinary to have attracted attention in the first place.

Mr Caplan: 'My learned friend said "movement of fingers". I assume he is still referring to the way the cards were held as distinct from some movement while the cards were held?'

Mr Goldblatt: 'The variation between fingers on one hand and the next is what I mean.'

Sir John Foster: 'Is it a permanent signal or one that was made at the beginning that is alleged?'

Mr Goldblatt: 'So far as I am instructed about this, the signal was held for the majority of the bidding, not for the whole of the bidding. It ceased when the play began, but it is fair to say that you will probably be shown one photograph that appeared in a magazine of an identifiable hand at the stage of the opening lead.'

This turned out to be a photograph from Time of June 4, taken when the opening lead had just been made on US 32. Schapiro in fact held a singleton heart on this deal and presumably it was going to be suggested that the way he was holding the cards corresponded to the one-heart signal. The photo, which was produced, was not very clear. Schapiro appeared to be gripping the cards between thumb and forefinger, but all four knuckles were together and on the same plane. It seemed to us that it could be interpreted as a signal for four just as easily as for one.

For the past 20 minutes Goldblatt had been attempting to move on to the next part of his case, that concerning inference, but had been recalled by further questions about observation. After some preliminary remarks about the nature of bidding he expressed the case as follows:

'Since knowledge of the heart distribution is only one factor out of many that determine a player's bid, it is fair for me to say that I cannot put forward any single hand on which I can say quite positively that unless they had known the hearts in each other's hand they could not have bid this hand the way they did. One cannot put it as high as that. What one can say – and what I shall try to demonstrate in going through the hands – is that in a number of hands the bidding seems to indicate as a probability some knowledge of the heart suit beyond what could have been gained by normal inferences. In some hands you may find the probability much stronger than in others.'

Counsel then made a somewhat surprising announcement. 'I have given a great deal of consideration as to the proper way to present the comments on the individual hands, he said. 'What I propose to do is to refer to particular hands in the course of my opening, to specify the sort of inference which I say is to be drawn, or to specify the bid which I criticise in the course of that hand. Then I propose to invite you, Sir John, to ask your assessors to advise you in saying whether that hand will or will not assist you. I have chosen this course in preference to putting the hands to experts who could give a much more authoritative view than I can, because it seems to me that it is only fair that the assessors should give their views impartially without any waiting or weighing of expert evidence about them.'

H'm. That brought us back to the point I had asked Caplan to raise when a new hand was put to Kehela. It would be impossible for the assessors to make any fair pronouncement without hearing our reasons for the action we took. You cannot analyse a bid at bridge in the impersonal way that you may be able to analyse a move at chess. Whether or not he perceived this, Sir John did not respond to the suggestion.

'Would you let Mr Caplan answer you and then we will discuss it, but not at the moment. We will just listen to what you have to say and have no views.'

Caplan indicated that he would bring forward expert evidence as to the significance of the bidding and play. It was agreed that the assessors would not be asked to give their opinions until a later stage.

Sir John then sought to discover whether Goldblatt intended, in his survey, to draw attention to inferences of the opposite kind. The essence of Counsel's reply was that he would think it right to draw attention to any contrary indications in the hands he put forward. 'But I am not proposing,' he said, 'to draw your attention to hands which apparently favour the defence, because my learned friend will be much more capable than I of making use of these hands in his clients' favour.'

Mr Caplan: 'It will be my duty to put those.'

Mr Goldblatt: 'I am sure my friend will do so as a matter both of duty and capability. I am prepared to concede that advantage.

It was clear that both Counsel looked forward to jousting on this unfamiliar ground.

Goldblatt intimated that he would begin with the hands that in his submission contained the strongest inference of additional knowledge about the heart suit. At the apex of his case he placed Italy 18, where at one stage Schapiro made a successful psychic bid of Two Hearts when holding only two small hearts.

We all had photocopies of the match records, but the bundles were awkward to handle and the less experienced bridge players naturally took a long time to comprehend the arguments advanced by Counsel. We had looked at only three hands, taking about quarter of an hour over each, when it was time to finish for the day.

When we met again next morning, Goldblatt resumed his analysis of selected hands. After the fourth example he said: 'The hands to which I am now going to pass are hands which I say raise suspicion but less strong inferences than the four I have dealt with.' From time to time he announced a further decline in the quality of suspiciousness.

The analysis continued up to lunch and when we returned from the interval we found Swimer in attendance. This was a slight shock because we had expected Butler to be the first witness and had planned, in the course of cross-examining Butler, to do some undermining of Swimer. Goldblatt had not finished his opening address, however. By the time the afternoon ended he had drawn the court's attention altogether to 21 deals. This was his introduction to the 21st:

'The last hand, if we can come to it, is Italy 48. This is the only hand on which I submit that the play beyond the opening lead may have been influenced by knowledge. Perhaps I should just interpose a comment as to why this is the only hand where one can find that the players have been influenced possibly or probably. The reason is that very often, by the time you come to play a hand, and after the dummy goes down, it is possible to work out the distribution of your partner's hand, even if you do not know exactly where the honour cards lie. The later one gets in the play the more one knows both as to the distribution and honour cards. It is often that by the second or third card one has a complete count of the two hands that are not in sight.'

Well, I don't know; I don't find the game as easy as that. It was one of the strongest points in our defence that the prosecution could point to only one hand out of 198 where we had apparently benefited; and analysis would show there was nothing in that hand either.

At the end of the session I spoke for a few minutes to Caplan and Leigh Howard on the landing upstairs. When we came down Boris was outside the waiting room.

'Swimer was still there when I went in,' he said. 'He told me he had been waiting for two hours. He has only just left. Look, it's pouring with rain. And he hadn't got an umbrella.'

In the next few days it was confirmed that the Americans would be over during the week beginning Monday, September 27. Sessions were fixed meanwhile for August 5 and 6. Swimer would be away but we expected to complete Butler's evidence during those two days.

When we assembled on August 5 we found that owing to an oversight nobody had told the General the date for this session. There seemed no alternative but to continue without him. Goldblatt thereupon resumed his catalogue of suspicious hands. From the way he had introduced the last hand of the previous session, I for one certainly thought he had come to the end of his list. However, I had observed him reading an article by Alphonse Moyse in the American Bridge World at the end of that session, and no doubt this supplied him with further ideas. The first of the new assortment was Italy 54, where I had the opening lead against a contract of 3NT. An exact knowledge of the inferences to be drawn from the Italian bidding was important here, and I was satisfied then and now that my choice of a heart was normal and correct. When it was represented as evidence of collusion I scribbled a note for Caplan, 'Ask him what I ought to have led.'

Mr Caplan: 'I wonder if my friend could help. As West has got to lead something, perhaps one would understand the point better if one understood what it is suggested he ought to have led instead of a heart.'

Mr Goldblatt: 'My friend can make what point he likes about that particular one. Probably the choice would be between hearts and spades on that bidding, but any one of the suits might have been selected for a lead.'

We repeated these tactics a little later when Boris's bid of Four Spades on Argentina 44 was criticised.

Mr Caplan: 'That is where I would be grateful if my learned friend would say what is the correct thing, if this is suggested to be a thing done by illicit information, which should have been done by North.'

Mr Goldblatt: 'I know that my learned friend would like me to put forward all the answers as well as all the questions in the course of my opening.'

Mr Caplan: 'I do not understand the criticism that says "you should not have done that" unless One understands what the player should have done.'

Sir John Foster: 'Well, we shall hear … In match points do honours count?'

Changing the subject, almost!

Boris's patience, never extensive, was stretched beyond its limits during this period. 'Why don't you tell him?' he kept whispering to me, meaning that I should prompt Caplan how to refute the prosecution's examples. But this was not the time, as a matter either of procedure or tactics.

'I now pass into my lowest category of hands,' Goldblatt said next, ignoring the smiles of those of us who thought he had already scraped the bottom of the barrel. 'My lowest category of hands, where the significance is less than in the ones I have been discussing and the action taken may be a perfectly ordinary choice by any of the players.'

In that case, how could it support the charge? Goldblatt was saying in effect: 'I agree that the bid or lead I am criticising was in itself reasonable. It is, however, a bid that a player knowing the heart distribution would be inclined to favour. Thus it is some evidence that the players did know the heart distribution.'

Caplan pointed out that this would be true only if the selection of hands were impartial and included all occasions where such a decision might arise. Goldblatt was for a time unwilling to accept this proposition. He made one singular remark:

'I would like to say that I have not carefully selected particular hands. I have been through these hands in an endeavour to find the ones which would give you, Sir John, the most assistance in the assessment of the value of the prosecution's case. The argument went on for quarter of an hour, Goldblatt maintaining that his examples established a pattern, and Caplan complaining of 'coyness' because Goldblatt would not address himself to the question: Was it contended that his selection of examples covered all the hands where a decision about the heart suit had to be made?

Eventually Caplan broke through.

Mr Goldblatt: 'I think I can deal with the question, because now I understand it. I thought I made it clear. I was leaving it to my friend to bring in for the defence the hands he suggests went the other way owing to lack of knowledge about the heart suit.'

Mr Caplan: 'This selection does not, then, show a pattern over the whole lot?'

Mr Goldblatt: 'We shall be able to see the pattern at the end of the day.

Sir John Foster: 'It will all come out in the wash.'

After his 35th example Counsel began his summing-up. Speaking of the degree of proof required to substantiate the charge, he said:

'If, at the end of the day, you come to the conclusion that the case on inference is, to put it at its lowest, consistent with the observation, I will invite you to say that the case has been clearly proved to the appropriate standard.'

Earlier he had put it differently, but now he seemed to admit that the case on inference must be, at least, consistent with the charge of illicit communication. We were hopeful that we would be able to convince the court that the evidence from the match records was not consistent with the theory that each of us always knew how many hearts the other held.

Nothing had been said so far about the form of the eventual judgment. Was there going to be a short verdict of guilty or not guilty, or a report in which the tribunal would set out its findings in more detail?

Mr Goldblatt: 'I think that concludes the matters which I want to cover in opening, unless there are any further aspects …?'

Sir John Foster: 'The only one is as to what form of report you want – or judgment? If you would like to reserve …

Mr Caplan: 'I have not considered it myself in detail. I would have thought that unless there is some useful purpose in making a decision now, perhaps ...

Sir John Foster: 'I see. One has to consider that the people who requested the Inquiry to be made are the British Bridge League. They may want it in some form.'

Finally Goldblatt informed the court that he had received an affidavit from von Zedtwitz. Sir John was inclined to think that the same test should be applied as in a criminal case, where such a document, giving no opportunity for cross-examination, would not be admitted. He asked Counsel to discuss the matter between them. Then we adjourned.

There were two main points that struck us about the opening speech. First, we were content that so much time had been spent on the internal evidence, the hands. If the prosecution had not brought these up, we would have had to. The second point concerned the manner in which the case bad been presented. When it was first announced that the BBL would be legally represented at the Inquiry we were given to understand that this was simply a matter of form – that Counsel would act as an *amicus curiae*, a friend of the court who would simply lay the evidence before the tribunal. Goldblatt first introduced the word 'prosecution' in this way: 'The prosecution's case – if I may call myself the prosecution, and I think it may be convenient for the purposes ...' It was soon apparent that the word was apt as well as convenient. We were quite willing to play it that way and I am sure Counsel acted with complete correctness according to his instructions. It could have been done differently, I put it no higher.

I remarked above that Goldblatt had possibly gathered some additional hands from the American Bridge World. I had been a fairly regular and, I think, a valued contributor to this magazine for about 20 years. Despite this, editor Moyse had written a completely hostile account of the affair at Buenos Aires. The ACBL Bulletin, which Dick Frey edits, carried a half-page advertisement for the Bridge World, exhorting the 180,000 odd League members to purchase the July issue and read 'The Case Against Reese and Schapiro'. Charming! I was not mollified by the fact that Moyse later published a counterblast by Rixi Markus. This, too, was to have dramatic consequences.

By contrast, Ewart Kempson, editor of Britain's *Bridge Magazine*, signified his distaste for the whole affair by declining to publish any reports on the 1965 World Championship. 'The sooner this contest is abandoned,' he wrote in his June editorial, 'the better it will be for the game.'

In September Kempson quoted some ecstatic comments by Moyse about the part played by Swimer and Butler. 'Before I go further, Moyse had written, 'I must pay due homage to the conduct of these British gentlemen, Swimer and Butler. Shocked, dismayed, perhaps even feeling besmirched, they carried on with dignity and honour.'

Ewart commented: 'We make soft woollen cloth in Yorkshire. It is known as flannel.'*

---

* Flannel is a colloquial term in some parts for empty flattery. Ewart Kempson, unhappily, died early in 1966.

6 'I'll be Judge, I'll be Jury'

THERE WAS STILL the afternoon before us when we broke up at the end of Goldblatt's speech and we expected to complete Butler's evidence during the next day and a half. But there was a slight hitch. When Boris and I returned from lunch and joined Eric Leigh Howard in the courtyard I could see he was much amused about something.

'There has been a new development,' he said as we approached. 'In fact, two new developments. First, Butler did not realise that he would be required tomorrow and will not be available. What is more important, he is unwilling to give his evidence at all today. It appeared that there were two reasons for this. First, Lord Bourne being absent, Butler was unwilling to deploy his talents in front of only one member of the tribunal. Secondly, he was unhappy at the prospect of a long interval between examination and cross-examination.

Goldblatt explained the situation to Sir John as soon as we got upstairs.

'Sir John, we are never free from trials and tribulations. I now understand that Mr Butler, though he is here today, is not free tomorrow. Secondly, he has raised a personal voice in favour of giving his evidence in front of both members of this tribunal and, so far as possible, consecutively. I suppose one ought to show some consideration to each of the witnesses in so far as possible, where they have personal viewpoints. That being so, I am now putting it forward.'

Caplan protested and Sir John remarked that it was for the two Counsel, not for a witness, to be concerned about the number of judges. Butler was asked in and Sir John said:

'Mr Butler, we are very anxious to have your evidence today in chief, and also it is such a discomfort for everyone else, so if you would not mind ...'

Mr Butler: 'I would like to put my point of view if I may, which is that I should like really to give my evidence before both members of the Court because obviously the impression which is made by a witness is of some value to the evidence.'

Sir John Foster: 'Your cross-examination will be in front of both.'

Mr Butler: 'Whatever impression I make upon you will not be made on behalf of your fellow.

Sir John Foster: 'The cross-examination will.'

Mr Butler: 'Not my evidence-in-chief, which seems to me of some value. Secondly, it seems to me that evidence I now give, if I am going to be cross-examined on it in eight weeks' time, I may have forgotten.'

Yes, that would be awkward.

Sir John pointed out that a shorthand note would be available and that in any case this was really a matter for the Counsel on both sides.

Mr Butler: 'I do not wish to incommode the Court.'

Sir John Foster: 'We are very grateful. You cannot come tomorrow?'

Mr Butler: 'No, I have put off something from today till tomorrow. I thought today would be sufficient. I was told it would be.'

Sir John Foster: 'Lawyers are longer than laymen. It always takes longer.'

Butler's evidence-in-chief

A provisional date, not too far ahead, was fixed for the next hearing, and Butler's examination began. The first five minutes were occupied by a recitation of his numerous offices. Then Goldblatt asked:

'When were you first aware of any allegations being made against Reese and Schapiro?'

Mr Butler: 'I was first notified by von Zedtwitz at lunchtime on Saturday, May 22 that Swimer wished to see me on an urgent matter. I went to his room and he said that Truscott was coming in to give certain information on an alleged charge of cheating made against Reese and Schapiro.'

Mr Goldblatt: 'What took place after that?'

Mr Butler: ' Truscott came in and said that the Americans had told him, in particular Jay Becker, that they had noticed some peculiar hand movements made by Reese and Schapiro on the Monday evening when they were playing against the Americans. Becker went on to say, so Truscott told me, that he had watched them again on Wednesday and had noted certain finger movements which he had not been able to interpret. But he had connected them with the heart suit. Truscott examined various hands on the Friday night and early on the Saturday morning he had discovered what he believed to be a code of signals. He then showed to Swimer and myself a number of hands which he said indicated that they had knowledge of the heart suit held by their partners. My first reaction was one of complete disbelief and I began looking at the hands in a critical way, thinking that these were, perhaps, coincidences.'

Mr Goldblatt: 'Did Truscott explain the code to you at this time?'

Mr Butler: 'My recollection is that he said there was signalling by showing the fingers on the outside of the cards, that one finger on the outside of the cards held showed one heart, two fingers showed two or five, three fingers showed three, and four fingers showed four. That was as far as he had got.'

There were differences between this account and the story outlined by

Goldblatt in his opening speech. In place of Hayden's 'discovery' (when she connected the two hands on which there was a singleton heart) we have Becker connecting the hand movements with the heart suit by some unspecified process. And there is no mention of any spreading of fingers to distinguish between two and five.

Continuing the examination:

Mr Goldblatt: 'What took place after that?'

Mr Butler: 'Truscott showed us a number of hands and two or three of them looked to me suspicious, although possibly they were capable of explanation.'

Mr Goldblatt: 'Do you remember which hands?'

Mr Butler: 'I cannot remember them, no. I did not keep a record of them. I had not got them before me. I merely saw them and made notes. I was tending to look for things to disprove the charge, but several hands did seem to give grounds for suspicion.'

Mr Goldblatt: 'In your mind?'

Mr Butler: 'In my mind. As a result of that, Mr Swimer and I agreed that we would watch Reese and Schapiro play that evening.'

The witness described how on the Saturday evening he arrived in time to make notes about the last nine boards, 126–134, played in the open room against Argentina. (In the open room the second half was played before the first – that is, 135–144 before 125–134.)

Mr Goldblatt: 'Where did you position yourself when you arrived?'

Mr Butler: 'In a seat reserved for the captain, which was immediately to the right of Reese and slightly behind him, at the corner of the table.'

Mr Goldblatt: 'Was the seat occupied when you came?'

Mr Butler: 'When I came in Swimer was sitting in it. I caught his eye; he got up and beckoned me over. I took his place.'

Counsel then took the witness in detail through the nine boards he had observed.

On board 126, said Butler, Schapiro showed three fingers and opened 1NT. Reese was showing two fingers and held five hearts. Butler was astonished when Reese responded Three Hearts, but Schapiro raised to Four and the contract was easily made.

On Butler's private notes, which were later produced, there was a query beside his record of what I was showing. Caplan contended in cross-examination that this meant the observation was uncertain.

Sir John asked several questions to determine whether Butler, from his position behind the player, could see what fingers I was showing on the other side of my cards. 'I want to know what you actually saw, you understand.'

Mr Butler: 'I could see three fingers on the inside and two, by deduction, were on the other side.

Sir John Foster: 'Well, in Perry Mason they say that is inadmissible, as being a conclusion of the witness. You see, we only want to know what you saw. We lawyers are funny people in that way.'

Mr Goldblatt: 'Passing on to 127, Mr Butler?'

Mr Butler: 'Schapiro showed three fingers. I was expecting him to have three hearts but in fact he had six hearts. Reese had four fingers out of sight. I could only see his thumb, which suggested to me that he had four hearts, but in fact he had none. I did not notice any other signalling.'

Mr Goldblatt: 'Can you tell us whether there was anything that you noticed about the way in which Schapiro's three fingers were deployed behind his cards?'

Mr Butler: 'I did not notice anything.'

Caplan made much of this passage later. In the first place it was indicative of Butler's state of mind. Already he was expecting to see three cards when he saw three fingers. Secondly, it was important that he had not noticed any spread fingers, which other witnesses were to describe as striking and unnatural. On 128 he could see only my thumb and I had four hearts. His view of Schapiro was 'slightly obscured by the intervening of the Argentine player, but he seemed to have three fingers showing'. Butler went on to say that he had not seen at the time how many hearts Schapiro held, as the play of the hand was not completed, declarer making a claim before the finish. When he saw the hand records later he found that Schapiro did in fact hold three hearts.

For an experienced player it is easy, especially with a sight of two hands (for remember that Butler was sitting between myself and the opponent on my right), to ascertain the distribution of any suit. Even if the play is not completed, the declarer must show his cards.

On 129 Butler's note read: 'Reese 2=5. Schapiro showed four fingers and held four hearts.

On 130 he had 'Reese 3?' He put the query because my fingers were slightly 'cockled'. In fact I held two hearts. Schapiro had four fingers showing again and held four hearts.

On 131 only my thumb was visible and I had a void in hearts. This time Butler noted that after some moments I lowered my hand onto the table'. He had not observed this gesture at any other time. Schapiro still had four fingers showing and held four hearts.

On 132 both players showed two fingers. I held five hearts. He had not made a note as to whether Schapiro held two or five.

Sir John Foster: 'You watched the play and I suppose you could count how many cards there were?'

Mr Butler: 'Sometimes after four or five tricks they say: "The rest are yours", or "I claim the rest." I do not know whether the hand was curtailed or not.'

It turned out that the play was recorded up to trick 11. The remaining cards would, of course, have been faced on the table.

On 133 Butler's note was that I showed three fingers and held three hearts. For some reason he had not made any note about Schapiro, who in fact held a singleton. 'He may have been obscured by the Argentine player. He may have altered the position of his hand.'

On 134 the signals corresponded, Reese showing four hearts and Schapiro three.

Asked what happened next, Butler described a meeting with Swimer in the corridor. Butler said, 'Have you anything to say? Swimer said, 'Yes,' and Butler, 'Well, I feel quite sick.' After this tentative opening they 'chatted it over miserably'.

Goldblatt asked whether there had been any duplication of observation:

'In the course of that chat did you discover whether or not Swimer had been observing any of the hands that you did from a different position?'

Mr Butler: 'I did not ask him. I thought he had left the room.'

Sir John Foster: 'You do not know now even?'

Mr Butler: 'I do not know whether he saw any of the same hands.'

Goldblatt cannot have expected this reply. We knew from Swimer's proof of evidence (exchanged between the solicitors) that he had watched some more of the play from further back. It seemed odd that the two should not have compared notes about hands they had both observed.

Mr Goldblatt: 'After your discussion with Swimer what further action did you take?'

Mr Butler: 'Nothing that night. I spent a sleepless night and then decided in the morning that the obvious thing to do was to call a meeting of the Appeals Committee, of which I was Chairman.'

Concluding his evidence, Butler confirmed that he had composed the official Report on the proceedings at Buenos Aires. 'I made various notes of course during the meetings and then compiled the Report on the following day.'

While Butler was giving his evidence in London, the American Contract Bridge League dealt a puny blow from Chicago. At a tournament there the League informed the press that the WBF committee at Buenos Aires had found us guilty. Papers all over the world assumed this to be a current finding and so reported it. One or two English papers fell into the same trap and later published apologies. The announcement from Chicago showed little respect for European members of the WBF who had shared in the decision not to publish any findings. The explanation given to a newspaperman by a League official was that the British press had represented the American players as the 'bad guys'.

When the Inquiry was resumed on Friday, August 13 the tribunal's attention was drawn to the American action. Sir John remarked rather wearily that it was a matter for the 'bridge societies' to sort out, and the BBL later issued a statement explaining why it could not act on the finding of the WBF report. The main reasons were: faults in procedure (people acting as judges of their own evidence); gaps in the evidence (hands referred to, but no details given); and inadequate opportunity for the players to defend themselves.

Butler cross-examined

We had plenty of material for Butler's cross-examination and Caplan made brilliant use of it during a session that lasted throughout the day. He began as follows:

Mr Caplan: 'Mr Butler, I suppose I may assume that you would never have been party to the selection of anybody to play for England against whom there was a breath of suspicion?'

Mr Butler: 'Quite so.'

Mr Caplan: 'And were you a party to the selection of Mr Reese and Mr Schapiro?'

Mr Butler: 'I was.'

Mr Caplan: 'And had been on other occasions?'

Mr Butler: 'Yes.'

Mr Caplan: 'It follows from that that there was no breath of suspicion against them?'

Mr Butler: 'Not to my knowledge.'

Mr Caplan: 'You were in an exceptional position to have knowledge of such matters by reason of the appointments which you have told us you held?'

Mr Butler: 'Yes.'

Mr Caplan: 'In fact, nobody could be in a better position?'

Mr Butler: 'Probably not, no.'

This was a valuable testimonial. Caplan went on to establish that we had been world-ranking players for something like 30 years.

Mr Caplan: 'They are both of them, are they not, in their different ways what might be described as colourful players?'

Mr Butler: 'Yes, certainly.'

Mr Caplan: 'As such, whenever they play they attract attention?'

Mr Butler: 'Yes.'

Mr Caplan: 'They attract, so to speak, a gallery?'

Mr Butler: 'Yes, certainly.'

Mr Caplan: 'The hands that they play are the subject of articles?'

Mr Butler: 'Yes, certainly.'

Mr Caplan: 'They are analysed and dealt with in books that are published by various writers on this topic?'

Mr Butler: 'Yes.'

Mr Caplan: 'Bearing that in mind, Mr Butler, do you not agree that it would be quite impossible for these gentlemen in the spotlight of attention in this way to have escaped a breath of suspicion if there had been any cheating by them before?'

Mr Butler: 'I would say so, yes.'

Counsel turned next to the general subject of accusations in top-level bridge. Butler agreed that such things happened, perhaps too frequently. 'Do you agree that the United States bridge players are particularly prone to be suspicious?' Caplan asked. Butler would not agree at first but later said, 'I think probably yes, they have been more suspicious than others.'

After referring to the incident at Lake Como, when the Americans had accused the Italians, Caplan asked:

'Do you agree that the Americans are the last people to choose to cheat against?'

Mr Butler: 'I do not believe it is right to cheat against any person.'

Mr Caplan: 'My question was not about propriety but whether the Americans were the last people one would choose to cheat against.'

Mr Butler: 'I would not know.'

Mr Caplan: 'You know it is alleged by the Americans that Mr Reese and Mr Schapiro cheated against the Italians?'

Mr Butler: 'I did not know it was alleged. I have not heard them say that. Some hands were shown to me. I do not know which matches they were from, whether they were against the Argentinians, the Americans or the Italians, except in the hands I was concerned to give my evidence about.'

Mr Caplan: 'Mr Truscott eventually showed you eight hands, did he not?'

Mr Butler: 'I do not know which matches they came from.'

This was a pretty astonishing reply, more so perhaps than Counsel realised. Italian bidding is almost in a different language from the bidding of other teams and naturally this has considerable bearing on everything that happens at the table when they are playing. Butler did not even know that six of the eight hands that led to his suspicions were played against Italy. It was as though a clerk at the War Office were to criticise the General's battle dispositions without enquiring who was the enemy or what weapons he possessed. Caplan continued:

'I will put those eight hands to you presently. Will you take it from me that six out of the eight were from the match against Italy?'

Mr Butler: 'I would accept that, of course, if you have evidence.'

Mr Caplan: 'The Italian team do not subscribe to the view that Reese and Schapiro cheated against them?'

Mr Butler: 'They have not told me anything about it. They have not told me anything.'

Counsel then began to take events in sequence to see how the matter was approached.

Mr Caplan: 'When you had the meeting after lunch did anybody produce to you any notes of any observations they had made up to that time?'

Mr Butler: 'Observations, no.'

This became an important part of our case. When Hayden gave her evidence she produced notes said to have been made on the Friday afternoon, but Truscott, according to Butler's recollection, neither produced nor mentioned any such notes.

Lord Bourne: 'Who is Truscott?'

Mr Caplan: 'Mr Truscott is a journalist who writes for a New York newspaper.

Mr Butler: 'Yes.'

Mr Caplan: 'And who had been the leading figure in making an accusation on another occasion in a tournament in Europe?'

Mr Butler: 'Perhaps you could refresh my memory about that? I do not know.'

Caplan refreshed Butler's memory of the episode at Vienna in 1957, when two Austrian players were accused. Butler agreed that Truscott had been a leading figure not in making, but in supporting, that accusation. He also agreed that if the libel action brought by the Austrian players had ever come to court he himself would have given evidence against them, saying they had cheated.

Mr Caplan: 'Although you had been a party, had you not, to clearing those persons from allegations of cheating at Vienna?'

Mr Butler: 'Yes, I was on the committee which passed a neutral verdict.'

This hardly gave an accurate picture. The conclusion of the committee had been that there was no case to answer, and Butler had concurred in that.

Caplan sought next to involve the witness in the following line of argument: When he first learned of the accusation he had been, in his own words, 'horrified, staggered, and unbelieving'; but after Truscott had shown him a number of hands he had decided there were grounds for suspicion. Did not that prove the importance of the analysis of the hands, and might not a further and more accurate analysis have shown that the suspicions were unfounded?

Butler was very guarded about the importance of analysis, and Caplan tried another tack:

'I am sure you will agree with this, that one of the reasons why it is so easy to make allegations of cheating is because so many things that happen at the bridge table are capable of being given a sinister interpretation?'

This seemed obvious but Butler answered flatly, 'No.' Caplan described a wide range of gestures with hands, cards, pencil, scorecard, pipe and so forth, to which a sinister interpretation might be attached by someone already in a suspicious frame of mind. Butler had to agree that the interpretations were legion. The next move was to examine the material that had caused Butler to become suspicious. As Butler could not remember the hands that Truscott had shown him, it was put to him that they were probably the same hands that Truscott had produced in front of the committee. These were Italy 22, 23, 25, 26, 54 and 117, and U. S. 30 and 36.

Mr Caplan: 'Mr Butler, these are the hands which I am suggesting Mr Truscott produced eventually before the committee in Mr Reese's presence, which you think were very likely the same hands which he produced to you on the Saturday afternoon.'

Mr Butler: 'Yes.'

Lord Bourne: 'Why is a journalist allowed to produce this sort of thing?'

Mr Caplan: 'I will come to that presently, because that is a very important factor in all this, as we shall see. I am very much obliged, General.'

Here Caplan was quickly taking up a cue, for this particular question was not raised again and anyway there was a fair enough answer.

On the first hand the question was whether, holding four hearts and five diamonds, it was natural for me to open One Heart or One Diamond. Position at the table was all-important and Butler could not remember whether Truscott had mentioned that I was third in hand after two passes.

Mr Caplan: 'Is this a hand which would begin to look suspicious to you?'

Mr Butler: 'May I say that I do not claim to be an expert on bidding? I do not set myself up to be an expert. I am a third-class player.'

In that case, why not call in a first-class player to assess the technical evidence? There were plenty around.

Butler eventually admitted that the first hand gave ground for no suspicion at all. To the second he attached 'very trifling weight', to the third 'some weight', though it was clear that the assessors did not agree with him. On the fourth, Italy 26, I had to lead against 3NT from:

♠ 8 6 5 4 3 2
♡ K 9 5 3
♢ 9
♣ 8 7

The Italian bidding had been strong and there were clear reasons for preferring a low heart to a spade, Butler thought a spade lead more natural and Caplan pointed out the danger of the suit being blocked, even if partner had something in it. Then a third suggestion was made:

Sir John Foster: 'Speaking as a player in the Eighteenth Class here – I want to ask you this – it looks as if spades are so much out against you –

while in hearts it looks as if they are not going to beat the contract. The only chance is perhaps there is only one stop in hearts, and so you play either your three of hearts or your king in the Eighteenth Class.

There is a Charge of the Light Brigade quality about that lead of the King.

Butler attached 'a small grain of suspicion' to this example, and so it went on. It was easy enough to show that Butler ought not to have allowed himself to be convinced of anything, but Caplan had a further point: the examples were so feeble in the sense attributed to them that it was difficult to understand how Truscott could put them forward as evidence to support the allegations.

Turning to matters of observation, Caplan asked: 'Would you be surprised to know that somebody was observing the same nine hands that you did, knowing the alleged code in more detail, and came to the conclusion that no code was being used during the nine hands that he saw?' After some argument between Counsel as to whether this put Kehela's evidence too high, Butler replied that he would be surprised, and why had Kehela not come forward during the inquiry at Buenos Aires? He added that he would find the evidence more credible if it were accompanied by notes.

Mr Caplan: 'You are not suggesting, are you, I am sure, that his evidence was given otherwise than in good faith?'

Mr Butler: 'I make no observation on that.'

Mr Caplan: 'May we assume, Mr Butler, that both his evidence and yours are given in good faith?'

Mr Butler: 'Mine is given in good faith, I cannot tell you about his.'

Mr Caplan: 'I am sure you would like to assume that his was given in good faith?'

Mr Butler: 'I am not going to comment.'

During his evidence-in-chief Butler had given some very stiff demonstrations of how we held our cards. Now Caplan showed him some photographs of Boris and myself in play and asked how he would interpret them. Some of his answers were unexpected. Caplan also held up cards himself, showing both back and front view and producing this exchange:

Mr Caplan: 'That would indicate to you?'

Mr Butler: 'I would put a query about that as to the number of fingers.'

Mr Caplan: 'That is what I want to get to, uncertainty of observation. You would not put that as two?'

Mr Butler: 'My eyesight is a bit bad.'

This remark was left suspended in the air for several seconds while Caplan's gaze swept the courtroom like the searchlights of a destroyer. He continued in a different tone of voice: 'We shall have to ask about that too in a moment.' And so he did. It was rather hard on the witness, for when

Caplan held up the cards he had his back to the light. Still pressing on the question of uncertain observation, Caplan said :

Mr Caplan: 'It is clear that on at least two out of the nine occasions the uncertainty was present in your mind?'

Mr Butler: 'Yes. I wrote it down at the time. 130 is a case in point.'

Mr Caplan: 'I suggest that it follows from that that in the other hands it was possible for you to have made mistakes?'

Mr Butler: 'No. When there were four fingers or two fingers showing, I was not making a mistake; but when there were three I was not sure whether it was three or two.'

Mr Caplan: 'This is where the mischief of the manner in which you allowed yourself to approach this investigation comes in. You approached this investigation with some suspicion in your mind?'

Mr Butler: 'Some suspicion, yes.'

Mr Caplan: 'If you approach it with some suspicion in your mind and you see that Mr Reese has three hearts in his hand, I suggest to you that you are very easily able to persuade yourself that it is three fingers that are showing on the other side whereas it might be only two?'

Mr Butler: 'I think it is clear from the fact that when there was doubt I put down the doubt that I was looking at it purely objectively and not with my mind made up before.'

That was a fair answer and one that set the limits on our cross-examination of Butler. From this point, however, he began to show an increasing stubbornness in his evidence. Caplan asked next:

'Do you not consider that the proper thing to have done was to have got somebody to observe completely objectively who had not already got a suspicion planted in his mind?'

Mr Butler: 'Certainly not. The fewer people who knew about it the better. If I could prove it had not taken place I certainly would not have pursued the matter further. I did not want to tell other people, obviously.'

Mr Caplan: 'Instead of which the observation takes place by somebody who already has a suspicion in his mind?'

Mr Butler: 'Yes.'

Mr Caplan: 'And the observation is of matters where there can be a degree of uncertainty, as is shown by the fact that in some cases you put the question marks?'

Mr Butler: 'Yes.'

Caplan mentioned the name of Harold Franklin, the chief tournament director of the English Bridge Union, and continued:

'Would it surprise you if Mr Franklin, with that experience of being chief tournament director, were to say that from his experience he knows that sitting in the position where you were sitting, it is impossible to be certain as to how many fingers are showing on the front of the cards?'

Mr Butler: 'It would surprise me a good deal.'

Caplan suggested next that Kehela, who according to his own account moved from end to end so that he could observe each player frontally, had a better view than Butler. The witness agreed that this would be so in theory but added: 'I would have said it was almost impossible to do that in that crowded room.' Later he spoke of 'a dense wall of people sitting on tiers of benches round the table'.

Here Butler made a bad mistake. I was sure from my recollection that the atmosphere during this last session against Argentina had been completely dead, with very few spectators.

Now came the most critical part of the cross-examination. Using every scrap of evidence, Caplan demonstrated that there had been some element of uncertainty in eight of the nine hands that Butler had observed. Either he had not known what was supposed to be the relevant code, or he could not be sure how many fingers I was showing, or he had not observed what Boris was doing. This was the climax:

Mr Caplan: 'Assuming that the fingers were spread, there are two at the most of the nine where there is coincidence between both, otherwise there is only one. Did you think at this stage that that justified you in being convinced that they had been cheating?'

Mr Butler: 'I was more than half convinced, I was not fully convinced.'

Mr Caplan: 'You were not yet convinced?'

Mr Butler: 'I was more than half convinced. There were two or three hands.'

Mr Caplan: 'But you were sick, you said?'

Mr Butler: 'I felt sick because even four or five coincidences with the code were enough to make me sick.'

Mr Caplan: 'There was only one hand, or at the most two hands, where both coincided?'

Mr Butler: 'Yes.'

Caplan sat back with the justified air of a man who had climbed a high mountain. He turned next to Butler's actions as an official.

Mr Caplan: 'Is it not normal in these matters for an official to disqualify himself from adjudicating when one of his own nationals is involved?'

Mr Butler: 'From adjudicating, yes, I should say so.'

Mr Caplan: 'You certainly did not do that, did you?'

Mr Butler: 'No. I felt that as Chairman of the Appeals Committee I could not let the matter rest where it was and I had then to call a meeting, but it would have been better if having called the meeting I had asked someone else to take the chair.'

Mr Caplan: 'Indeed, that is exactly what I was going to suggest. Not only, Mr Butler, did you not disqualify yourself, as you agree is normal, but you went beyond and acted as a witness and as presiding over the tribunal?'

Mr Butler: 'For the Appeals Committee, yes. Then I realised that it must go through a higher tribunal, which was the World Bridge Federation of which I did not act as Chairman, of course. I am not Chairman.

Mr Caplan: 'But you acted upon it?'

Mr Butler: 'I sat on the committee, yes.'

Mr Caplan: 'And voted?'

Mr Butler: 'And voted, yes.'

Going back to the time of observation, Counsel asked whether it would not have been better to have a neutral observer who had not been argued into a state of suspicion beforehand. 'I think not,' said Butler. 'Are you serious?' Caplan asked. Butler was serious.

Counsel reminded the witness of his famous remark to me at the committee meeting (Butler's version): 'You have an ingenious mind; you invented the Little Major and now you have invented the Little Heart.'

Mr Caplan: 'So you have not only acted as witness and judge, but also as sarcastic commentator?'

Mr Butler: 'Reese was arguing that the findings were not fair and I suggested that they were fair.'

Mr Caplan: 'You also said, of course, that he had an ingenious mind?'

Mr Butler: 'Yes.'

'Let us see what flows from that,' said Caplan. He invited Butler to agree that to signal with the fingers and to keep the signal in view throughout the bidding was extremely crude. The argument continued at cross-purposes, for Butler persisted in saying that the idea of showing length in hearts as opposed to general strength or something obvious of that sort was 'very simple' and so might have been thought undetectable. He would not address himself to the question, Was not the method of signalling crude?

Caplan put it to him that both Boris and I had extremely fine records with other partners. We had both won events at world level, the Mixed Teams Olympiad and the World Par Olympiad, when not playing together. Still apart, one or the other of us had won the Masters Pairs, the most testing event in Britain, in 1963, 1964 and 1965. Boris had won the Gold Cup ten times, a feat that may never be equalled. This year with our respective partners we had finished first and second in the international trials. All this was important evidence, for when players can win events only when playing together they are more open to suspicion. Thus the question arose, Why had we not done better in the critical match at Buenos Aires?

Mr Caplan: 'Britain went down to a crashing defeat against Italy, did they not?'

Mr Butler: 'Yes.'

Mr Caplan: 'Enormous?'

Mr Butler: 'Yes.'

Mr Caplan: 'What was it?'

Mr Butler: 'I just know they played badly.'

Mr Caplan: '121 match points. I suggest to you as a matter of commonsense, Mr Butler, that if two of the world's greatest players are also cheating, this kind of result is unthinkable?'

Mr Butler: 'It should have been, but they played badly and at the inquiry Reese admitted he played badly during the week. I am just saying what Reese said to me: "We played badly."'

This was the most wounding remark I had heard this year. The player is not born who will admit he played badly in a long match. What I had said was that Boris and I made a number of mistakes that were inconceivable for a pair using a cheating system. Butler had another explanation for our non-success: the 'system' had broken down; we had failed to get the benefit we had expected, This was somewhat at variance with the analysis of his Counsel, who had produced a large number of hands on which we were said to have profited.

Caplan took the witness through some of the events that preceded the accusation. Butler agreed that Swimer had twice been disappointed after previous trials and that the selection committee had been divided about appointing him as captain. The letter I had written in January, stating that I did not want to play with Boris or to be subjected to any pressure to do so, was produced. Butler had no knowledge of any unpleasantness at Buenos Aires either towards, or within, the team. 'As far as I know they were a perfectly happy unit of six,' he said.

Caplan took one slightly false step at the end – it was my fault for not warning him. Knowing that Perroux, who had abstained from the vote against us, was a criminal lawyer, Caplan led up to the point he was intending to make by asking:

'On your committee of inquiry, whatever you call it, was there any person who was trained in assessing evidence?' Unlucky! Butler was able to tell him that at least four members of the committee had legal training.

Butler re-examined

Goldblatt began his re-examination by giving Butler a chance to speak of his own high motives and of Truscott's impartiality.

Mr Goldblatt: 'At any time while Truscott was explaining the allegations to you, did you hold the view that he was trying to win you over?'

Mr Butler: 'Not at all. I think he was giving me the case objectively.'

Some of us had not received quite that impression. Butler was digging in his heels now, as another answer showed.

Mr Goldblatt: 'Did you find, on going through the eight hands that were analysed with you in cross-examination, any more or any less reason for investigation, or about the same?'

Mr Butler: 'About the same; as I said, each hand, most of the hands, added one further grain of suspicion into my mind, or doubt.'

So the careful explanation of many matters of which he was admittedly ignorant had not altered his view of the significance of the hands.

Goldblatt asked about Kehela's observation and Butler expanded on his previous account:

'The point I was not allowed to make in my cross-examination was, I was told that Kehela was standing on the back of the row and went to the other side of the room during the bidding, and in my opinion it is impossible, physically impossible, to do so. He would have to clamber down four steps, taking a big stride down, climb over a rope, run round the other side, climb up four steps on the other side, and it all takes half a minute to do. That is what made me doubt about Kehela's evidence, it put a doubt in my mind, because he said he saw things and from different positions which, in my opinion, he could not have reached.' Almost an obstacle course. The witness was then re-examined about his own observation.

Mr Goldblatt: 'Was there any finger display which you observed from either Reese or Schapiro which appeared to you in any way to contradict the code which you had been told about?'

Mr Butler: 'Only the one on board 127, when Schapiro showed three fingers but had, in fact, six hearts. I had not known the code for six hearts and I made a note of it at the time.'

Mr Goldblatt: 'Looking, for example, at hand 128 …

Mr Caplan: 'I am sure the witness does not want to do himself an injustice. He might look at 127 and 130 – Reese.'

Mr Goldblatt: 'My friend might save himself for comment at a later stage.'

Mr Caplan: 'I thought you might like to avoid your witness having strictures passed upon him in case he has made a mistake.'

Mr Butler: 'I have "Reese 3?=2".'

Mr Caplan: 'That is right, exactly.

Finally, Goldblatt referred to Swimer:

Q. I want to ask you about Swimer as a person. Has he, to your knowledge, any reason whatever for animosity against either Mr Reese or Mr Schapiro? A. Not at all. I think he has an affection for both of them.

Q. In your dealing with Swimer prior to the meetings of the Appeals Committee and the Executive Committee, did you find any trace of partisanship against either Reese or Schapiro? A. No, he was completely heartbroken, as I was too. I did not sleep at all that night.

Lord Bourne: 'Who was heartbroken?'

Mr Butler: 'Swimer was, and so was I.'

7 The Triumvirate

THE DAY APTER Butler's cross-examination I turned up some photographs taken during the Saturday evening session against Argentina and soon found one that made a mockery of Butler's assertion that Kehela would have had difficulty in moving from end to end. Two spectators were standing near the table and the benches behind them were empty. That was two small points gained: Kehela's evidence was unshaken and Butler had not been careful in his recollection.

Meanwhile, I felt we were losing ground in public estimation. Some American and continental papers had referred to 'secret photographs' and many people had the idea that some sort of film had been taken. In addition, the know-alls and rumourmongers were busy. I heard of one typical conversation. Four Crockford's members were dining with friends in a restaurant and when the case was mentioned a fifth person said, 'I have a cousin who was in Buenos Aires and he told me that Flint and Konstam knew all the time.' You see how four people were slandered in seven words, 'Flint and Konstam knew all the time'? Not this story, perhaps, but others like it oozed and dripped around the country.

The European Championship was being played at Ostend in the middle of September and I went over for three days, partly to watch the play and partly to speak with some continental experts whom we might want to call in our defence. They had reported favourably on the match records and could testify about similar accusations in recent years. While I was in Ostend the American party of Truscott, Hayden and Becker, later called by Kehela 'the triumvirate', arrived in England. Swimer took them to the Hamilton Club one evening to play a match. This caused much turmoil as Boris had been a prominent member of the club for many years. Later in the week the triumvirate went to Ostend for three days, arriving the day after I left.

Boris was not well at this time and did not attend any of the sessions the following week. The first witness when we met on Monday, September 27 was Alan Truscott. Truscott is able and has a good brain. His career in England, possibly because of a gauche manner, did not reflect his capabilities. He emigrated to the United States in 1962 and a year later succeeded Albert Morehead as bridge editor of the *New York Times*.

Truscott's evidence-in-chief

Truscott began by describing how Becker had called him aside on the Thursday evening and told him about the varying finger positions he had observed. On the Friday afternoon Truscott sat behind me, opposite Schapiro, when we played the Italians. He was immediately struck by the peculiar way in which the cards were held.

Mr Goldblatt: 'You used the word "peculiar"?' A. Peculiar in the sense of unnatural, that usually one holds the cards in as easy a way as possible. It is very tiring hour after hour to keep holding cards and you will often see players put their cards down on the table because they are tired of holding them.

It had not occurred to me before that one needed the strength of Samson to support thirteen cards. I have seen frail old ladies of ninety do it.

In the present case, Truscott went on, the way in which the cards were held was stiff and unnatural. Sir John observed that it was difficult to understand what the witness meant, and Caplan said he would provide a pack of cards later and ask in detail about this.

An important question and answer followed:

Mr Goldblatt: 'From where you sat did you observe anything from Reese's manner of holding the cards or not?' A. No, I was sitting immediately next to him and it was very, very difficult. I was sitting practically like this, and if he is holding his cards like this I cannot really see behind them, so I cannot say anything about the way in which his cards were held.

Butler and Swimer, watching from the same angle, had been confident of their deductions.

At the end of the session, the witness continued, he took away copies of notes made by Hayden, collected the hand records of the session, and compared the two. He spent some time trying to establish a connection without success. He was joined later in a restaurant by Hayden and Becker and then came the 'Hayden discovery'. She suggested that they look at all hands where one finger was recorded. The first such hand contained a singleton heart and Hayden recalled a previous deal from another session where one finger was showing and there too the player held a singleton heart. A quick test of other hands convinced them that they had found the solution. As they had noticed that the fingers were sometimes together, sometimes not, they formed a provisional hypothesis that two fingers apart meant five hearts, three fingers apart meant six hearts, and so on. The only inconsistency arose from the fact that Hayden and Becker, from where they were watching, sometimes could not be sure whether I was showing three fingers or four. On such occasions they marked 3D, the D standing for a drooping little finger.

It was past 4.00am when they left the restaurant and Truscott spent another hour in his hotel looking through match records. Having retired to bed presumably at about 5.30 in the morning he was up bright and early at 9.00, telephoning Gerber to give him the momentous news. It now turned out that Gerber too had taken notes of four or five hands he had watched during the same session. Apart from one 'mistake' the notes fitted in with the hypothesis. As Becker and Hayden wanted to rest before playing in the afternoon, Truscott acted as the spokesman at future meetings. He explained the situation to Butler and Swimer in 'considerable detail'. Swimer asked to see more hands and together they looked through a further selection.

In the afternoon Truscott watched Flint and myself play in the open room and observed that the cards were now held in a perfectly natural manner. As he described it, I had two fingers of my right hand across the cards, the third and fourth fingers somewhat below.

Q. Was there any noticeable variation between one board and the next in the way in which Reese was holding his cards while playing with Flint? A. I did not watch very long. I only watched two boards and as far as I could see there was no change.

Two boards seemed a rather short period in which to establish a different pattern of behaviour, especially as he had not previously observed me from the front. Perhaps he wanted to rest after his exertions during the last 24 hours.

The witness was asked next about the hands to which he had attached significance. He made much of the two hands on which Schapiro had made a psychic bid in hearts, ltaly 18 and 127.

'Psychic bids in a world championship,' he told the court, 'are very, very rare indeed. I can remember only two psychic bids of any kind in Buenos Aires by any player of any team, and they were both made by the pair we are considering and they both related to the heart suit. Psychic bidding is a very dangerous weapon which, used with a partner who has no special knowledge, is liable to recoil and cost a considerable number of points.'

This last sententious remark was like saying that it is dangerous to drive a car at 100 miles an hour. So it is, in general, but not for a racing driver on a racetrack. The statement about the infrequency of psychic bids in world championship matches could easily be refuted.

'The last matter that I want to raise,' said Goldblatt, 'concerns photographs. Have you any photographs?'

Truscott had two. One was the photo from Time where Boris had a singleton heart and it was difficult to see whether or not his index finger was extended. There was nothing in the least strained in the way he was holding his cards. Truscott had an explanation for this:

'In this particular picture the hand is slightly more relaxed than I remember seeing it normally. But this is not surprising. When the photographer comes into the room the players cease to think about bridge. They wait until the flashlights have been shot off. They tend to be more relaxed.'

Lord Bourne: 'How do you know that?'

Mr Truscott: 'When the photographer comes in, the players feel they must get it over.'

Mr Goldblatt: 'That looks as if it was a deal in which Schapiro was displaying one finger.'

Mr Truscott: 'It looks to me like that, but it is not too easy to see. However, the other photograph which I have is a better one. Have you seen this one?'

This one was a print of the photograph that had accompanied the announcement about Hayden's forthcoming book, Diary of a Scandal. It was taken at the point of the opening lead and meant nothing, for I would have put down my cards to enter the contract on my scorecard.

That concluded Truscott's evidence-in-chief. The early part had been well organised and well presented. Later on, it seemed to me, especially when discussing hands, he had pressed the case too hard.

Truscott cross-examined

Caplan began the cross-examination with a reference to Vienna.

'This is not the first experience you have had, is it, Mr Truscott, of supporting an allegation of cheating?'

When his mind had been brought to bear, the witness described the circumstances in which he had formed his conclusion:

'I had had the code explained to me by somebody who claimed that he had decoded it, and he stood with me on the following day and watched the players.'

Not a very fair method of approaching the matter.

Caplan set out next to establish the close relationship between Truscott, Becker and Hayden.

Mr Caplan: 'They are both friends of yours?'

Mr Truscott: 'Mrs Hayden is a friend of mine in the sense that we live in the same area. She does checking for my column and I occasionally play in tournaments with her.'

Mr Caplan: 'You have a number of connections with her?'

Mr Truscott: 'Yes; we have family connections. We see each other's children play together.'

There was a long discussion about the way in which the cards were held. Caplan demonstrated that it was perfectly simple to hold the cards with any number of fingers showing without looking at all unnatural. 'Yes,' replied Truscott, 'but if you are seeking to convey a message that will be picked up at a quick glance, you may hold them in a less natural way.'

At this point there was an adjournment. Over coffee with one of the assessors, Lord Bourne descended sufficiently far from his judicial position to observe that this Mr Truscott seemed to be something of a busybody.

When we resumed, Caplan asked the witness why he had taken no notes on the only occasion he had watched Boris and myself playing together. Truscott gave three reasons, none of them very powerful: he had been sitting close to me and might have been overlooked; he did not have a pencil; and he was so shocked by the whole affair that he did not think of taking notes.

Many questions followed about the exact positions of the various observers, the certainty or uncertainty of their observations, and whether or not they had noted down the exact hands on which the fingers were observed to be spread or not spread. Working valiantly, Caplan made some dents in the testimony but it was clear that sooner or later we would have to make a more frontal attack.

Passing next to the technical evidence, Counsel invited Truscott to agree that hearts was the suit in which psychic bids were most often made. After some debate the answer was: 'No, I do not think so. I think I have seen more psychic bids in spades than in hearts.' The witness was insistent that the eight hands he produced before the committee in my presence were not the strongest he knew of at that time but a random selection from 16 or more which he had noted.

Each member of the triumvirate exploded a small bombshell at some time in his evidence. Truscott's came when Caplan enquired about the frequency of psychic bids.

Mr Caplan: 'Is it not perfectly well recognised that Mr Reese and Mr Schapiro do make psychic bids?'

Mr Truscott: 'Yes, I would say that in the course of the last 15 years they have made more psychic bids than any other leading British pair.'

Mr Caplan: 'That being so, do you consider that two psychic bids by Reese and Schapiro out of a total of 198 boards represents a high proportion of psychic bids when these two are playing together?'

Mr Truscott: 'This now leads to the question of whether, on previous occasions, they did or did not have special understandings. In my opinion a pair who psyche as often as they have in international championships – I now think they have had special understandings on previous occasions.'

It will be noted that this answer was what the lawyers call 'non-responsive'. Truscott had been asked simply whether two out of 198 was a higher proportion than usual. If he wanted to bring out that in his opinion we had been cheating for years he should have told his solicitor and waited for a direct question which might or might not have been put. Also, it was not in the least true that we make an unusual number of psychic bids; more than some partnerships, less than others. Caplan observed dryly that there had been other evidence about our past record.

Up to now Counsel had dealt mainly with side issues. In the central part of his cross-examination he developed three lines of argument:

(1) If Hayden had taken notes during her observation and Truscott had copied them on to the hand records, why were these notes not produced at any time, either when Truscott was seeking to convince Butler and Swimer, or in front of the committee? This was one of numerous questions and answers on the same point:

Mr Caplan: 'I want to suggest to you that if there had been a complete record in the hand of Mrs Hayden of finger positions seen during a session, you would have put that in the forefront of what you were saying to Mr Butler, saying, "Look, there in writing by Mrs Hayden is a record of what finger positions she saw." That would, I suggest, have been in the forefront.'

Mr Truscott: 'No, I do not think so. That is something I would think of and you would think of, if it is a question of a formal inquiry lasting a number of days, but I do not think it is something one thinks of when trying to arrive at a solution to a difficult matter quickly on the last day of a tournament.'

That, said Caplan, accentuated the point he was trying to make. If you want to show quickly and conclusively that there is justification for what you are saying, surely you produce the scorecard with the written notations? He appreciated that the committee might not have wanted to disturb Hayden on the morning of an important match, but it would hardly have disturbed her to hand her scorecard to someone else to take downstairs.

(2) Counsel drew attention to many discrepancies between Butler's narrative of events in the official Report, countersigned by Solomon, and Truscott's account. Truscott took the sting out of this attack by saying that the Report was about 25 per cent right and that he had read certain passages with astonishment.

(3) We were more successful with a third argument. According to Truscott's account, the spread fingers theory had been worked out at the Saturday morning session and had been explained as part of the code to Butler and Swimer; but those two, in their statements and in Butler's evidence, had denied any knowledge of the way in which two hearts and five hearts were supposedly distinguished. Truscott answered only: 'Well, Mr Butler was absentminded, I do not know; but he was certainly told at the time.

In re-examination there was one of those little flurries between Counsel that I always found engaging. Goldblatt was asking questions about the Report.

Mr Goldblatt: 'Reese asked to see the evidence and (says the Report) "Truscott was called in with his analysis which he had previously shown to the Chairman and Swimer". Would you say this, Mr Truscott … ?'

Mr Caplan: 'Please do not lead. "Would you say this?" must be the preliminary to a leading question.'

Mr Goldblatt: 'It may be my friend's preliminary, it is not mine.'

Mr Caplan: 'There is no question which can follow which would not be leading. "Would you say this?" must be a preliminary to a leading question.'

Mr Goldblatt: 'It may be my friend's style of advocacy, it is not mine.'

Mr Caplan: 'There can be no question about it.'

Sir John Foster: 'Let us hear him; he has been warned!'

Mrs Hayden's evidence-in-chief

Mrs Hayden is a fair, good-looking woman in her early forties. She began demurely, answering 'yes, sir' and 'no, sir' to her Counsel's early questions. When she first heard of the allegation she had been resistant. She had always thought of Reese as 'a very superior person'. (I am used to that word in a derogatory sense, but here it was meant to be complimentary.) The way we both held our cards on the Thursday afternoon was graceful and quite natural-looking but she soon concluded that Becker had been right. She became convinced that it was a 'distributional thing'. Thinking about it made her play badly in that session. Up till then, she assured us, she had played very well.

The special characteristic of her evidence, delivered in a flow that lasted for half an hour almost without interruption, was the little details she put in which gave, and according to Caplan were intended to give, verisimilitude to her story. Here, for example, she describes her emotions when playing a slam hand (US 63) on bridgerama:

'We all picked up our cards but we could not bid until the buzzer sounded. You will see that I have a very big hand, and if I find my partner with some kind of a heart or diamond fit and a decent hand there is even a possibility of a slam. This was just flipping [flitting?] through my mind, all the things that flip through your mind as you look at a hand and it is not time to bid. I believe I was the opening bidder. I took a look to my left and Reese was holding his cards with two fingers showing and I thought, 'Ho, ho, no slam, Reese has got two aces, and then I thought, Isn't it ridiculous, to think you can think you are off [i.e. down] in a slam and that the opponents have two aces before even the bidding has begun. I really almost smiled, chiding myself mentally that I could be so silly to think of that.'

Haunted by the fear that I might hold two aces she later bid an injudicious Blackwood 4NT(asking partner to show by a conventional response how many aces he held) and landed in the wrong slam contract.

After this session they told Truscott and also Gerber of their suspicions, on the strict understanding that these two would not pass it on without Becker's agreement. This was her description of the time when the famous notes were allegedly taken, on the Thursday afternoon:

'I now felt that I could retire. I felt it was off our hands. We had told our two witnesses; Gerber and Truscott were now responsible and I could relax. However, I am not the relaxing type and I thought, Well, I'll just go check to be sure they are handling everything correctly, and I went myself to the pit [her with-it name for the open room] and took a look. I saw Truscott sitting right next to Reese, closer than I am to Mr Pugh, between the two of us like so. I thought to myself, How stupid, why didn't he sit between Reese and Shapiro where he could have seen both of their hands because where he is he will only be able to see Schapiro's hands? However, I was confident that he was taking notes, at least of Schapiro's fingers. I then looked around and up on top of the grandstand behind Schapiro I saw Gerber standing where he could see Reese's fingers. I thought, Well, that's good. Then I thought, Perhaps as a safety play, I know these men are both taking notes and they will be very accurate about it, but just as a safety play in case they do not take sufficient notes I will take notes. So I climbed up. By the way, it was very crowded, I could not get a seat close. I could not get a seat at all, but I climbed up the back of the grandstand behind one of the Italians and I stood on the very top, and as I got there the announcer was calling out Number 119 and I put on my glasses so I could see carefully and I could see 119 board number on the table. I could see only Schapiro. I watched, and as Schapiro took his cards he quickly looked at them and put them in this position so that four fingers showed. I took a note. I opened my pocket book and found an old score-sheet which I believe has been presented to you gentlemen.'

It was gripping stuff, as they say in the theatre, and Hayden had an attentive audience. The code-breaking session was described with equal verve. Much was made of the fact that Gerber had broken his word and spread the story. She came next to the Saturday night, when the Butler-Swimer observations were made. Italy was playing North America on bridgerama and she and Becker were left out of the team. On the third or fourth board of the session the Americans had a calamity, doubling their opponents into game. At this point Kehela came out of the bridgerama hall and told her the match was lost. With the tension relaxed, the two went for a walk. During this, Kehela revealed that Gerber had told him about the allegation, saying he wanted his deputy captain to know in case he died tomorrow. 'That makes no sense,' commented Hayden, 'in case he dies tomorrow. Gerber wanted to tell, he enjoyed telling people.' Now came the bombshell. Kehela told her he had watched me play and knew the charge to be true. He added, 'If anybody asks me about this I will deny it. I will deny there was sufficient evidence.'

There was something wrong with the timing here. Kehela had watched the second half of the Britain-Argentina match, so he could not have had this conversation with Hayden three boards after the beginning of a session that began about the same time, or at most half an hour later. The witness had made at any rate one demonstrable error.

Hayden's evidence-in-chief ended at midday on Tuesday and we adjourned until the following morning. Caplan's chambers are only a short walk away from Sir John's and he asked Leigh Howard and myself to go with him. I knew what he was going to say.

'We have reached a critical stage in this case,' he began, 'and I have to ask for further instructions. I cannot say that all these witnesses are just mistaken. It won't wash. The alternative is to attack them as to credit. Before I follow that course I must have instructions from Schapiro and yourself.'

'Is there not something between the two extremes?' I asked.

'Maybe they were genuinely suspicious at first and later found themselves in a position from which they could not withdraw. I have known that happen in other cases.'

'No,' said Caplan, 'that amounts to the same thing. Either their evidence is honestly given or it is not.'

'I still don't quite see your difficulty, I replied. 'We didn't do what they are suggesting. So surely you must put it to them that their story is false?'

'Of course I will,' he said, 'but there are different ways of doing that. I can challenge them formally and let our defence speak for itself; or I can cross-examine more fiercely as to credit.'

Mrs Hayden cross-examined

During her evidence Hayden had made much of the reluctance of Becker and herself to create a public scandal. We had read about her forthcoming book and we knew they had both appeared in a radio programme. We also knew that Hayden had appeared in a 'Bridge Forum' where, according to the ACBL Bulletin, she had been warmly applauded after giving a 'blow-by-blow' account of her part in the affair. Caplan began his cross-examination by casting doubt on her sincerity.

Mr Caplan: 'You have been at pains to tell us of your desire not to – 'crucify' was the word you used – Mr Reese and Mr Schapiro. Am I right in thinking that you are engaged in writing a book about this particular matter?' A. I think you are wrong. Would you like me to tell you about the book?

'You tell me about the book, yes,' said Caplan incautiously.

We were told at length about a book she had contracted to write some time before and a plan to add a chapter called 'Nine Days in May'. She was sorry about the misleading announcement in a magazine but had not taken any steps to publish a disclaimer.

Caplan passed next to the general nature of her evidence.

Mr Caplan: 'Mrs Hayden, when you came here you realised that what you were required for was to give a factual account of what you say you saw?'

Mrs Hayden: 'Yes.'

Mr Caplan: 'One noticed that in giving a purely – as you realised that you were supposed to give – factual account of what you saw, you – and I hope you will forgive the expression – slipped in a tribute to the high ethical standard of Mr Truscott; you slipped in a tribute to Mr Becker being the sort of person who never accuses anybody of cheating; you slipped in a reference to your having heard that Mr Reese and Mr Schapiro had cheated on other occasions; and you slipped in at some length a reference to Mr Kehela being a person who admitted he would tell a lie. Did you do all that deliberately?'

Mrs Hayden: 'Yes.'

Caplan was quite funny about her detailed description of the hand where she saw two fingers on the back of my cards and was nervous of bidding a slam lest I hold two aces. 'One thing you could discard immediately, could you not, was that one finger showed one ace, two fingers two aces, and so forth? You had seen on several hands one player showing four fingers and the other also showing three fingers or four fingers. Did you suppose that you were playing with a pack containing seven or eight aces?'

'Let me deal with another matter,' he went on, 'where I suggest something has been invented in detail to give apparent verisimilitude.' Truscott, obviously an intelligent and ingenious person, had according to the story been given 19 notations to compare with the hand records. He had spent so long trying to find a correlation that when joined by the others it took him 40 minutes to explain what he had been doing. 'If anybody of the meanest intelligence seeks to crack a code of that sort, what is the first thing he must do? Is it not to look at all the hands where one finger, or two fingers, are showing and see what they have in common?'

The witness had to agree that this was elementary and Sir John nodded assent. There was another point that Caplan might have made about this. If you look at a row of figures like 3, 3, 4, 2, 4, etc, surely it is not a long journey to associate those numbers with length in a suit?

The next question was why Hayden and Becker had chosen Gerber as a person to whom to communicate their suspicions.

Mr Caplan: 'Let us consider another aspect of your evidence in regard to this. You told us how with the delicate sensibility which you had in regard to Reese and Schapiro you and Becker wanted to confine the knowledge of this alleged cheating to as few people as possible. In order to do that you told two persons, one of whom was Gerber, whom you say you know to be a person who would enjoy telling others?'

Mrs Hayden: 'We did not have much choice. Truscott seemed to be a natural. We were perhaps a little in doubt about Gerber but we realise now we did not know him then as well as we knew him subsequently. He lives in Texas. That is a bit of a way from New York. Do you think we should not have told Gerber? Is that your point?'

Caplan's main point was that they had told the one person who by virtue of his position as captain of the American team was bound to take official action.

Finally, Counsel put it to the witness that the account of her conversation with Kehela was untrue.

Mr Caplan: 'I suggest to you that you could not and did not have any conversation with Kehela at the time you said you had?'

Mrs Hayden: 'The time may have been slightly different. It was dark out. I know this much.'

Mr Caplan: 'Is that the answer you are giving because you may have exposed yourself by the evidence you have so far given precisely in regard to the time?'

Mrs Hayden: 'No, at the time I gave it I said to you that I was not certain at what time this was. I am not too sure what you are driving at.'

Mr Caplan: 'That will be heard in due course. Thank you.'

Becker's evidence-in-chief

Becker sat with his arms folded, the corners of his mouth turned upwards in a fixed half-smile, and spoke in a calm, unemotional voice. After playing a few boards of the first Monday evening session, he said, he looked to his right and saw that I was holding my cards in what seemed to be a peculiar manner. He gave a demonstration, awkwardly holding the cards with two fingers of his right hand in a V formation. Then he happened to look to his left and noticed that Schapiro was holding his cards in more or less the same way. As the play progressed he noticed other variations and by the time the session ended he was convinced that signals were being exchanged. It was two or three hours before he said anything to Hayden and he warned her not to let it affect her concentration next time she played against us.

Nothing more was done before the next Thursday. (I thought, listening, What self-control with such an exciting secret!) The first session on Thursday was disastrous for the American team and in the short interval he admonished Hayden about her play: 'Dorothy, you are not playing bridge; you are worried about these fingers; can't we possibly get back on the track. Simply play the best we can, there is nothing we can do about it at this point. Please play bridge. What impressed him most during this session was when the cards were held with one finger. 'This struck me as a tremendously unusual way to hold cards.' So it looked, the way the witness demonstrated, with one short finger pointing up to twelve o'clock.

Then came the familiar story of the calling in of Truscott and Gerber, the observation on Friday afternoon, and the late-night code-breaking session. Like Hayden, Becker made much of his desire to confine the matter. 'The only person I was able to think of who, I felt, would not feel any necessity to divulge, this was Gerber.' Gerber, the captain with a duty to perform and a man noted for his outspokenness, not to say his truculence! Like Hayden, Becker had a conversation with Kehela to report. Before the final session on Sunday night Kehela had said to him, 'I know the charges are true but I beg you not to insist on claiming the match against Britain and so causing great publicity.' The General was puzzled about this insistence on claiming the match:

Lord Bourne: 'Can I be quite clear which way this insistence of yours was before this final session?'

Mr Becker: 'I was insisting that the United States could not lose in this match, whatever settlement was made, whatever the outcome was. I was firm. I had been firm all along and I did not weaken my position when I was talking to Kehela.'

Becker cross-examined

Caplan began the cross-examination with a reference to Como:

Mr Becker, if in the course of my cross-examination I have to suggest that you have fabricated evidence, would it be the first time to your knowledge that anybody has ever suggested that you have fabricated evidence in regard to a bridge matter?'

Becker agreed that it was not the first time. His description of the affair at Como was that only one of the American team had openly accused the Italians of cheating. In the public mind they all became associated with the charge and in that limited sense he, like the others, was held to have fabricated evidence by European experts who disbelieved the accusation.

Mr Caplan: 'I shall take it a bit further than that. That is the only sense in which anybody has ever accused you of fabricating bridge evidence?'

Mr Becker: 'To the best of my knowledge, that is.'

Mr Caplan: 'I shall put something much more specific than that to you. This matter of "we must win at practically all costs" is very much the American bridge team feeling, is it not?'

Mr Becker: 'No.'

Caplan put it to the witness that the American team had been responsible for the remarkable scene at Como when the players of both teams had been required to hold their cards below the table during the bidding.

Mr Becker: 'Would you leave out the word "remarkable"?'

Mr Caplan: 'Very well, "scene". You do not think it remarkable?'

Mr Becker: 'Well, I think it rather remarkable that the opponents should have a way of sending messages to each other; that is more remarkable to me than that we should ask or try to so prevent them from sending messages to each other.

Mr Caplan: 'This means that you were of the opinion, and are of the opinion, that the Italians were cheating on that occasion?'

Mr Becker: 'Yes.'

That was Becker's bombshell. Later he was more precise, saying that all six members of the American team had been convinced, simply by the nature of the plays made against them, that one of the Italian pairs had been signalling. I was amazed at this. For one thing, I was at Como and knew all the hands on which the allegation was based; for another, the many triumphs of the Italian players since then, in a great variety of partnerships, seemed fully to prove that their early successes were based on merit.

Caplan introduced a new matter at this point but returned to Como later to show what he had in mind when he spoke of fabricating evidence. We had turned up the April 1958 Bridge World in which a syndicated article by Becker had been reproduced. This described a hand on which an Italian player was said to 'go into a long huddle' and make 'an extraordinary return'. The implication was very plain and Becker did not deny that for tournament players the article suggested malpractice. We also had a copy of a letter sent to the *Bridge World* by the Dutch player, Herman Filarski, who had been scoring at the time of the incident. Filarski insisted that there had been no 'long huddle' at all and gave a rational explanation for the play. The *Bridge World* did not publish his protest and he sent a copy of the correspondence to the secretary of the European Bridge League, who circulated it to the delegates.

The other main strand of the cross-examination concerned the different accounts of the development of the affair in Becker's article for the Journal-American and in his evidence. Becker's reply was that the article, while based on a telephone call and a cable he had sent, was partly rewritten by a reporter on the paper. This he was able to substantiate later.

When asked how he reconciled his description of the awkward way in which we held our cards with Hayden's 'very graceful and natural-looking', the witness made a strangely exaggerated remark. He thought our way of holding the cards was awkward because since Buenos Aires he had observed one thousand people holding cards and had yet to see one who did not hold them with four fingers touching some portion of the back of the cards. Towards the end of the cross-examination Caplan referred to Kehela:

Mr Caplan: 'You and Mrs Hayden are both of you aware, are you not, that Mr Kehela has given evidence in this Inquiry?'

Mrs Hayden: 'Yes.'

Mr Caplan: 'Did not both you and Mrs Hayden agree to throw in some pieces of evidence which you hoped might discredit Mr Kehela?'

Mrs Hayden: 'Yes.'

Caplan gave his rendering of one who in his entire career had never heard such a damaging admission. Sir John subtracted from the effect a little by remarking, 'It does not shock me as much as it does you, Mr Caplan.' Sir John also made the point that Kehela, at the time of the alleged conversation with Becker, might not have precisely formulated his doubts.

Becker's re-examination carried us into Thursday morning. Although the Inquiry was private, important news tended to reach the people concerned. In a letter to Rixi Markus Kehela reaffirmed the evidence he had given at the Inquiry, observing (as if we hadn't noted it) that the triumvirate were set on making out their case.

8 'Dear Me'

IT HAD BEEN DEPRESSING to listen to the triumvirate all telling the same story, and Swimer, the non-playing captain of the British team, was still to come. Caplan, while full of fight, did not conceal that he regarded the case as difficult; a little like a doctor who, talking to the patient's relatives, manages to leave it in the air that only professional skill lies between death and recovery.

Our solicitor, Eric Leigh Howard, was more encouraging. 'Don't worry that Caplan has problems,' he said. 'Counsel are often like that in the middle of a case. Of course this has been a bad time, listening to all their witnesses, but this case has one special feature. As a rule, the critical moment for the defence is when the principal defendant is in the witness-box. Often the prosecution will not seem to have made out its case, but then the defence is blown apart by cross-examination. Nothing of that sort can happen here. So far as the observation side is concerned, the fact is that you did nothing and you know nothing. They won't be able to shake you on that. The evidence about the hands is more argumentative, but here you have a strong case and obviously you will have the advantage in any technical discussion. Once the prosecution's evidence is over, things must begin to go our way.'

If the American witnesses had confined themselves to a plain statement of what they alleged they had seen, it would have been still more difficult to diminish their evidence. Fortunately for us, Truscott and Hayden especially had identified themselves with the prosecution by making many aggressive statements and so raising the question of malice. Truscott had spoken in a most exaggerated way about some features of the technical evidence and Hayden had 'slipped in', as Caplan put it, many remarks that went beyond observation of actual events.

In the next few weeks we had further indication of the way these people were acting. At Ostend they talked to any member of the bridge press who would listen to them. The French tournament director, de Heredia, said in a letter to me: 'Je ne cache pas que la qualité de vos accusateurs et leur virulence, voire leur assurance, ont terriblement impressionné le public du Bridge.' (I will not conceal from you that the quality of your accusers and their virulence, that is to say their assurance, have made a tremendous impression on the bridge public.) Heredia recalled a similar case in France when the violence of the accusations made against a certain pair at one stage caused him wrongly to believe them guilty.

There was also a meeting of the World Bridge Federation at Ostend early in the championship, and some of the American members were ready to express their view of the case. All this had one serious consequence. A continental witness who could have been most valuable to us, someone who had personal knowledge of several matters we wanted to bring in, and who had already given a most favourable report on the match records, withdrew his support. He wrote to me frankly enough, saying he had been overwhelmed by the combined pressure. He was willing to testify by means of an affidavit about certain incidents but would not appear in person. His lawyer and his editor had both advised him to stay out. 'If you are innocent,' he ended cheerfully, 'you will easily establish this at the Inquiry.' I did not argue with him but I could not resist pointing out that as a witness his function was simply to testify to matters within his own knowledge, not to judge the case in advance.

Another potential witness from Europe defected at the same time. 'For reasons not connected with the case,' he said in a brief letter. His testimony would not have been as valuable as that of the other, but the blow was greater because this was a personal friend of long standing, someone to whom Boris and I had both shown some kindness in the past. I mention these matters, not in reproach, but because they are part of the story.

Another development was the issue of a libel writ by Swimer against Rixi Markus. This matter has not been determined as I write, so all I can say is that it was widely believed to arise from an article entitled 'The Case for Reese and Schapiro' which had appeared under Rixi's name in the Bridge World. This was the background when we met on November 15 and 16 for Swimer's evidence. Sir John's chambers had been redecorated since our last visit. 'In case we have to admit the press,' he quipped.

Swimer's evidence-in-chief

Swimer's evidence-in-chief added little that was new. Up to Saturday, when he first heard of the accusation, he had often watched us play from the captain's chair and had noticed nothing unusual about our play or our methods of play. On the Saturday morning he came back to the hotel shortly before lunch and found a message asking him to go to MacNab's room. There he found MacNab, von Zedtwitz, Gerber and Truscott. They told him of Becker's suspicions and gave him the details of the alleged code. It was said that one finger on the back of the cards meant one heart, two fingers either two or five, three fingers three, four fingers four. That was all.

Mr Goldblatt: 'After you had been told the code, did you say anything or did you listen to some more?' A. I said it seemed quite ridiculous that they should think this sort of thing was possible, and what else did they have? They brought several hands to my notice where they said that it rather looked as though they might have had advantage from this showing of the number of hearts. I went through quite a lot of hands with them in order to try and find some which pointed the other way. It seemed to me that was possible, and finally I did find one hand.

The significance of this speech, for us, was that the Americans had sought to persuade him, not with any notes of observations, but with hands.

After this interview Swimer decided to confer with Butler. Butler could not be discovered for some while but Swimer eventually found him in his, Swimer's, room with – guess who – Truscott. The two officials decided that they would keep observation themselves in the evening. In the afternoon Swimer watched Schapiro play with Konstam and noted that he held the cards always in the same way, with four fingers showing and only the thumb on the inside. (Boris would contest this, as his natural method is to hold about two fingers on the cards, not more, and such photographs as were available supported that.) Describing his observations in the evening, Swimer maintained that he could easily see how many fingers I was showing, although he was sitting behind me. He produced notes of what he said he had observed. After ten hands he left the room for a short while. When he returned, Butler was in the captain's chair, so he went high up on the platform behind me and made some more notations. On a few hands he could not see what I was doing. His note of the two hands where I held a void, 127 and 131, was that at some point in the bidding I had changed my cards from the left hand to the right.

Goldblatt then read out the actual heart holdings, to point the correspondence with Swimer's notes. Lord Bourne asked a few questions to establish that Becker and Hayden had not been present at the meeting in MacNab's room. Swimer said he had not seen either of them before he went in for observation. That concluded the evidence-in-chief.

Swimer cross-examined

Caplan began the cross-examination by asking about the meeting to which the General had just referred. Swimer had understood that Truscott, Becker, Hayden and Gerber had all taken notes of observations.

Mr Caplan: 'There is not the slightest doubt that Truscott said he had taken notes of the finger positions he had seen?'

Mr Swimer: 'That was what I was told at the meeting.'

Mr Caplan: 'As captain of the British team you would presumably be very concerned about this accusation?'

Mr Swimer: 'Naturally.'

Mr Caplan: 'Presumably the first thing you would require would be a sight of the alleged notes that had been taken by Gerber and Truscott?'

Mr Swimer: 'Why should I? Why should I want to have a sight of them?'

Mr Caplan: 'Here is an accusation of cheating against two of the members of the team made by people who say they have taken notes of observations. In your concern for your team members do you not want to see those notes of observation?'

Mr Swimer: 'No. I should not think so. If they tell me that they have these notes, why should I want to see them? How would that help me? What difference would it make to me at the time?'

Mr Caplan: 'Would it have made any difference to you if when you had asked for Mr Truscott's notes he had said he was sorry but he did not have any?

The witness did not answer directly. All he would say was that it was obvious they had made notes.

Caplan then quoted, without giving the source at first, some passages from an article by Truscott in the *New York Times* which referred to the study of match records by Truscott and Swimer together. 'It appeared,' said the article, 'that Mr Reese and Mr Schapiro had an almost perfect record in bidding situations relating to the heart suit.'

Mr Caplan: 'Is that what appeared to you and Mr Truscott when he was putting matters before you?'

Mr Swimer: 'That was the time when I examined some of the records to see if what they were trying to say was accurate.'

Many of Swimer's answers, like this one, were not directly addressed to the question he had been asked. Caplan pressed him strongly to say which of the hands that were shown to him tended to support the charge of illicit knowledge. 'I do not know, several of them,' he replied. Truscott had given him a list of about 19 hands but he had not studied them since. Caplan asked him to look at them overnight so that he could tell the tribunal next day what was the material that in his view tended to show that his colleagues had been cheating.

Then Counsel turned to a different subject:

Mr Caplan: 'Did you have any discussion as to how they differentiated between two and five?'

Mr Swimer: 'Not to my knowledge, not so far as I can remember, I do not think so.'

It seemed unlikely that no-one would have asked about this. Caplan continued:

Mr Caplan: 'Mr Truscott says he told you ...'

Mr Swimer: 'Perhaps he did.'

Mr Caplan: '... how the differentiation was made. What?'

Mr Swimer: 'Perhaps he did.'

Caplan pounced on this answer. 'Do you mean he may have done and you took no notice?'

'I was under a strain at the time,' said the witness, 'and possibly it did not sink in.'

This led to another question:

Mr Caplan: 'If you did not know how they differentiated, when you saw two fingers showing you would be keeping a pretty good look-out to see what else was being done, would you not?'

Mr Swimer: 'How do you mean by "pretty good look-out"?'

Mr Caplan: 'Do you not understand that?'

Mr Swimer: 'What do you mean by a pretty good look-out? What would I be doing?'

Mr Caplan: 'You are not allowed to ask me questions, but if you have any real difficulty about the meaning of a question you may ask me to rephrase it.'

Goldblatt intervened: 'Perhaps my friend would be kind enough to treat the last answer as a request to rephrase the question.'

Mr Caplan: 'Keeping a pretty good look-out – you do not understand what it means? You want me to rephrase it, is that right?'

Sir John Foster: 'He is not sure what you meant by it.'

Mr Swimer: 'I do not know what you mean by "a pretty good look-out". I either see or I do not see.'

Mr Caplan: 'You have never heard the expression "keeping a look-out" for something? I want to know if you are fencing with me, Mr Swimer. Have you never heard the expression?'

Mr Swimer: 'I have, yes.'

A definition was agreed upon and Caplan asked:

Mr Caplan: 'Were you not looking for the point of differentiation?'

Mr Swimer: 'No.'

Mr Caplan: 'You were not? Why not?'

Mr Swimer: 'Well, it showed up almost immediately. I mean, it would show up by the time a hand was being played.'

Of course, this was not an answer to the question, 'Were you not looking out for the method of differentiation?' I quote the passage, not because it had any special importance, but because it illustrates that there was some acerbity in the exchanges. Swimer was having an uncomfortable time. This possibly had a bearing on some later developments.

A long and confusing passage followed in which Swimer was invited to read Butler's Report and see whether, in his view, it contained inaccuracies. Nothing very significant emerged, but Swimer was tiring. Caplan then put it to him that the fair way to observe is for two observers to sit opposite the players they are observing and make no notations as to fingers in regard to any hand where they see the face of a card. It took time, but eventually the witness agreed that this would be a fair way.

At the end of the session Caplan asked whether there had been anything awkward or ungraceful in the way I held my cards.

Mr Swimer: 'No.'

Mr Caplan: 'Is that right?'

Mr Swimer: 'Yes, that is right.'

Mr Caplan: 'Having got a point of agreement with the witness, that seems to me a very good moment to come to a stop.'

On the way downstairs Caplan murmured, 'Bricks without straw, bricks without straw.' It was true, this type of evidence was very difficult to refute. We had the impossible task of proving a negative – of proving that nothing had happened.

When we resumed next morning Swimer was asked which hands he had picked out as most tending to show that there had been illegal passing of information in the heart suit. Italy 25 and US 50 were the ones he had selected.

Reverting to matters of observation, Caplan held up a hand of thirteen cards and asked Swimer how many fingers were showing on the opposite side. Might be one, two, three or four, Swimer replied.

Mr Caplan: 'Thank you. That is exactly what I am putting to you, that in fact it is not so easy as you are trying to suggest to be certain how many fingers are showing on the other side.'

Sir John Foster: 'One can hold the cards in a way that makes it clear perhaps; you have not explored that.'

Swimer gave some demonstrations of what he claimed to have seen. They were all quite laughably awkward.

Mr Caplan: 'That looks easy and graceful, does it?'

Mr Swimer: 'I think so.'

Caplan tackled the witness about some other inconsistencies between his narrative and Butler's. There were differences in the account of when they met to discuss the accusation and who was there, at what point Butler had taken over the observation from Swimer, and what happened on the two hands when I held a void.

Mr Caplan: 'Now I want to ask you about some matters concerning the occasion when you say you watched Boris Schapiro.' Intending to comment on his client's nervous agitation, Caplan looked round. His client was fast asleep! (It is fair to say that his occupation at Quents kept him up very late at night.) Caplan continued: 'Although he does not look it at the moment, is it right that he is a rather fidgety person?'

Counsel asked some questions about the personal relationships within the team. Was it right that I had not wanted to play with Schapiro at Buenos Aires? Swimer agreed that was so.

Mr Caplan: 'Let me remind you of a conversation. Did Mr Reese come to you and say words to this effect, "Am I thought to have the worst judgment of anybody in London? Not once have you asked my opinion about the line-up"? Do you remember his saying that to you?'

Mr Swimer: 'No.'

Mr Caplan: 'Anything like it, just think?

Mr Swimer: 'I remember that he was peeved. I do not remember his using those words.'

Mr Caplan: 'Peeved with you?'

Mr Swimer: 'Yes.'

Mr Caplan: 'Why was he peeved with you?

Mr Swimer: 'Everybody was peeved with everybody from time to time.'

That was a fair epitaph on the week, I dare say; better than Butler's 'a happy unit of six'.

Caplan asked Swimer about the trials for Baden Baden when he had played with Boris:

Mr Caplan: 'Was he very critical of your play?'

Mr Swimer: 'In the last week-end, in the final session, he was, yes.'

Mr Caplan: 'Did you attribute your non-selection for the international team that year to Schapiro's criticism of your play?'

Mr Swimer: 'Yes, I think that was the main reason why I was not selected, because he was rather, again, vocal with his criticism. Everybody became aware of any kind of error that I made.'

Finally, Swimer was asked about the '110 per cent guilty' remark that he was reported to have made at the Executive Committee meeting. His reply was:

'I do not remember using that kind of phrase. It is not a phrase I am likely to use. I do not remember using it. But I was in an emotional state. I cannot see how they [i.e. the press] got it anyway.'

I could have told him that. Gerber spoke about it to Flint, and no doubt to many other people as well.

Swimer re-examined

In re-examination Counsel's questions are limited to matters that have been raised in cross-examination, and usually nothing of great moment arises. This was to be an exception.

Goldblatt's first questions were directed to showing that Swimer had not been influenced primarily by the hands but by his observations later in the day.

Mr Goldblatt: 'At the end of that [first] interview were you leaning in any particular direction as to whether the allegations of cheating were or were not true?'

Mr Swimer: 'I was fairly sure that this could be a sort of trumped-up story.'

Mr Goldblatt: 'What, if any, parts of the case that had been put to you at that time did you regard as being fairly surely trumped-up?'

Mr Swimer: 'It seemed to me that this finger business was so crude. It seemed to me that these people did not need this sort of thing and it just did not make sense to me.'

We were happy with both these last two answers. Shortly before the adjournment Sir John returned to the 'trumped-up' suggestion:

Sir John Foster: 'I am a bit intrigued by the trumped-up charge answer. This sort of line strikes me as a little curious, that Mr Swimer should think that A, B, or C would trump up a charge. That is what is going through my mind.'

Mr Caplan: 'I have already asked him about whether they were known to be prone to making accusations.'

Sir John Foster: 'Perhaps Mr Goldblatt will elaborate on that. It is the sort of thing I am curious about.'

Returning from the luncheon interval we observed Swimer in earnest conversation with the BBL solicitor, John Pugh. Goldblatt continued the re-examination.

Mr Goldblatt: 'I have been invited to ask you to elaborate your belief at the end of the first interview that the allegations against Reese and Schapiro may have been trumped up. What reasons did you have for supposing that?'

Mr Swimer: 'There were not any reasons particularly, but I thought they might be mistaken. I did not think they just thought of the whole thing. I thought it seemed so crude that it just did not seem something that was probable.

Sir John Foster: 'Trumped-up is to my mind a bit more than just a mistake.'

Goldblatt asked next about Swimer's relationships with members of the team.

Mr Goldblatt: 'It was also put to you that you had some resentment in your mind against Schapiro. Did you on accepting the captaincy of the British team at Buenos Aires entertain any resentment against any of the six players in your team?'

Mr Swimer: 'So far as Schapiro is concerned, this is very, very far from the truth because I say that Schapiro was more responsible than any other one member of the team for my accepting the captaincy.'

Mr Goldblatt: 'What do you mean by that?'

Mr Swimer: 'He was the one who repeatedly approached me, telephoned me and spoke to me to try and persuade me to take on this job.

Counsel asked the witness at what point in time he had made the notes of his observations.

Mr Goldblatt: 'Were the pencilled columns of figures, and in one case words or symbols under the letters R and S in each of these documents, all inserted by you prior to the end of the Argentina session that you were watching?'

Mr Swimer: 'Do you mean each of these?'

Mr Goldblatt: 'Yes.'

Mr Swimer: 'They were put in during the play of each hand.

I looked up with interest and whispered to Caplan. Swimer quickly added: 'That means immediately after the bidding.'

Sir John Foster: 'Before the play even?'

Mr Swimer: 'Before the play started.'

Mr Caplan: 'His first answer was "during the play".'

Twice during the re-examination Swimer had spoken of being under a strain. Once was when Truscott had been explaining the alleged code at the first interview and the second occasion was during the meeting of the Executive Committee.

'What was your strain at that time?' Goldblatt asked.

'That was at a time shortly after I had spoken to Schapiro, at a time shortly after he had confessed to me that they had been cheating.'

That is how it happened, the most sensational moment of the trial so far; smooth and totally unexpected. Sir John, who had left the table to take a drink from a carafe of water on the mantelpiece, turned sharply round. I could sense Boris, a few feet away, seething like the lid of a boiling kettle. If Goldblatt was taken by surprise he did not show it. Caplan sat up very straight and said:

'This is a most extraordinary piece of re-examination.'

Mr Goldblatt: 'It certainly is an extraordinary time for this to come out. We shall probably all have to develop this. I think perhaps, that having been said, it would be as well if I dealt first of all with other matters and then came back to that. Probably my friend will want to cross-examine further upon it.'

Some more questions followed about the exact nature of the observation, particularly the two occasions when I held a void. Everybody was waiting for more news of the alleged confession. As it was a new matter it became 'further examination'.

Swimer further examined

Mr Goldblatt: 'Mr Swimer, I think you had better tell us when and how you came to talk to Mr Schapiro.

Mr Swimer: 'May I first of all say that this is something I had hoped I would not have to disclose to anybody, but the way things have developed it would seem that the proceedings of this Inquiry will not only affect my welfare and my family's welfare but a lot of innocent people. Therefore I came to the conclusion that it was the proper thing for me to do.'

Sir John Foster: 'Could you perhaps say, Mr Swimer, how you see it that it would affect your welfare and your family's welfare?'

Mr Swimer: 'I think there has been a tremendous amount of criticism of my behaviour.'

Sir John Foster: 'During this Inquiry?'

Mr Swimer: 'Not during this Inquiry, outside, from a lot of different sources.'

The witness then gave his account of what happened on the Sunday morning at Buenos Aires, between the two meetings. He had been in front of the hotel with his wife and Albert Rose. Schapiro had come out of the hotel alone and had called him over. 'I think he was about to say a lot of nonsense, but I said, "Boris, don't waste your time. I saw everything for myself." He said, "Will you believe me, this is the first time it has ever happened." Then he said, "Will you forgive me?" By this time I had actually broken down. He said, "Will you forgive me?" I said to him, "How could you do such a thing and how could you – I am supposed to be your friend – let me become a party to this?" He said, "Will you believe me, it was that evil man, he made me do it. I wouldn't play the Little Major and he made me do it." Then he kept saying, "What shall I do now?" I said to him, "I suppose you'd better deny it" sort of thing.'

After a question about the time of the alleged conversation and why had he kept silent at Buenos Aires, Swimer went on:

'I missed out something. Mr Schapiro said to me, "You won't tell anybody, promise you won't tell anybody." I did not promise and I did not say anything to that, but I did not intend to tell anybody about it.'

Mr Goldblatt: 'When did you change your decision about this?'

Mr Swimer: 'Yesterday, last night, yesterday afternoon when I was being examined. When I got home.'

Swimer added that he had told three people what had happened but did not wish to disclose who they were.

Mr Goldblatt: 'Sir John, I think I shall leave the question. My friend ought to cross-examine on that.'

Mr Caplan: 'I should imagine there could be no doubt about that.'

Mr Goldblatt: 'There is no doubt.'

Swimer further cross-examined

Mr Caplan: 'Mr Swimer, when did you form the decision to give this startling piece of information to this Inquiry?'

Mr Swimer: 'Yesterday.'

Mr Caplan: 'Did anybody in this room know about the decision that you had made?'

Mr Swimer: 'This morning, yes.'

Mr Caplan: 'I am going to suggest to you that this is all a lot of made-up rubbish. You have already spoken about your own interests in this matter? Mr Swimer: 'Yes.'

In the next part of the cross-examination there were references to the writ that Swimer had issued. Later:

Mr Caplan: 'I am going to ask you a little more about this story that you have suddenly produced. You said you had hoped that you would never have to disclose it?'

Mr Swimer: 'That is right.'

Mr Caplan: 'You were so tenderly concerned about Schapiro, however, that you were satisfied to see him branded as a cheat?'

Mr Swimer: 'How do you mean "so tenderly concerned"?'

Mr Caplan: 'You have said you hoped you would never have to disclose it, which I imagine was intended to show some concern for him, and that you had no reason to talk about it to the Bridge Federation. The fact of the matter is that at the meeting you were quite satisfied to see Schapiro branded as a cheat, were you not?'

Swimer's answer to this was that there was sufficient evidence and he did not want to bring out the confession. That argument would be more plausible, I thought, if at any time he had done anything to mitigate the consequences of the scandal. If the situation was as he represented it, and if he felt some concern in a personal way, the obvious solution was to admit nothing, withdraw the team, go home and make a confidential report to the British authorities. Also, if one person had confessed, surely it would have been natural to go to the other and say, 'The game's up. Now let's consider what's to be done.'

Caplan left a number of obvious questions unspoken at this moment. Sir John asked one of them:

'Does it not seem rather ambivalent to say "you had better deny it"? It makes nonsense of the whole thing, does it not?' Swimer replied that we had to deny it in order to survive. Sir John commented: 'If somebody has committed a murder and says he has not done it you do not tell him to go on denying it. The truth must appear now and then.' And Lord Bourne asked: 'If they were in fact considered by you to be international cheaters did you want them to survive?' Rightly or wrongly we felt – our legal advisers and ourselves – that Swimer's story of a confession had not damaged us. On his own showing he had withheld vital evidence that ought to have been put in much earlier. He could hardly have improved his standing in an evidential sense.

In the half-hour that remained Caplan made his opening speech for the defence. I am leaving that over till the next chapter, as the present episode was not ended. A couple of days later Eric phoned me and said:

'There has been another extraordinary missile from the other side. Swimer now says that while at Rio (this would be three or four days after the events at Buenos Aires) he wrote a letter to himself in London which is still unopened. He wants to be recalled and to open and read the letter in court. I haven't spoken to Caplan yet, but I imagine he will object.'

When we met for the next session on November 26 Goldblatt informed the court that according to his instructions there was in existence an unopened envelope which Swimer had addressed to himself from South America. It contained an account of what he said had occurred at Buenos Aires some days before. It was felt proper that Swimer should attend with the document in his possession so that the tribunal would have the opportunity of investigating it and seeing what, if anything, it added to the material already before it.

What was in everybody's mind, of course, was that the letter would probably contain some reference to the alleged confession. That would establish, not that the story of the confession was true, but that it was not concocted for any purpose connected with recent events.

In the legal discussion that followed, Caplan said simply that the document was inadmissible. 'No witness can substantiate his own evidence in any way whatsoever by a document which he himself has produced.' He had opened for the defence, he did not want to waste time examining inadmissible documents for their authenticity, he wanted to proceed with his case.

Goldblatt contended that the time at which, according to the defence, the story of the confession had been concocted was a live issue in the case. The document might have a bearing on that and so was material at which the tribunal was entitled to look. Caplan said there was no authority for such a proposition. Sir John observed: 'We are at liberty as a tribunal to disregard rules of evidence unless they are founded on good sense.'

Finally, Sir John and the General were left to confer privately. When we were recalled, Sir John intimated that he would not look at the document if Caplan would withdraw the suggestion that the confession story had been concocted because of recent happenings. On that understanding, Swimer, who had been waiting downstairs, was not recalled.

Like the story of the confession, the significance of this new development could be argued either way. Sending oneself a letter in another continent – was it the action of a person anxious to set down the facts while still in mind or did it fit in with the picture of someone who had given doubtful evidence and foresaw the possible need to bolster up his story?

The unopened document became known in defence circles as the 'Dear me' letter. We wondered, Did it begin, 'Dear me,' and end, 'Hoping this finds you as it leaves …'?

9 A Thought for Christmas

AT THE CONCLUSION of the prosecution's case Goldblatt referred to the affidavit from von Zedtwitz. We had seen this and in my opinion it amounted to very little. Before it was suggested that any code had been broken, he had observed one hand where I held the cards with two fingers separated, and in his recollection he associated this with a hand where I held five hearts. We had the right to object to any evidence that could not be tested by cross-examination, and we did so object.

Opening speech for the defence

Caplan's opening speech was brief and effective. He began with some comments on the background:

'One of the features of this case up to now has probably been that you, Sir John, and General Lord Bourne have had a glimpse into another world entirely, a world which you may think turns out to be of a rather unexpected character, that is to say the world of top-class international bridge. It is a world in which, I venture to suggest the evidence has disclosed, there are extremely strange passions and extremely strange antagonisms at work. That is the background of this whole Inquiry, this peculiar world. It is a world in which there are few, it appears, if any, great players who are not subject to envy and malice by other players who have not reached their heights. It is a world where the weapons of that envy and of that malice have been found not infrequently to be the false trumped-up accusation of cheating. That is the corner of that world which is the subject of this Inquiry. It is a world especially in which Mr Reese, who is by very common acknowledgement in that world to be regarded as perhaps the very best player in it, and in which Mr Schapiro, who is hardly perhaps greatly inferior as a player, have been almost magically free from accusations of this kind, notwithstanding their pre-eminent position and notwithstanding the kind of jungle this world is.'

Why, Caplan asked, even if you start from the assumption that great players might want to cheat, why should they exchange only the marginally important information about the heart suit when there is much more important information that could be exchanged in a simpler way? If it is said that they have been actually detected only in the one form of cheating the answer must surely be that if two brilliant players were cheating all along the line they must sweep the board. Nobody could stand against them.

Then there was the improbable method: 'When one considers all the ways in which cheating can be done, one thinks, Is it really credible that two clever men should do it in this crude fashion, so crude that it is alleged by some witnesses that they were holding their hands in a way which was so awkward that others could not fail to notice the awkwardness?'

Counsel spoke of the 'cruel dilemma' in which we found ourselves on that 'horrible Sunday' when we were separately charged before the committee. 'Fortunately my clients are not obliged simply and solely to resort to bare denials, because in this game of bridge, when there is an accusation of cheating, the experts recognise that the cards talk: the cards talk very loudly. What has been played by these people who are said to have cheated is regarded as of great importance. It is no good Mr Truscott or anyone else coming here to say that the reason why he produced hands was of secondary importance. The reason why the hands were produced and the reason why everybody was looking at the hands was because everybody recognised that the hands cannot lie. I am going to put before you a number of instances where, as the hands cannot lie, it is just impossible for there to be cheating taking place.

Sir John Foster: 'Meaning they would have done better?'

Mr Caplan: 'They would not have called this, they would not have done that. It is impossible. You may say, "Well, can that really be right? Are we to take notice of things of this sort when we have the evidence of people who say they saw the signals?" It is a good question. May I endeavour to answer it in this way?'

Caplan's way was clever, and his own idea. He asked the court to imagine a big money game where the bystanders at the end of the session claim to have observed the passing of signals denoting length in the heart suit. However, on one hand a player held:

♠ A K Q
♡ A K 10 x x x x x
♢ A K
♣ —

The bidding ended in Six Hearts and it turned out that the partner held three cards in hearts. Knowledge that partner held three hearts would make the grand slam a demonstrable certainty. In face of such evidence, who would believe that the players were signalling to one another on that hand?

This, said Caplan, was an extreme example of how the cards could speak with a loud and clear voice. We would bring forward many hands, not so extreme as this hand obviously, where the same sort of inference could be drawn. After instancing two such hands (US 35 and Argentina 34), he concluded:

'I thought I would just indicate the line of argument and why it is that such emphasis will be placed upon the hands, because there is nothing else that innocent persons can do when faced with this kind of allegation except deny it and then rely upon the way the cards speak.'

Sir John Foster: 'A guilty person would deny it too. '

Mr Caplan: 'On the other hand I put before you the psychology of it, that if you had two guilty persons, separately tackled, who had been guilty of a crude fraud, and had each been told that half a dozen people had seen them do it, the most likely result psychologically is that one of them would say, "Well, I've been found out; that's too bad." '

Reese's evidence-in-chief

The session following Caplan's opening address began with the discussion about the possible recall of Swimer. Then I was called as the first witness for the defence. Caplan took me through the events that have made up this story, beginning with my record as a player, the selection of the team for Buenos Aires, and my relationship with the various people involved.

When Caplan asked about cheating methods in general I chose my words carefully.

Mr Caplan: 'I want to ask you about this kind of thing, cheating and so on. First of all, if bridge players are cheating, is it information of a particularly valuable kind for them to convey to each other how many hearts they hold?'

Mr Reese: 'Yes, it is valuable. It is not the most valuable, but it is valuable.'

Mr Caplan: 'It is valuable, but will you tell us what information of greater value they could convey to each other, if they wanted to cheat?

Mr Reese: 'It would depend on how complicated a system one was going to use, but let us say that I just spoke to you for a minute before we went into a tournament. I would suggest, perhaps, two signs for you. The first would be a simple one to show whether I was good, medium or strong for the bid I last made.'

Taking it at one mile an hour, I explained how one could bid in halves or even quarters, calling in effect 'Two-and-a-quarter spades' or 'Two-and-a-half spades'.

Mr Caplan: 'Is this more valuable than just the knowledge of what hearts …?

Mr Reese: 'Oh, it is of a different order.'

Mr Caplan: 'Is it much more valuable?

Mr Reese: 'Yes, much more valuable. The other thing I was going to mention – and again this is something I could put to you in half a minute if you and I were going to play in a tournament next door – was just having one simple sign, maybe the angle at which you hold the cards, for spades, hearts, diamonds, clubs. Then at any time you can suggest a lead from partner, either an opening lead or a lead later in the play. With those two signs of incredible simplicity, and quite undetectable because they cover such a small area of ground, I would say that I could play with somebody not among the first 200 players in the country and probably play world championship bridge with them, just with those two simple signs.'

A little later Caplan asked:

'Mr Reese, if you had turned your mind, or wanted to turn your mind, to cheating, would you have had any difficulty in devising undetectable ways of cheating and conveying far more valuable information than the heart suit?'

Mr Reese: 'I think no difficulty at all. It is the sort of thing I could very easily turn my mind to as an intellectual feat, very easily.'

Goldblatt looked up at Sir John and started to write busily. One could foresee the question: So you would find it easy to devise ways of cheating which you thought could not be detected?

Caplan asked about my previous relationships with American players and Sir John seemed to be tickled by my description of the qualifying round in the 1964 Olympiad. 'We were playing on bridgerama. We had a wretched little room downstairs; it was a sort of boiler room. In the session of 18 boards one or other of us was sent out of the room about ten times while his partner was explaining what he understood by the last bid.'

Perhaps the most significant passage in my evidence followed. I related several incidents which could not have failed to arouse suspicion had we been engaged in any malpractice. First I described how Becker turned full face to look at his opponent during the bidding.

Sir John Foster: 'It leads to the other person pretending to be something else in order to defeat that?'

Mr Reese: 'Not necessarily, but it is not part of the game to look at an opponent to see how he is reacting. One American player once said of another, "I'm not going to bid till ***** takes his eyes out of my lap," and I was frankly surprised to see Becker doing this, because he is certainly a man of good reputation.'

Goldblatt made a note of this remark too. It was agreed that studying an opponent's demeanour was more suited to poker than to bridge. Then Caplan asked:

'Were there some other surprising things you noticed?'

Mr Reese: 'There were a number of factors – this is how I would put it – which, had we any nefarious intent, certainly could not have failed to attract my attention. Now it was very peculiar, in the middle of the week when I was playing in the open room, to see members of another team like Becker and Hayden and Gerber come to watch us play, especially as they stood far away from the table and not in a position where they could follow the play intelligently. One would expect them to be more interested in their own team playing on bridgerama.'

Lord Bourne: 'Of course, people watch each other at international tennis at Wimbledon. A fellow goes and watches the other semi-final with very great care. I do not expect that is necessarily so in bridge – I accept that.'

Mr Reese: 'They do not in bridge, General, because you are playing in a long, relatively tiring tournament. You can, if you are very interested, get behind someone and watch the play, but it is exceedingly rare and it is much more interesting to watch on Bridgerama – that is the basic point.'

On Saturday there had been at least two surprising occurrences. First, it was peculiar, and had annoyed Flint and myself, that Swimer should make a point of my playing with Boris for the last session against Argentina. Swimer knew that Flint and I liked to play together whenever possible, and this was an obvious opportunity. In the evening it struck me as an excess of duty when Swimer took the captain's chair to watch the end of the match. Then came the strange phenomenon of Butler clambering over the ropes to occupy the captain's chair. 'As it happened, I was declarer on the first two hands after his arrival and after each I said to Boris with mock gravity, "Did I play that all right, partner?" Not very funny, but the sort of thing that passes for a joke between us.' I added, which was perfectly true, that I had glanced at the notes Butler was making and had seen strange symbols like 'R S 3'.

My evidence-in-chief lasted for two more days after this. At the next session I described the events on the Sunday – the two meetings, the committee's announcement, the way the story was circulated to the world's press. Then came the long task of dealing with the technical evidence. First I had to comment on the 35 hands where it was alleged that our bidding or play had been, or might have been, influenced by knowledge of the heart suit. Everything had to be taken very slowly because Sir John was attempting to follow all the points I made and conscientiously wrote them down in his book. It seemed to interest him, and progress from one hand to the next was often held up while he asked a question about the bidding at the other table. I had intended, when advancing the hands favourable to our side, to address my comments in effect to the assessors, but now I changed my plan. I cut down the number of new hands, omitting the more delicate examples and painting the picture in broad colours.

To change the pace during the recital of hands, Caplan gave me a chance to comment on the photos from play that had been put in by the two sides. A few weeks earlier our solicitor had asked a colleague in

Buenos Aires to obtain for us as many photos as possible, taken at the table. Our man in BA replied darkly that he had encountered some difficulty and had put a detective on the job. Eventually we received a dozen or so, of which two or three were relevant and useful. One, taken during the bidding, showed both Boris and myself holding the cards in a way that controverted the alleged signals.

Finally, I made a point about Truscott's octet – the eight hands he had produced to the committee in my presence. Truscott had maintained in evidence that they were not the strongest he knew of at that time, but a random selection from a larger group. I submitted that it was clear, from the position of these hands in Goldblatt's list, that they were a specially selected group.

The current hearing was on December 8 and we were not due to meet again until January 11. Asked when he thought the defence would be concluded, Caplan forecast the end of March. 'When I took this on they told my wife it would last about a fortnight, remarked the General wistfully. Priday observed that the British Bridge League was hoping for an early conclusion. Apart from other considerations, the cost of the Inquiry must already have exceeded the original estimate. The English Bridge Union, more affluent than the BBL, had said at the outset that the League could call on it up to £500; I believe this was later increased to £1,000.

Before we dispersed, Goldblatt left us with a thought for Christmas.

'I would like to give notice to Mr Reese,' he said, 'that the first question I intend to ask him when we resume is whether, having heard the number of the witnesses who have given evidence against him, the direct evidence they have given us as to the observations they made, and having had the opportunity through his Counsel to test all that evidence by careful and protracted cross-examination, he feels that any purpose is to be pursued by the further time and trouble involved in maintaining his and his colleague Mr Schapiro's denial of the charges against them. I shall ask that question right away next time.'

One has heard of defence Counsel submitting that there is no case to answer, but seldom, I think of the prosecution presuming that there is no answer to a case. Legal etiquette forbade me, while under examination, to consult Caplan about the best way to deal with this. The question contained various assumptions – for example, it implied that our situation had deteriorated since we first acceded to the proposal for an Inquiry. A number of debating points could be made about that.

There were two interesting developments over the Christmas period. I had sent a photocopy of the match records to Heredia, in France, and I received now a very encouraging report from him. His conclusion, and he spoke as an expert regularly appointed by the French Federation to inquire into allegations of cheating, was that there was nothing in the records to suggest illicit knowledge of the heart suit and abundant evidence pointing the other way. With Gallic flamboyance he was prepared to stake his reputation as a tournament director, and much else, on the proposition that we had not exchanged signals about hearts; or, if we had, we must be complete children at the game, and he was not prepared to accept that either. Leigh Howard was in Paris at the end of the year and he obtained from Heredia an extremely strong proof of evidence. The second development occurred in America. The following paragraph appeared at the head of a column by Herb Caen in the *San Francisco Chronicle* of November 13:

> The Hilton Hotel, scene of the current big contract bridge tournaments, is abuzz with rumors of another cheating scandal a la the Terence Reese-Boris Schapiro bomb that burst in Buenos Aires recently. Two sizable names are involved.

That was all, but the sizable names were – Becker and Hayden!

Our first intimation of this came from an American at Crockford's who, playing in a private game in New York, was told by someone who had been at San Francisco that it had been common knowledge ('buzz-buzz at every table') that Becker and Hayden were being, or had been, watched. As the story was pieced together, it appeared that some other players in the trials had expressed suspicion and had requested that they should be monitored. No official statement was published and it was expected that a minute of the next meeting of the directors of the ACBL would say that the charge had not been substantiated. 'All that can be made of this,' one American journalist wrote to me, 'is that two or three players dislike B and H.' In the current Bridge World there were letters from Harrison Gray and Rose, both deploring Rixi's article in our support. Gray spoke of his mounting sense of nausea. 'This rushing into print,' he said, 'well-intentioned though it may be, can only defeat its own object.' Rose observed that in his opinion Butler and Swimer at all times had the interest and welfare of the team, and its individual members, foremost in their minds. The next meeting, on January 11, began with the usual inconclusive discussion about future dates. We were somewhat pressed because Flint had a plan to go to America for six months early in February and we also wanted to have Heredia's evidence quite soon. Only one more day was possible in January, but there were chances of a consecutive run in February. Then the cross-examination began.

Reese cross-examined

Mr Goldblatt: 'Mr Reese, I warned you in advance of the first question I was going to ask you. Now let me repeat it. Having, over the many sessions for which this Inquiry has already lasted, listened to the evidence of various people who have told of their observations upon yourself and Mr Schapiro, and having had the opportunity of testing that evidence at great length and in great detail through your Counsel, are you going to continue with the time, trouble and further expense of this Inquiry by continuing to resist the allegations which are made against you.'

I had decided that if I answered in a sentence he would have to break up the question, so I replied:

'You have turned a number of corners in that question. The brief answer is yes.'

Mr Goldblatt: 'You appreciate that I am not asking you to admit from your own lips that you cheated. That might be a very difficult thing for a person to do. I am merely asking you whether you are prepared at this stage to bow to the inevitable and to abandon your further resistance to these allegations.'

Mr Caplan: 'That is a question I object to. I might very well have objected to the first one. How Counsel in the position of prosecuting Counsel dare to put to a person who is in the position of the accused, "It is inevitable that you are going to be found guilty," I do not know. It is most improper.'

Sir John seemed disposed to agree. He suggested that in answering I should take the word 'inevitable' out of it.

Mr Reese: 'The question contains a statement that the Inquiry is bound to, or likely to, end in a particular way. Since I do not agree with that statement, the subsequent part of the question becomes meaningless. If you will take it in two parts I will answer it.'

We left this, and Counsel turned to matters of a more evidential nature. His first question, wrapped around and enclosed from four sides as is the legal habit, was this: What conclusion would I draw if during two consecutive sessions I observed that each of my opponents displayed varying finger patterns at the back of his cards?

Mr Reese: 'I would simply draw the conclusion at that point that the man held his cards in different ways at different times.'

Mr Goldblatt: 'Perhaps I did not make the question quite clear, because your answer contained the words "the man". I am postulating that throughout the 14 boards of each of these two sessions each of your opponents is observed by you to hold his cards during the bidding in these changing ways. What conclusion would you draw?'

Mr Reese: 'I would conclude at that point that both the opponents were in the habit of holding their cards in different ways at different times. I would draw no firm conclusion from that.' Mr Goldblatt: 'Would you draw any tentative conclusion from that?'

Mr Reese: 'No, I would not. As I have said, I have for 30 years held the cards in different ways at different times, and there is evidence of that.'

This wasn't taking us very far and Counsel asked next how Schapiro normally held his cards and what it would mean if he were observed to change the finger patterns in the way described by Becker and Hayden. Mr Reese: 'As I said, it would have no meaning whatsoever, so far as I am concerned, and if indeed it happened where Schapiro was concerned – I do not by any means accept that it did – it would not mean anything to me.'

Mr Goldblatt: 'Are you shutting your eyes to what that sort of variation of finger pattern does in fact mean?'

In fact? This, surely, was for him to prove. I answered:

'Goodness me, you might as well say, supposing you watch somebody and you observe that in 14 hands sometimes he has the cards in his right hand and sometimes in his left hand; sometimes he rests his chin on his hand and sometimes he does not. There are innumerable variations of behaviour which are bound to occur within a two-and-a-quarter-hour session.'

Counsel then approached the same question from the viewpoint of Becker and Hayden. The evidence had been that Becker on the first Monday at Buenos Aires, and Becker and Hayden on the Thursday, had observed the changing finger patterns of both opponents. Did I agree that this might have been so in respect of myself? Quite possibly, I said, with the qualification that there might also have been changes during the bidding of a single hand, and that there could be different interpretations of any way of holding the cards.

Did I contend, Goldblatt asked, that any of the evidence given by Becker and Hayden about what they saw during those first two sessions was either incorrect or dishonest? I replied:

'I cannot be certain that it was dishonest. It is conceivable that they watched and observed this phenomenon to which you have referred and that they believed, although I think it was most unreasonable of them to believe, that they had at some point grounds for suspicion. I am not in a position to say that was not so.'

Goldblatt then handed round copies of a document which reproduced all the observations and notes provided by the various witnesses. It was an elaborate display, adorned with sundry asterisks and obelisks. 'I am going to devote a certain time to asking you about this,' he said.

As the defence did not concede that the notes were a true and accurate contemporary record, there could not be much point in questioning me about them. However, I did not interrupt while Counsel explained his document to the court. Several points arising from it were discussed and it was not until 20 minutes later that he asked if it was my contention that dishonesty had crept into the evidence by this stage. 'Certainly,' I replied.

This disposed of the ornamental chart for the time being, but it exposed me to some difficult questions about the timing and extent of the dishonesty which the defence alleged. We were attributing an unlikely course of action to our opponents, and it was easy for Counsel to highlight some of the improbabilities. I suppose I could have stonewalled and declined to advance any theories about their actions. However, I can generally be trapped into expressing an opinion and I put forward my interpretation of how the whole affair had developed. It was not necessary, I said, to presume a deliberate conspiracy, planned in advance. Perhaps Becker, Hayden and Truscott saw something happening which they thought might be an exchange of signals. They spoke about it to Gerber, and within a few hours came unexpected support from Swimer and Butler. The Americans flew a kite and it caught the wind.

Butler, I pointed out, had come to observe in a suspicious frame of mind. He took up a position immediately behind me where he could see every card I held. He was a person, I suggested, who was capable of being affected by subjective influences. His way of conducting the observation, although he might not have realised it, was by no means the fairest.

As for Swimer, he had gone to Buenos Aires in an unhappy frame of mind. His captaincy had been markedly unsuccessful. He was very conscious of that, I suggested, and very sensitive about it. Then the Americans came to him with their story. He was shown a rubbishy set of hands and at that stage, I contended, he ought to have told the Americans that he wanted to hear no more about it. Instead, he enters into an arrangement to spy on his own team-mates. Having reached, as he said, a certain conclusion, he consults no member of the team but plans with Butler to concede the matches against US and Argentina.

It was the first time the word 'spy' had been introduced into the case and I knew it would create a small flurry. Goldblatt asked a little later:

Mr Goldblatt: 'Mr Reese, you have used the word 'spying' in relation to the conduct of Swimer and the actions of Butler. Would you still have so considered it if these two had watched this Argentina session in precisely the way they did and had come away saying there was no truth in the allegations? A. Your question is, Would I say they had spied? The definition of spy, I imagine, is to observe secretly with a view to obtaining information.

Mr Goldblatt: 'So you would still have called it spying?'

Mr Reese: 'I certainly would.'

Goldblatt suggested that if Butler and Swimer had announced a different conclusion, that would have disposed of the allegations against us. I said it would be naive to think that. Once these accusations reach a certain stage, it doesn't matter how many people deny them. The accusers would simply say that of course it leaked out. One had seen this often enough in international cases.

Counsel pressed the point about the duty of a captain in a situation:

Mr Goldblatt: 'Mr Reese, let me ask you this: Specific allegations having been made against two of his players, would you or would you not regard it as the duty of the captain to attempt to ascertain for himself whether there was any truth in those allegations?'

Mr Reese: 'That is a difficult question, of course, which I was expecting. I quite agree that different people might interpret that in different ways. I personally, if I were captain of a British team and such a thing were said about two members of my team, would have said I was sorry they thought that and would have told them we would not continue to play. I would have taken the team home and arranged for an inquiry, knowing that the match records would establish the truth one way or the other. I think that is the proper way to handle such a matter.'

This, now I come to look at it, was quite an adroit answer, combining a broadminded outlook, dignified patriotism, humane consideration, and trust in the internal evidence.

The next set of questions related to the testimony of Becker and Hayden. Goldblatt's point was that even if the Americans might have had some motive at Buenos Aires to discredit Schapiro and myself, it was absurd to suggest that they should have pursued the same course after all their presumed objectives had been gained – after Britain had conceded the match and the committee had found us guilty. Not absurd at all, I replied. Their credit was still at issue. 'It was not only a matter of persuading this Inquiry. They have done a great number of other things with a view to convincing the world that they were right. Indeed, following out the logic of your question, why should they go to Ostend and hold a press conference there and try to persuade people of the truth of what they had said?'

Sir John asked about Ostend, and I told him what we knew so far about the interview they had given there. I mentioned also that some continental magazines had recently published the entire American story. Goldblatt said with a slight edge of sarcasm:

'I am sure you have been as active as anybody could have been in finding out about all the articles that have been written about these allegations of cheating?'

Mr Reese: 'I have not been in the least active. In the natural course of events I receive the American Bridge World and a Danish magazine, a Dutch magazine and one thing and another. I never go out to find anything about it. Nor do I go out to persuade people one way or another. I did not hold any press conference.'

The next thrust was from a slightly unexpected angle. Turning to the evidence of Kehela, Goldblatt suggested that the number of times even this defence witness had observed coincidence between fingers and hearts was above normal expectation. When some kind of premise had been agreed the matter was left to the mathematicians. Hiron assured us later that we had nothing to fear from this quarter.

Departing at length from matters of direct observation, Goldblatt challenged my evidence about the method of conveying information by finger signs. I had no difficulty in maintaining my point that there were many simpler, more undetectable and equally clear ways of communicating. I was also able to restate my argument that information about heart length was less valuable than about certain other features, my point having been that a winning advantage could easily be established in a less elaborate way. As the day ended, Goldblatt was asking me about the Little Major. It looked as though he was going to follow out Butler's train of thought – that the cheating system with Boris was in some way a substitute for the intricacies of the Little Major.

Before the next session we learned that Truscott had sent a communication to Pugh about the Becker-Hayden affair at San Francisco. What was significant, in relation to our case, was that a small committee had been set up to study the internal evidence. We could perhaps quote this as further proof of the importance of such evidence. However, Caplan considered that we ought to wait until the case had been officially determined before we made any reference to it at our own Inquiry. We had to avoid anything that might appear in the end to be an unsubstantiated attack on credit.

When we resumed a fortnight later, Goldblatt developed his theme about the Little Major. He began by suggesting that the alleged cheating code gave me 'a somewhat similar pleasure and advantage'. I replied that it would not be in any way a similar advantage because the one is an exceedingly complicated intellectual affair, whereas there is nothing intellectual or interesting in exchanging knowledge about the heart suit. I could see no relation of any sort. Goldblatt continued:

Q. One of the points that has been put, Mr Reese, is that it is a very delicate matter for somebody to broach to a partner the possibility or desirability of using a cheating system during a championship match. I think you will agree with that?

Mr Reese: 'I do indeed.'

Mr Goldblatt: 'What I put to you is, having regard to the relationship between yourself and Schapiro, with Schapiro wanting to play with you and you reluctant to play with him, it was an easier matter for you in your position to broach to Schapiro the terms on which you would play, that is to say you would play if he would cheat?'

Mr Reese: 'That is a suggestion which I reject. I do not see any logical basis for it.'

Mr Goldblatt: 'In what light do you regard cheating at bridge, Mr Reese, with horror, detachment, or somewhere in between?'

Mr Reese: 'There are things in life which I consider much more horrible, certainly. I think I regard it with contempt, and also with mystification, because really people want to do well at bridge in order to satisfy themselves that they are cleverer than the other person. If you take that pleasure away, such as it is, I personally cannot see any pleasure in winning at all.'

Soon after, Goldblatt turned to the hands. First he invited me to say what, in my view, was the overall probative effect of the hands. I replied, truly enough, that we had been extremely lucky. Schapiro and I make a number of tactical and irregular bids in the ordinary way and there might easily have been three or four which would appear strong in the context of the allegation. As it happened, there were none that afforded any substantive proof. On the other hand, there was an absolutely remarkable number of hands pointing the other way – far more than I thought possible when I began the analysis. I ended: 'Since you put the question to me, I would say that the hands prove absolutely conclusively to any judge of the game that signals were not used.'

Counsel began with the 15 or so 'defensive' hands that I had put forward in my evidence. His usual method was to secure my acceptance to some general proposition, such as the desirability of maintaining certain standards for overcalls, and then try to bring this down like a blanket on the point we wanted to make about a particular hand. I stressed all the time that the proper way to approach the matter was to put oneself in the position of the player possessing the illicit knowledge and consider what action he would be inclined to take, bearing in mind, of course, that he must not do anything capable of arousing suspicion. It went on for about three hours, neither side giving any ground. Goldblatt concluded:

Mr Goldblatt: 'Do you not agree, now that we have discussed all these hands in detail, with the number of other factors brought into consideration, that all the decisions you say are so obvious are intensely arguable?'

Mr Reese: 'No. I do not think you have made the slightest dent in any of the arguments I put forward, not the very slightest.'

Mr Goldblatt: 'Would you have accepted any dents I have made, or did you come to this cross-examination determined to maintain that attitude?'

Mr Reese: 'My opinion was naturally clear on these hands. You did make one or two small points which I conceded, although they did not touch upon the arguments I put forward. You did not touch my principal arguments on any of these hands in a way that would cause me to rethink them.'

My mulish attitude came in for criticism again when we reached the last hand of the day. Goldblatt had begun on the prosecution hands now and was discussing Italy 22, one of Truscott's octet, mentioned in Chapter 6. According to Truscott, I had a nefarious reason for opening One Diamond on K-9-8-x-x instead of One Heart on K–Q–J–x.

Mr Goldblatt: 'Do you agree that apart from any other consideration an opening bid of One Heart has value for lead-directing purposes, if you find yourself defending and not playing a contract?'

Reese: 'It has a slight advantage in that respect, yes.'

Mr Goldblatt: 'I think that is an advantage with which you did not deal in your previous analysis of the hand?'

Reese: 'I was rebutting your points on the hands. It was not my duty to add to them.'

Mr Goldblatt: 'You would say, would you, that, in giving an expert view as to whether a hand does or does not point towards cheating, it is not the expert's task to take into account all the factors, whether pointing for or against?

Reese: 'I cannot imagine it is my duty to do more than reply exactly to the points you have raised.'

Mr Goldblatt: 'Is that your attitude of mind in dealing with these matters, that you will reply exactly to those points, and if there are others which, from an expert's point of view, would reinforce them, you would be silent about those, because you have had the good fortune not to have them mentioned? A. It would certainly be my view. If you put these hands up against me, and produce various arguments with the assistance of your advisers, it is not my duty to correct you either on the way you put them or to add to them, and subject to any instruction that is the attitude I would maintain.

Caplan and Sir John both joined in. Sir John thought it was a fair question. It could be a trap, he said, a test of credibility. I said I had not suggested that it was an unfair question, only that it was a most unrealistic one.

By the time my cross-examination was continued over two weeks later, the whole of Flint's evidence, and part of Heredia's, had been interposed. This caused some changes in the situation, so I will deal with these events in order.

10 'Written in the Hands'

JEREMY FLINT BEGAN his evidence on the afternoon of Wednesday, February 2, little more than a week before he was due to leave for America. Three more sessions had been arranged for the following week, and we hoped to complete the evidence of Heredia as well.

Flint's evidence-in-chief

Caplan began the examination with questions about the week at Buenos Aires. These were the witness's answers on a number of matters (not necessarily consecutive):

Mr Caplan: 'Having played for England on other occasions, how did you find the atmosphere at Buenos Aires on this occasion?'

Mr Flint: 'I would say that in many ways, in many respects, there was a coldness, and particularly in the social field it was a hostile tournament.'

Mr Caplan: 'What happened when you and Reese played together on bridgerama on the first Monday?'

Mr Flint: 'Schapiro was very critical of our performance and said that we were making a ludicrous spectacle of ourselves and, in fact, some of his comments were very forthright.' (The tribunal was to learn later what 'forthright' meant in relation to comments by Schapiro.)

Mr Caplan: 'How would you describe the relationship between Reese and Schapiro at that time?'

Mr Flint: 'It had not been good for the past three months and, culminating with these hostile remarks, I would say it was almost at breaking point.'

Mr Caplan: 'Prior to the tournament, what indications had Reese given as to who he wanted to play with?'

Mr Flint: 'Reese had always indicated that he wanted to play with me, from about three or four months previously. We were developing a highly complicated system and we were both very keen to do well with this, and he wanted to play with me.'

The witness made a point of the fact that during our long discussions about the Little Major I never made any sort of suggestion, however indirect, that might tend to our obtaining an unfair advantage. This would be extremely easy to do under cover of a system which the opponents would not fully understand. Tournament players will know what I mean.

Caplan then turned to the allegations of cheating. He asked first about the advantage conferred by illicit knowledge of the heart suit. The witness said the advantage would be considerable but mentioned other types of information that would be still more valuable. With such information, he said, a pair like Reese and Schapiro would be invincible.

Mr Caplan: 'Speaking in general terms, what was their performance like in Buenos Aires?'

Mr Flint (after a pregnant pause): 'Disappointing.'

Sir John Foster: 'Have you taken into account that, in a cheating system, you perhaps could not be invincible altogether because you have got to do some things that look so strange that people would deduce you were cheating? Have you taken that into account?'

Mr Flint: 'Yes, I have not been unconscious of that.'

Sir John returned to this point a little later. If the players are clever enough, he suggested, they can give themselves an advantage by always making the right choice when the decision is close and the bid they want to make is within the 'tolerance', i.e. non-suspicious. That was Goldblatt's argument about pattern. Flint replied that we had many opportunities for advantageous calls that could never have been criticised, and Caplan observed that if a pair was using illicit knowledge throughout a long match the results in the heart suit would surely be better than normal. Here he was anticipating some later evidence that we proposed to call.

After about an hour of discussion on general matters Flint began an analysis that included all the hands advanced by the prosecution, all additional hands mentioned in my evidence, and a few new hands, a total of about 50. First, we made a determined attempt to exclude the circular argument that Goldblatt had used on so many occasions.

Mr Caplan: 'There is no hand where it has really been said, "Here is a call which could never have been made but for knowledge of the heart suit"; but what has been said over and over again is, "Here is a bid which is consistent with illicit knowledge of the heart suit." What do you say to that type of presentation of the case?'

Mr Flint: 'I would say that where these hands are, in fact, in accordance with the known methods of Reese and Schapiro, I cannot see that they show anything, and certainly if I were serving on an expert jury and were asked to consider those hands, I would suggest that they should be immediately struck out.'

Surely that was right, and well expressed, yet on the very first hand (Italy 1) Goldblatt, cross-examining on each hand as it came up, had recourse to his ancient theme, saying in effect, 'It may be, as you say, that Three Spades is a correct bid at this point. But if Schapiro knows that his partner holds two hearts, is it not the only bid he can consider making?' Thus it was made to appear that a demonstrably correct bid was part of the pattern whereby the call that suited partner's hand, in the light of illicit knowledge, was invariably chosen.

In the hour that remained we finished only three hands. Caplan would put the example to the witness, adding, if it was a prosecution hand, what point had been made about it. At Sir John's suggestion, Goldblatt cross-examined at once and then Caplan re-examined. As time went on, the discussion became more general, with the assessors joining in. It took altogether two and a half days (the legal day being a short one of about four-and-a-half hours) to complete the full list.

Jeremy's answers were always concise and very well reasoned, but progress was slow for various reasons. Sometimes the assessors would indicate that they were satisfied with the witness's reply to a prosecution hand, but Goldblatt was not readily deterred from putting all his points. Here he had Sir John's support. One of the objects of cross-examining, he remarked at the end of the first day, is to test the witness, to see if his answers on related matters show him to be 'too much a champion'. Caplan also did not hurry things along. He saw himself as the link man between the tribunal and the experts and would often embark on a summary, beginning, 'I suppose one could say this ...' Often one could not, but meanwhile the witness was given a chance to restate his point and the ball was kept in play. Sir John's remark about being too much a champion was not a direct attribution but Jeremy may have taken it as a slight warning nevertheless, for after the first day he was careful not to be too definite. Where I had been curtly dismissive of Goldblatt's less likely suggestions, Jeremy would listen gravely and after a few moments would say, 'I am not sure I can altogether go along with that. You see ...' He was also extremely good at explaining matters to the tribunal. During my evidence Sir John and the General probably thought to themselves, Well, of course this fellow can win bridge arguments with Counsel; that doesn't prove anything. But now there was a change, we made real headway in establishing this part of our case.

At lunchtime on the third day of Flint's evidence only two more hands remained, so we hoped to make a start with Heredia later in the afternoon. When we met after lunch, the General was missing at first. During the interval he had been seen writing busily in another part of the building and we had wondered if he was engaged on a summary of the morning's highly technical evidence. It turned out that he was writing up, not his bridge notes, but notes for a speech on China. Somebody remarked that the two were possibly interchangeable.

When the outstanding hands had been disposed of, Caplan asked Flint about Swimer's reactions when he was left out of the team after the trials for Baden Baden in 1963. The witness described them as bitter. Finally, Caplan turned to the situation when the rest of the team, without Boris and myself, went from Buenos Aires to Rio de Janeiro to play a friendly match.

'The atmosphere in the English camp was really most unpleasant,' said the witness. 'Swimer had been most evasive in any questions that I put to him about the whole matter. He had suggested, as I told you, that we should not have any dealings with Reese and Schapiro, and I was not happy about this. I was not happy to have someone else's say-so that they were guilty. So I asked to see the records and Swimer rather contemptuously said I would not find anything there, and I said, "I prefer to be the judge of that." That is when I started to go through them, a little at Rio and a considerable amount on the aeroplane coming home.'

Flint cross-examined

Goldblatt never hesitated to walk into examining. He began:

Mr Goldblatt: 'Mr Flint, in your earlier evidence you were critical of Swimer's way of dealing with the accusations at Buenos Aires. Could you help me as to why you criticise him?'

Mr Flint: 'Yes, certainly. Here is an inexperienced captain and two of his players are accused of cheating. This is the first time he has been captain of the English team and two very, very famous players who to the best of his knowledge are completely innocent are accused of cheating, and what does he do? He does not consult two elder statesmen who are present, Konstam and Harrison Gray; he goes along and – I cannot use another word – he snoops, and conducts a sort of spying campaign on his own players, and when they are arraigned before a tribunal he does not, in fact, give them any support. He also tries to cut them off from their own team-mates by suggesting that they are to be incommunicado.'

Mr Goldblatt: 'I want you to assume that an English captain, having heard accusations made against a pair in his team, made a decision to observe that pair in action, did observe them, and as a result of his observations reached the conclusion that the accusations against them were well-founded. If an inquiry subsequently took place, what do you say the English captain should have done?

Mr Flint: 'I think he would have to attend that inquiry, and I suppose he would have to give evidence to that effect.'

Mr Goldblatt: 'If, therefore, in this particular case, Swimer did – and you appreciate this is a hypothesis, there is great dispute about it – observe matters which appeared to confirm allegations of cheating against Reese and Schapiro, you do not seek to say that he should not thereafter have told the people enquiring into it at Buenos Aires about what he had observed?'

Mr Flint: 'No, I do not think – I see that once he has gone so far, it is like the primrose path, he was too far in to draw back from it. Yes, I accept that.'

Mr Goldblatt: 'Would you accept this much, too, that if an English captain receives allegations against a pair in his team whom he has no reason to suspect, one course he may decide to take is to go and see for himself whether there is anything in these accusations at all?'

Mr Flint: 'I can only comment that I think it would be a very ill-judged course to adopt.'

Sir John Foster: 'You should not tip them off, I suppose?'

Mr Flint: 'Well, that is another matter. I think there are many people who, you know, might have said, if they had thought there was any possible truth in the accusation, "Look, you two, if you are doing this thing, for goodness' sake stop it, whatever it may be."'

Mr Goldblatt: 'What about Butler taking the same course of action? What do you say about that?'

Mr Flint: 'Well, he rather reminds me of the character, is it not in Alice in Wonderland, of judge and jury, accused and prosecution, and every other possible role he seems to have fulfilled in this matter.'*

It was a feature of Goldblatt's cross-examination that he always gave the defence witnesses every chance to declare themselves on critical matters. Whether this was done so that his fairness would be evident, or because he thought the witness might overreach himself, I was never sure. He asked next:

'You have it very firmly in your own mind that there is no truth whatever in the allegations against Reese and Schapiro?'

Mr Flint: 'As far as I am concerned, from what I have seen, observed, or in any way seen from the records, I can see no truth in it.'

Mr Goldblatt: 'Would it be fair to say this, Mr Flint, that your analysis of the hands has been directed at finding hands which point against cheating by Reese and Schapiro?'

Mr Flint: 'No, when I looked through the records originally I did so with both points in mind, either to find supporting hands, or hands that tended to show they were innocent.'

Mr Goldblatt: 'How high do you place the general conclusion on the hands with which you have dealt?

Mr Flint: 'I would say, as far as I am concerned, I am totally satisfied that if Reese and Schapiro were cheating in the way that has been alleged, then they are either not as good players as the world supposes, by a very, very long chalk, or they made an imperial muddle of their cheating. When I say "not so good", I mean on occasions they played like nincompoops.'

Counsel suggested that using a cheating system would make the game excessively complicated, especially if the players had to bear in mind

---

*'I'll be judge, I'll be jury', said cunning Old Fury:
'I'll try the whole case, and condemn you to death.'

always that their bids must be within the area of tolerance, i.e. non-suspicious. Jeremy did not accept this. Any cheating system, he remarked,must be a simplifying manoeuvre for the players. (There are really two aspects of this, which were not sufficiently distinguished. Obviously a pair could encumber itself with too many signals and so lose concentration; but to know a single factor like the length of partner's heart suit must make the game easier.)

Caplan re-examined briefly, leaving about three quarters of an hour for Heredia to begin his evidence.

Heredia's evidence-in-chief

Irénée Bajos de Heredia made two separate appearances, with other witnesses intervening, but it is convenient to take all his evidence together. The stylish flow of his patronymic is a little misleading. He is stocky in build, with spiky hair and a countryman's complexion. His manner and speech are blunt, with none of the flowery attachments one usually finds among Frenchmen of his class. A yellow Gitane invariably dangles from his lips. It comes as a slight surprise to learn that he is the father of seven daughters.

Heredia speaks no English and Leigh Howard undertook the role of interpreter. It was not an easy task, for the witness often went off at a rate far beyond interpreter or shorthand writer. However, as I could generally follow what he was saying, everybody else must have done. Setting aside the question and answer form, this was his early evidence:

'I have for many years been the honorary international referee appointed by the French Bridge Federation. I have directed many big international tournaments. I am a writer and journalist and as a player I have won many French championships. 'My feelings in regard to the ethics of bridge playing, and those who break those ethics, are very severe. I have been officially concerned in all French cheating cases. Sometimes the people accused have been acquitted, sometimes not.

'In such investigations examination of the hand records is the most important aspect, because people think they see things, they think they do not see things. One has seen, another has not seen. But the analysis allows conclusions to be drawn. We have had a case in France where nobody had seen anything at all, and the analysis alone established there had been cheating. Another case was exactly the opposite. This was an affair "passionelle". It started like the present case. Three people alleged that they had seen cheating going on. A tribunal was appointed to consider the affair and I was president of the technical jury which examined the hands. The accusation was rejected.'

Mr Caplan: 'On the strength of the analysis of the hands?'

Mr Heredia: 'The French phrase is that the proof had not been brought of what was alleged. The accusers were unable to satisfy the tribunal of what they had seen.'

Mr Caplan: 'From your experience, do you believe it is possible for two people to cheat over the course of a championship without an examination of the records revealing that fact?'

Mr Heredia: 'In my opinion that is absolutely impossible. If people cheat, a pattern [loi de tricherie] establishes itself. You will find that they always deal with a certain type of situation in the same way. This pattern shows up in the analysis. You see many things in the analysis.'

This last answer was very important for our case and Caplan let it hang in the air overnight. Only a morning session was possible on the following day. When discussion turned to the present affair, the witness said:

'I have known Reese and Schapiro for about 15 years. We have passed the time of day at tournaments where I have been directing and they have been playing, but I have not had any close personal relations with either of them.

'The accusations received great publicity in France, both on radio and in the press. I saw Reese for a short while at Ostend during the European Championship in September, but I did not mention the case as I thought it might be embarrassing for him. Soon after, Le Bridgeur published a number of hands from the world championship which had been put forward as supporting the charge of cheating. For myself, and for many people in France, this led to a renewal of the affair. Till then we had assumed that what everybody was saying was true. But after I had seen these hands, I at any rate said to myself, "This does not make sense." I wrote to Mr Reese, asking whether there were other hands on which possibly an accusation could be based. I received in due course the complete dossier from his solicitors. As soon as I had time I embarked on a complete analysis. For about six days I had sessions all by myself, two or three hours at a time.

Mr Caplan: 'In examining all the hands, did you find any hands which, in your view, gave support to an accusation of cheating?'

Mr Heredia: 'I shall reply to you first by a preliminary. If a pair plays well, there will always be hands that could support an accusation. Suppose, for example, the suggestion is that my partner and I signal aces. When one day I lead from K x and find my partner's ace, this hand could be held against me without my being able to reply to it. Or suppose that you, Leigh Howard, play with Reese and I accuse you of knowing the holdings in diamonds. In a long match I would surely find eight or ten hands which would go well with the accusation. But the conclusion is completely destroyed when I find others which show the contrary.'

Mr Caplan: 'Having analysed the whole of these hands, is there anything in them which supports an accusation of cheating in hearts?'

Mr Heredia: 'Nothing. I would even frankly say there is not a single abnormal hand, I should perhaps tell you in what spirit I have examined these hands. As in all inquiries of this kind, I have not studied the bidding in a technical way but have put myself in the position of one or other of the players, thinking that I knew how many hearts my partner held, and in that situation I considered what I would do; or what did that player do in an analogous situation on a previous hand.'

These last two answers, it seemed to me, were a model of clear thinking on a difficult subject which most people approach in quite the wrong way. The witness made another shrewd observation in reply to this next question:

Mr Caplan: 'Were the results of the Reese-Schapiro partnership at Buenos Aires above, at the same level, or below the level of their normal play?'

Mr Heredia: 'A little below normal, too many poor contracts. Indeed, the order of events in this whole affair is most surprising. Ordinarily, the reason why a pair is suspected and watched is because its bidding and results are thought to be abnormal. Here there is nothing peculiar in the results. Before you look to see how a pair cheats you must first be satisfied that its performance is what you would expect of a cheating pair.'

Caplan passed next to details of Heredia's technical evidence, particularly the new hands. Some of the witness's points were very good, some did not greatly impress the assessors, either because of the differences between French and British bidding styles, or because some of the bids he suggested would have been outside the 'tolerance', a factor which Heredia tended to underestimate. When Caplan saw that an argument was having little effect he immediately dropped it. No harm was done, for the occasional misconceptions established that the witness had made his analysis quite independently.

Heredia continued his evidence a fortnight later, taking a plane from Paris that reached London airport at 8.30 in the morning; a notable feat for anyone, positively heroic for a bridge player not even engaged on his own affairs.

When he had finished with the analysis of hands, Caplan asked: 'Have you heard that at Buenos Aires this allegation of cheating was investigated without direct reference to the tournament director? From your great experience, what do you say about that?'

'That is what does not add up in this affair. Most of the big scandals are just a "nothing", because of the emotions involved. It is not difficult for an impartial tournament director to determine whether a pair cheats. It would have been sufficient to place one official opposite Mr Schapiro and another opposite Mr Reese. They would take notes of the finger positions and compare them later with the match records. If they find substantial coincidence, then the charge is proved. That is what ought to have been done, without a scandal or anything. I ask myself, Why was this procedure not adopted?'

'And what answer do you get?'

'I must tell you, this type of affair is full of emotion. One finds that the people concerned in it have a strong interest. The need for scandal surpasses the need for justice.'

'Is it in any way possible that Becker, Hayden, Truscott and Swimer – would none of those know the correct procedure to adopt?'

'I do not know what they knew or what they did not know. But the procedure is so normal. If you have a complaint you take it to court, you do not try and deal with it yourself. I might make an exception for Mr Swimer, who has perhaps a duty to deal with matters concerning his team.'

'Lastly, if the committee had been told that Becker and Hayden had made notes, what would have happened?'

'In my view, if the notes were the basis for a decision, the committee would have asked for them. One must ask people for the basis of their accusation.'

Heredia cross-examined

Goldblatt began:

'Mr Heredia, do you take the view that if a complaint had been made at Buenos Aires to the tournament officials, and a period of observation by officials had followed, and on about 15 to 16 observed hands fingers were seen to correspond with heart holdings in the vast majority of cases, then the accusation would be proved and no investigation of hands would be necessary?'

It was not the easiest of questions to render immediately into another language. When Heredia understood it he answered that if this were done, and strictly proved, an analysis of the hands would not be necessary, but on the other hand an analysis of the hands would have shown in this case that the observation was faulty.

Most questions and answers during this period were less accurately recorded, for the proceedings became somewhat disorganised. The best I can do is to set out Counsel's more pertinent questions and the nearest answer that can be extracted from the transcript, with sometimes two or three people assisting in the translation of the witness's remarks.

Mr Goldblatt: 'Is it your experience that in all cases where an accusation of cheating is made, the precise code and precise manner of signalling the code is unknown?'

Mr Heredia: 'People always think they see something but in this case I understand that people thought they saw something and afterwards it was stated that it related to hearts.'

Mr Goldblatt: 'You find it is typical, do you, that accusers think they see suspicious movements or signs?'

Mr Heredia: 'Yes. They do not know what the signs mean, or whether they are signs, but they imagine they are.'

Mr Goldblatt: 'Have you personally had a case in which, before the end of a tournament, you have been told both the signals and their meaning?'

Mr Heredia: 'Yes. One checks up, and if the charge is confirmed the players are advised to give up the game.'

Mr Goldblatt: 'Would you agree that where there is an accusation of cheating, with the code and signals allegedly known, the best and most obvious way to prove or refute it, if the tournament is still in progress, is for observations to be made on the accused player?'

The witness had said in his evidence-in-chief that it would be proper for impartial officials to conduct such an investigation. He added now that even if it was found that the conduct of the players corresponded with the suspicions against them, it would still be necessary at some stage to prove that the messages allegedly sent had been received and made use of. 'One must prove that the crime shows a profit, that people have benefited from it.'

This last remark raised a philosophical point of considerable importance to our case. Many people had said from the first that if the court accepted the evidence that signals were made, it would follow that the charge of cheating was proved. That may sound right, but consider a parallel situation: four witnesses say that a boy taking a history examination had a crib giving the dates of the kings and was seen to use it; yet in his examination papers many of the answers are wrong. Where would that lead? One would presumably conclude that there was something wrong with the observation.

There were other areas of speculation. While it might be difficult to reconcile the two propositions – signals made, but signals not used – was it utterly impossible? Could it be some mad or defiant caper on the part of the players, or some protective device to be used only if the opponents were doing something improper? Unlikely, of course, but the vagaries of human nature have a wide range. 'You must admit,' said a Canadian friend, looking me straight in the eye, 'that there are a couple of oddballs at the centre of all this.'

The remainder of Heredia's cross-examination was concerned with the new technical evidence. The witness was very firm on all the points he had made.

Heredia re-examined

Mr Caplan: 'I have only one question. If observation of players appears to confirm that they are cheating, but the analysis of the hands does not support that, which in your view is to be preferred?'

Mr Heredia: 'I have a very precise view about that. If one does something, the trace is left. Take a nail from a tree and a mark is left. So with cheating at bridge; what is done is written down in the record.'

Mr Caplan: 'Sir John, for the sake of the record, would I be wrong in taking the answer to the question as being that one would prefer the results of the analysis of the hands to the evidence of the alleged observations? If not, I would like Mr Heredia to answer.'

Mr Heredia: 'Yes, absolutely.

Mr Caplan: 'That is what I thought.'

Lord Bourne: 'What he said was, "It is written in the hands."'

Ortiz-Patino's evidence-in-chief

Next morning we called our third witness during this fortnight, Jimmy Ortiz-Patino. When Jimmy first appeared on the bridge scene, at Amsterdam in 1955, he was anybody's idea of an international playboy, night indistinguishable from day. Now that was past and he came before the court as a director of many companies, actively engaged in the management of his family's worldwide concerns. Despite his present responsibilities he retains the effervescence of a youthful Gary Player, whom he resembles a little in physique (allowing for the fact that Jimmy pursues less athletic occupations) and in the determination he brings to any enterprise in which he is engaged.

Early questions established the witness as a regular member of the strong Swiss team and as a player who had a special interest in allegations about cheating.

'The first major post-war scandal concerned a pair who had played at Montreux, close to my home, in 1954,' he said. 'I was very interested to examine the situation because there were allegations going on practically every year about certain leading players. On several occasions I was mixed up directly in allegations, particularly when at Como the Americans made again – because it was not the first time – allegations of cheating against the Italians. They asked me to sit in on one of the matches and see if I noticed anything strange in the behaviour of the Italians. The accusations were proved to be unfounded and the Americans had to apologise.

'Because there is no indication that these allegations of cheating will stop, we in Switzerland have suggested that a screen be put between the players so that you cannot see your partner during the bidding or opening lead. Our idea is more aesthetic than the diagonal screen that was once tried out in Italy. It consists of a solid cube which descends on the table like a lampshade. You push a button to light up your bids, but the light does not appear until the opponent on your left has also bid. Thus the partner cannot tell who has taken a long time. Because a player can take as long to think out a pass as a bid.'

Sir John Foster: 'That is clever.'

Jimmy added that at Deauville the previous year 16 world champions playing in a special event had answered a poll about the desirability of experimenting with such a screen. All signed in favour except the two Americans present, who voted against.

Mr Caplan: 'I have asked for these details to establish you as a person who has made a special study of these matters. While we are dealing with this expertise of yours, would you be good enough to tell us anything you like to tell us about the Americans and allegations of cheating?' Mr Ortiz-Patino: 'The Americans have frequently accused European champions of irregularities in play. It is, I think, important to realise here that in America bridge is a very big money earner. It has become like golf or tennis for them. They have a vast number of players. The professionals syndicate their articles in hundreds of papers. They sell tours and cruises with great publicity. You can go for a three weeks' cruise to the Caribbean playing bridge on the way out and bridge on the way back.'

Sir John Foster: 'You need not bother to get off.'

Lord Bourne: 'I suppose it is air-conditioned and no windows.'

Mr Ortiz-Patino: 'Bridge is big business, and to maintain their prestige the Americans expect to win the world championship with so many players to choose from. Until 1954 they were unbeatable, but since then they have lost regularly.'

Caplan asked about ways of holding cards and the witness gave this important testimony:

'Many people do not observe these things, but I do. I am always watching for things at the table. I have not noticed anything special about Mr Schapiro except that he is continually putting down his cards to relight his pipe.

'I can speak very definitely about Mr Reese. I have noticed that he never holds his cards for long in the same hand. It is rather strange for someone who is so calm and otherwise so even in all his gestures, tones, voice, and everything. It may come from his habit of showing his cards to the gallery when he is playing. Apart from this mannerism, to play with him is like having a stone wall in front of you. Mr Schapiro is more volatile; I feel more communication with him at the table, but he is completely ethical in every way. When I have played against them it has always been a very pleasant game, one feels always a very fair and friendly atmosphere.

Caplan asked about ways of conveying information and Jimmy demonstrated what he thought was the method adopted by at least one pair in the past. It consisted of a system of spacing between the cards. A small, perfectly natural space between, say, the third and fourth cards from the right would convey a message about strength or distribution. It would be completely undetectable.

Sir John then put this point: 'Imagine two very good players who cheat and give themselves a 1.5% advantage. If they keep to that, using it only when there is a marginal choice between one bid and another, it will not show in the records. As they are very good players, the fact that they do well will not lead to suspicion.'

Jimmy replied that Boris and I had played actually below our normal form at Buenos Aires. Also, we were among the quickest players in the tournament game, always finishing ahead of the official schedule. Careful sifting of the illicit knowledge would surely slow up the game, even for us. As Sir John's question had been put to the defence at large, Caplan commented on the self-discipline needed to restrict the advantage to so few occasions; an argument worth developing, I thought.

There was a reference to Heredia, and Jimmy testified to his high standing and his reputation for bearing down on players who were in any way incorrect. Did he agree with Heredia, Caplan asked, that where there was a conflict between what people said they had observed and what appeared in the records, one would prefer the evidence of the records? 'Yes, absolutely,' the witness replied.

Jimmy ended his evidence-in-chief with a valuable addition to the technical analysis. He had made a study of all occasions where at an early stage of the play we had led a card that gave some picture of length in the heart suit, in accordance with the convention known as 'fourth best'. He had found ten occasions where there was an opportunity to lead at the first or second trick a conventional card in hearts. Only once (Italy 20) had we played an irregular card, and then there was a sound technical reason. On the other nine occasions we had played a true card.

Mr Caplan: 'And false-carding in hearts with illicit knowledge is a thing which cannot deceive one's partner but can deceive one's opponent?'

Mr Ortiz-Patino: 'Exactly.'

Mr Caplan: 'A very useful thing if you are cheating in hearts?'

Mr Ortiz-Patino: 'Exactly.'

Mr Caplan: 'And this was done just once in ten. Just for the sake of completeness, are there in fact only three instances of false-carding altogether by these two players?'

Mr Ortiz-Patino: 'Yes, I found two other instances, both leads of the fifth best card, once in diamonds and once in clubs. That is very little, much less than by most other pairs.'

Mr Goldblatt: 'Italy 19 and US 69 are the two?'

Sir John Foster: 'You must have a wonderful analysis system, Mr Goldblatt.'

Mr Goldblatt: 'Well, I had a complete list of opening leads but I have lost them just at the time it would have been most useful.'

Mr Caplan: 'It is terrific, I would like to see this some time. Mr Goldblatt would obviously have made a very good staff officer.'

Ortiz-Patino cross-examined

Goldblatt began with questions about the witness's observation of players. Jimmy repeated that he had not noticed anything particular about how Boris held his cards, only about his pipe.

Mr Goldblatt: 'So you cannot help me as to whether you would expect to see him in the ordinary way with one or two or three or four fingers behind his cards?'

Mr Ortiz-Patino: 'No, but if he had held them with one, then two, then three, then four, I would have noticed it. That would have struck me as very funny.'

There was some misunderstanding about this until Jimmy explained that what would attract his attention would be movement during the bidding of a single hand, not variation between one hand and another. 'What registers with me,' he said, 'is what you do with the cards when you pick them up from the board, what you do during the three minutes of bidding.'

Mr Goldblatt: 'So that if one had a code which did not require the fingers to be moved during the course of the bidding, but merely required the setting of the fingers to be changed from one board to the next, that would be a less crude method of signalling than moving the fingers during the course of the bidding?'

Mr Ortiz-Patino: 'I do not know that it would be less, but it would still be very crude.'

The trend of Counsel's next few questions was not altogether clear to me. 'I expect you would describe Reese as the most disciplined player you have come across,' he said, 'possibly the nearest thing there is to a bridge computer?' Jimmy replied that he had meant disciplined in the sense of being ethical. I was not a mathematical type of player: others might work out problems in more detail, whereas I would take the straightforward course on a difficult hand and so play more quickly.

Sir John, always ready to extend his knowledge of our strange pursuit, asked whether there was any time limit in bridge. It was explained that, as in chess, there was no limit for a single bid or play, but one was supposed to complete a session within a given period.

Mr Ortiz-Patino: 'There is a system of penalties. The first time it is a yellow warning, a yellow flag. The second flag is a red warning. Then you get penalised a number of match points.'

Lord Bourne: 'I wonder you do not have this in the House of Commons?'

Goldblatt returned to the point he had been developing:
'You were talking of players who analyse more deeply than Reese does?'

'At the table, yes.'

'In your experience, Reese does not always spend the time on analysis that he may do afterwards?'

'I do not know what he does afterwards.'

Counsel was implying that I had given more study to my evidence than to my bidding at the table. It was not a very profound suggestion. I spend a large part of my professional life answering queries about bidding and the arguments relating to them come very readily to mind.

Goldblatt sought to establish next that even if the Americans had made similar accusations in the past, the circumstances were different in that the signals had not been intercepted and exposed. Jimmy said it came very close to that at Como, where the Americans had required their opponents to keep their hands below the table.

The remainder of the cross-examination was on the chart of conventional leads which the witness had submitted. Lacking the advice on this occasion of his instructing solicitor, who was absent, Goldblatt examined each hand in turn. What advantage could there be here, he asked, in misleading the declarer about the distribution of the hearts? Would a false lead have made any difference to the result of the hand?

As Jimmy said, that was not the point. A player making a false or true lead cannot know at the beginning of a hand what effect it will have. The object of a false card (this was the point that had to be explained to the tribunal) was not simply to mislead about the suit led, but to give the declarer a wrong count which might cause him to misjudge the distribution of another suit. Apart from that, it would unsettle the opponents not to know what was going on. 'The basis of all this is that if one could sow the seeds of doubt in the opponents' minds as to what we are going to play, how we are going to lead and discard, then one has gained a great advantage.

Caplan did not re-examine. Jimmy shook hands with everyone in the room in continental fashion, then left to catch the afternoon plane for Geneva and the world of affairs.

11 Ringing the Bell

I WAS STILL GIVING evidence on the hands, it may be remembered, when we broke off to interpose Flint and Heredia. We met next on Tuesday, February 15. Heredia was not due to complete his evidence until the following week, so I went back into the witness chair.

Reese cross-examined (second part)

'We were on Italy 22,' announced the General unexpectedly, enjoying the sensation caused by this remark. We had not supposed that he was so well up with the technical evidence.

Throughout the prosecution's case on the hands it had been argued that whenever there was a choice we had made the bid or play that conformed to knowledge of the heart situation. Goldblatt threw this disputed question into the cauldron again when he asked:

'Did you agree with Flint on the two or three occasions when he concurred with my suggestion that whatever the reasons for a particular lead or play or bid which was under discussion, they were made much easier if you did know partner's heart holding?'

Mr Reese: 'I think there is a logical fallacy in the whole approach, but that is not perhaps what you are asking me. I don't know, I don't think myself it is easier to open One Heart on A-K-Q-x-x because you know that partner has got J-10-x-x. There are hands on which you are entitled to suggest that if your partner has got such and such a holding, then the bid which is proposed is more likely to succeed. That is an accurate way of putting it. But to say it is easier is not, in my opinion, an accurate way of putting it.'

Mr Goldblatt: 'An easier choice, if you like.'

Mr Caplan: 'Then we have to look at the hands; that is the whole point, to see if there is some other choice.'

Sir John Foster: 'I think what Mr Goldblatt is saying must be right if there is an even choice and you have got two alternative bids. It is easier to make the right choice if you know the other side. I do not know if it advances us very much?'

Mr Reese: 'The game does not consist of a series of even choices. When a chess player opens P-K4 or P-Q4 he does not regard it as an even choice, he considers that one move or the other is better suited to his style of play. In the same way at bridge you look for what you consider to be the best bid and all this talk about alternative choices is misleading and tending towards a false and unfair conclusion.'

Sir John Foster: 'It depends on the premise, does it not? You do not think an opening bid might be this or that?'

Mr Reese: 'The choice between two alternatives may be theoretically close, but a player knows from his experience how to arrive at a conclusion and what he normally does in that particular situation. He seeks to make the best bid in all the circumstances. My basic point, which I developed at the beginning of my evidence, is that provided it is reasonably accepted that the player made what at the time he considered was the best bid, then no argument can be founded on that whatsoever.'

Caplan stressed again that it was essential to examine individual hands on which a choice was supposedly made, and Sir John summed up by saying in effect: If there were a succession of even chances Mr Goldblatt's argument would be right, but in Mr Reese's view there is not.

After a few more questions about earlier hands Goldblatt came to the final point of his cross-examination.

Mr Goldblatt: 'We have had some evidence already from Butler and from yourself about your reaction to the charge of cheating at Buenos Aires. Both were to the same effect, that you were – one might describe it as undemonstrative – when the charge was put to you?'

Mr Reese: 'I do not remember Butler making any comments, but I made that comment, yes.'

'One of the things you did know after the first committee meeting was that Swimer had got up to give certain evidence against you?'

'Yes.'

'Up to that time you had been on reasonably good terms with Swimer?'

'Neutral terms.'

'If you were innocent of this charge, Mr Reese, I suggest to you that you would have been inwardly seething at what Swimer had done to you, before that committee. Were you inwardly seething?'

'I am not an inward seether by nature.'

'You see, Mr Reese, here is an English captain who has not just betrayed two members of his team but has betrayed them by giving evidence against them in committee, and you heard it. Did that not cause you to seethe inside?'

'It is just not very greatly my nature to seethe inside about that sort of thing. There are one or two occurrences in life which do cause one to seethe inside, but that sort of behaviour by someone for whom I had no respect whatsoever did not in fact cause me to seethe inside. I had other emotions more prominent perhaps. Even if I had seethed inside, as you put it, I do not expect I would have shown it.'

'You say you were not seething. Were you angry?'

'I was more contemptuous than angry. One treats accusations whence they come. I also had many other problems to consider. I had other things to think about than being angry with him.'

'You see, Mr Reese, what I put to you is that if you had been innocent, the one thing you would have done, having heard Swimer at the first committee meeting, was to buttonhole him outside, take him aside and have a blazing row with him. You say that is entirely foreign to your nature?'

'I do.'

'It is my suggestion that you acted as you did because you were guilty and knew it?'

'It is very easy for guilty people to put up a great show of indignation, they usually do in life.'

'Was there anything to prevent you taking him aside and having a row with him in private, had you so wished?'

'I am sure he would have taken great pains to avoid such a situation from arising. Anyway, I had many other things on my mind at the moment this committee meeting ended. I had my morning's press work to deal with, I had got many things on my mind.'

'Your morning's press work? What! Commitments in your capacity as a bridge journalist?'

'Yes, I had to get an article written by midday.'

'To that work the accusation against you – the false accusation of cheating at bridge – had to take a subsidiary role?'

'However that may be, I had a deadline for an article and I take a possibly perverse and mistaken pride in fulfilling my professional obligations at a time like that. Perhaps I did it to calm my mind; I know quite well I went off to the press room and typed an article before lunch. After lunch, goodness me, I had many things to deal with, the reaction of other people in the team and so forth. I did not understand, naturally, that the thing would reach the proportions it eventually did. I thought it would probably collapse. You have got to remember that when Swimer came out he did not say anything about not playing for the rest of the day. He said, "I don't want you two to play till this matter has been settled," something of that kind.'

'What did you say to him then?'

'I hardly answered him. I might have said, "Oh, very well," or something like that. You see, at the first interview the thing was not put in anything like as brutal or detailed a fashion as it was at the second interview. The 't's were not crossed and the 'i's were not dotted to anything like the same extent, and it did not penetrate that the thing was going to be put to us in the form that it was later.'

'There could not be any doubt about it at all, could there? You had been told at the first meeting that Swimer had watched for about ten hands and

Butler for the remaining ten hands, and each felt quite sick because the signals fitted the code. That is what is reported to have been said at the first session. That is right, is it not?'

'Well, Swimer spoke very little at the first session. I do not know that he made more than about one little speech from the back of the room, and it did not impinge on my attention to quite the extent you may think it did.'

'Let us have a look.'

Goldblatt was generally very much master of the facts and developments in the case, but here he stubbed his toe somewhat. The detailed account of observations made by Swimer and Butler was given before I came to the meeting. After we had turned up the Report:

Mr Caplan: 'This is where my learned friend's question is misleading. What is at the bottom of page 2 and onwards is not Swimer giving evidence in the presence of Mr Reese. All this detail by Swimer is not in the presence of Mr Reese. At page 4 you will see that Mr Reese was called in and denied the charge. He asked to see the evidence and the evidence that was provided for him then and there was Truscott being called in with his analysis.'

Mr Goldblatt: 'I am obliged to my friend.'

Mr Caplan: 'The whole of my learned friend's questioning for the last 25 minutes has been made on a fallacious foundation.'

Then later on, Goldblatt persisted, when the picture was clear, why did I not take some action to have it out with Swimer? 'You never saw Swimer yourself apart from the one occasion when he told you he did not want you to play on?'

Mr Reese: 'No, he remained rather in the background. I did not run to his room to find him or anything like that. I continued to go to our players' dining room and behaved quite normally. I do not remember seeing him.'

Lord Bourne: 'Did you have it out with Butler, because he gave evidence at that first Appeals Committee?'

Mr Reese: 'Yes, he did. You cannot talk to Butler, he would be too much on his dignity. Being president of this and chairman of that committee, he is not the sort of person you could possibly speak to. Swimer I could have spoken to.'

My evidence had extended over three months and seven separate hearings. After I had been re-examined on a few matters, Schapiro took the witness chair for the first time with about 45 minutes to go before the luncheon adjournment.

Schapiro's evidence-in-chief

Boris gave his early evidence in a faint, extremely weary, but distinct voice. He still managed to be quite funny at times, mostly at my expense. Describing his tournament successes:

'The Gold Cup I won ten times. That is the major British championship. I won that ten times, of which eight times were with Reese. He has in fact won it eight times, and twice I won it without him, so I won it ten times. A subject of great annoyance to him.'

Caplan asked about previous relations with Swimer and the witness described the trials before Baden Baden when he played with Swimer and made various comments, and Swimer was left out of the team. Then in the trials before Buenos Aires Swimer had finished third with Rose and again, after Boris had communicated his views to the selectors, Swimer was the only player of the leading six to be left out. The debate about the captaincy followed, when some of the team were willing to have Swimer but Konstam and Boris himself did not agree:

'This was common knowledge, that I was objecting to Swimer as captain and that I wanted Dr Lee, who was a very good captain the year before in New York.'

I remember saying to Boris at the team meeting, 'The reason you want Sidney is that he listens to your nonsense and dispenses free whisky.' To which he answered, 'Yes, and what's wrong with that?'

'Incidentally,' he added now, 'I heard Swimer say in evidence that I telephoned him and persuaded him to accept the captaincy. I did not even know the man's telephone number, and I was absolutely against him from the start.'

Sir John Foster: 'What was your objection to Swimer as captain, I did not quite get it.'

Boris informed him. Then:

Mr Caplan: 'Now we come to Buenos Aires, and I want to ask you about something which happened on the first day, which Mr Reese said he heard about but which you will know about directly, in connection with one of the Americans?'

'Gerber. Well, it was a most mysterious thing, I do not know to this day what it was all about. The only thing it showed me was that he sort of hated me and all of us. I did absolutely nothing – Konstam says I made one of my facetious remarks.'

'Was Konstam present?'

'Yes, he was. But I did not even make a facetious remark at all, if I remember rightly I said something like "Have you a cigar?" He turned on me as if I had done him the most terrible injury and said he did not want to talk to me, he did not want anything to do with us, the way we behaved in New York, how we did this, that and the other; I was absolutely flabbergasted, I do not know to this day what it was all about.'

Lord Bourne: 'What did you say to him, to upset him?'

Mr Schapiro: 'To upset him, I did not say anything. I mean, I sometimes make joking remarks but I did not in that case, if I remember rightly I asked him something about whether he had a cigar to spare, or, these

Americans, these cheap cigars sticking out of his pocket, have you got one of these to spare?'

Yes, we were beginning to get the picture. We should hear Konstam's version of the incident in due course.

Boris's relations with me were the next topic, and here he gave full play to his theme that I was 'obsessed with that idiotic Little Major system'.

Mr Caplan: 'Mr Schapiro, let me ask you about this. If a player of your proven ability and a player of the proven ability of Mr Reese were playing together and had the advantage of cheating methods, what kind of results do you say you would get?'

'It would not be possible to lose any match. That is my profound conviction. It would be utterly impossible to lose a match.'

'That is, with your ability plus cheating?'

'Yes, impossible. Provided we had a reasonable pair in the other room. You and Denis Poore would do!'

Denis Poore is (or was) a director of Crockford's, better known for his financial acumen than for his prowess across the green baize.

The witness was invited to comment about ways of cheating – what would be the most useful information to exchange and how it could be done. He was a bit vague about the second part, recalling that according to the Italian newspapers he had signalled with his pipe. As the session ended, Caplan was asking about the situation when we played against Argentina on the last night.

Mr Caplan: 'Did you see Mr Butler come to that session?'

'I could hardly fail to.'

'Tell us in your own words exactly what happened.'

The witness described Butler climbing over the ropes, taking his seat, and producing in turn his spectacles, his notebook and his pencil. 'It reminded me of what goes on at home, at the trials, and I sort of made a facetious remark to Reese about it.'

Mr Caplan: 'While he was there, making these notes, did you see where Swimer had gone to, who had formerly been sitting in that seat?'

'Yes, I did, he went up at the top, behind Reese.'

'Was that usual or unusual?'

'Unusual. We were, I do not know how many, 180 match points up. What was he doing up there? No interest in the hands.'

'And Butler in the so-called captain's seat, was that a usual or unusual thing?'

'Most unusual. That was the first appearance he made all the week. I had not seen him before.'

(Butler was in fact visible in one of the photographs taken earlier in the week.)

'If you had been cheating, there were sufficient unusual things going on?'

'I think we would have stopped by then. I should have thought so, yes.'

As soon as we got outside, Boris said to me:

'Well? How was I? Better than you expected, wasn't I? What? Be honest now! Did I make a good impression?'

'You made a strong impression,' I said tactfully, as we stepped into the frosty courtyard.

After the adjournment Caplan asked the witness about his previous experiences against American teams. The effect of his reply was that Americans were unwilling to accept the obvious reason for their defeats by European teams during the last ten years. Asked next about his alleged fidgety ways at the table, Boris emphasised that as a matter of habit and training he kept his eyes on the cards and did not look at his partner. Then Counsel came to events on the critical Sunday at Buenos Aires.

Mr Caplan: 'What was the first intimation you had on the Sunday of anything amiss?'

'I am not quite sure. I am very vague about Monday or Sunday.'

'Sunday is the day when everything fell in.'

'Oh, I see. That morning I was walking about in the foyer of the hotel. Swimer came up to me and said, "You're wanted in here." I had no idea what it was about, and he conducted me into a room where this committee was sitting. Thereupon I think it was Butler who recited the charge. I was absolutely flabbergasted; quite flabbergasted. I denied it. I was a bit dazed at the time. I could not understand what was happening for a few minutes; and then they asked me to leave and wait in another room. I subsequently learned they now summoned Reese.'

'According to the note which was made [the Report] you, as you said, were brought in first, and the chairman – that is Butler – said it was alleged that by finger signals you were communicating your heart holdings to each other. When you were asked if you had anything to say you made a blank denial and said the charge was absurd.'

'I said more than that. I remember saying to Butler, "I think you must be quite mad."'

'Had you any opportunity of talking to Mr Reese before he went in?'

'No, none whatever.'

'What was the next thing that happened after that?'

The witness had to be reminded of the external course of events. Then he continued:

'I was waiting outside and Reese went in and was interviewed on his own. When he came out I was naturally very agitated. I am very highly strung and I get very agitated and very excitable. I went up to him. This was the first opportunity I had had of seeing him. I forget exactly what I said to him, but I remember distinctly thinking the man must be completely mad because he said ...'

'Who are you talking about?'

'Reese. He said, "I have got to go and dictate an article," and "I have got to go and have my lunch."'

'He was taking it very calmly?'

'Very calmly is not the word. I thought the man was completely … I always thought he was a bit mad, but there I saw he was mad. He obviously saw my agitation. He said, "It is no good being agitated. You have done nothing, keep calm, go and have lunch, go for a walk, don't worry me, I've got things to do."'

Goldblatt had interpreted my coolness as a sign of guilt. Now one saw that Schapiro had been equally baffled and had reacted quite differently himself. He went on:

'I was in a pretty bad state indeed. By this time a lot of people knew about it. Two or three of the Italian team came up and tried to console me. They told me they did not believe a word of it. They tried to take me into the bar to have a drink. I went with them and the daughter of an Italian duchess was there, who is an old friend of mine. Her daughter of 17 was there, and she said, "Calm yourself. Come out and have some fresh air." It is very difficult to describe the state I was in. She practically dragged me outside. I went out with her, and as we crossed the road to a patch of green I saw Swimer. I walked up to him and he saw me and walked towards me. The girl was left standing and I said to him, "How could you associate yourself with these American gangsters?" That was the expression I used. He looked uncomfortable. He did not look me in the face. He looked like that and then he said, "I thought you did it," whereupon I called him [such and such], interlaced with one or two adjectives which I cannot use in view of the presence of this young lady here [the shorthand reporter]. I also called him a miserable specimen of humanity. He never said a word. The next thing I saw, he was standing there, how can I describe it, he was blubbing and wringing his arms. It reminded me of the wailing wall in Jerusalem. It was sickening. He was standing there blubbing and wringing his arms like that. I felt a wave of nausea come over me. I thought if I stayed there another second I would start vomiting. I turned round and walked away and rejoined the girl on the other side of the road. That was the last I saw of Swimer. That is the last I ever want to see of him. That is presumably the time when he told you that I confessed to him.'

The General asked when this encounter had taken place in relation to the two committee meetings. It was between the two, but there was some confusion as to whether it was before or after lunch. Schapiro said:

'As far as I was concerned, there was no lunch and so it did not matter. I remember this little girl took me upstairs and got me a drink. The state I was in can hardly be described, I was in a ghastly state, not like Mr Reese who was dictating a bridge article to his secretary.'

When Caplan passed to the second meeting, Boris's recollection of events was so hazy, and so much intermingled with what he had heard since, that he was unable to contribute very much. Caplan read from the Report, asking him whether he remembered various remarks I was said to have made. This passage had the effect of reminding the court that the main lines of our defence had been advanced immediately the charge was made.

Caplan turned to the hands next and Boris made some good and original points about his own calls. When the analysis was continued at the next meeting, a week later, he took an early opportunity to introduce a point he had been brooding on. This was that, being a quick, non-analytical bidder, he would not be capable of distinguishing between what would and would not be suspicious.

'I bid quickly and hope it turns out right. That is my attitude. If I were cheating, the records would be littered with evidence of it, absolutely littered.'

When he had finished with the hands Caplan asked the question that had already been put to Flint and myself:

'In your view, what ought to have been done by an English captain to whom Americans come and say the sort of things they are supposed to have said to Swimer?'

'You mean a decent captain? I would have thought the attitude of Signor Perroux would have been the adequate one. He was asked this question in my presence. He said, *"D'abord je les aurai assommé, puis j'emmenerai mon equipe."* ("First I would have slaughtered them, then I would have taken my team home.") In my view, that is what Swimer should have done. But let us suppose that he decides to investigate the charge. Then either he himself, or at his request the Americans, should have told the chief tournament director. This tournament director is well supplied with assistant tournament directors and scorers. It is up to them to make an unbiased examination and not for Swimer and Butler and these Americans to spy on us.'

This speech, with its neat picture of the chain of officialdom in the tournament world, anticipated evidence that Heredia was proposing to give later.* It was a very obvious point and anyone more constitutionally minded than Boris and myself would have brought it up much earlier. However, it made an impression now.

Sir John Foster: 'The tournament directors would have been entitled to watch?'

Mr Schapiro: 'There is a head tournament director. He could have watched. His assistant could have sat down unbiasedly and investigated the whole matter. It was not for Butler to do that, or Swimer.'

---

*The last stage of Heredia's evidence, described in the previous chapter, took place after this part of Schapiro's evidence – TR

Sir John Foster: 'You would not have any objections to being spied on by these people?'

Mr Schapiro: 'They are officials, it is their job.'

Lord Bourne: 'How could all these Appeals Committees – we have heard of two committee meetings taking place on the Sunday – be run without the tournament director knowing about it and insisting on being present?'

Mr Caplan: 'He was not. You have seen the Report, he was not even there. He was not even present.'

Lord Bourne: 'Does he not have a statutory duty?'

Mr Caplan: 'He may have, but we have the names of the people who were present.'

Mr Reese: 'Lerena [the official in question] may have been present at the Executive Committee meeting, the second one, but he certainly was not present at any of the Appeals Committee meetings.'

Mr Goldblatt (studying the Report): 'He is not recorded as being present at the Executive Committee meeting.'

We were content to leave it there.

Schapiro cross-examined

Goldblatt began the cross-examination with one of his more involute questions:

'Let me come to the question I have already asked Reese at one stage, Mr Schapiro. If you did observe two opponents during two 14-board sessions of a world championship match, and you did notice that each of your opponents was, as between one hand and the next, varying the manner in which he held his cards, by sometimes holding them with one finger behind the cards, sometimes with two, sometimes with three, sometimes with four, and occasionally the fingers spread, and you also noticed that when a particular manner of holding the cards was adopted for a particular hand the cards were held in that manner throughout the bidding, what inference would you draw?'

'Mr Goldblatt, I am not a statistician or a psychiatrist, and I cannot answer questions like that.'

'Do you find that a difficult question to answer?'

'That is the way I answer it. You ask me what bids were made, what inferences I got, what I said to Swimer and what happened, and I will tell you, but it is no good asking me questions like that because I cannot answer them.'

'Then perhaps you will try and help me about this, Mr Schapiro …'

'I am not going to try and help you at all.'

'Is that going to be your attitude throughout?'

'No, but if you ask me questions like that, yes. Ask me anything else and I will tell you frankly what I bid, why I bid it, but do not put statistical questions because I cannot answer them. My mind is not capable of doing so.'

'Do you regard that as a statistical question?'

'I do.'

'Perhaps I have not put the question very clearly?'

'Perhaps not. I cannot answer questions like that.'

Goldblatt tried again, breaking up his main question into separate parts. It proved difficult to direct the witness's mind to the questions he was asked. Boris was not just being cussed. For a year he had been under intense nervous strain, he was tired and he knew it. He expressed his attitude openly enough in reply to another question.

Mr Goldblatt: 'Are you telling us that you have not taken sufficient notice of the way in which other people hold their cards at the bridge table to be able to answer a question on what inferences you might draw from any variations you saw?'

'My dear Mr Goldblatt, in answer to that, I will put it quite plainly. You are a lawyer and you are trying to trap me into saying something incriminating, which in my foolishness and impulsiveness I might do. I do not propose to do it. I do not know anything about these things. I did not cheat in Buenos Aires, and I am quite willing to answer any questions with regard to what I did and what I did not do, but I do not see why I should answer these questions. If Sir John directs me I will answer you in the best possible way, but I do not know what all this amounts to, honestly I do not.'

Sir John Foster: '"Have you noticed, playing bridge, how people hold their cards?" was the question. The answer seems to be no.'

Mr Schapiro: 'I have sometimes, I have not made a specific study of it. I do not look around, not like Mr Becker who looks everywhere.'

Mr Goldblatt: 'When have you noticed that Becker does it like this and like that?'

'When I play him.'

'But you said you always keep your eyes right down on your cards?'

'I am holding my cards like that, and he goes like this and like that, and you say I cannot notice – really!'

'It is no more difficult … '

'It is a damn sight more difficult.'

'What was I going to ask you?'

'I do not know, but you said how could I not miss it.'

'How could you give an answer "a damn sight more difficult" when you do not know what the question was? Perhaps we will get on a bit more easily …'

'You and I, Mr Goldblatt, will not get on at all, from your attitude from the beginning of things. I'm warning you about that.'

Sir John Foster: 'You must not be too much against, or at all against, Mr Goldblatt personally. First, he is a lawyer. He is only a porte-parole. Secondly, you do have the report of the meeting at Buenos Aires, which we were asked by the Bridge League to inquire into. Therefore, in order to get a contradictory statement we have to put Mr Goldblatt on one side and Mr Caplan on the other. Do not get at Mr Goldblatt personally.'

The witness replied with spirit, mentioning various matters which had aroused his ire. He referred in particular to one incident so trivial that I did not mention it when describing my cross-examination. Goldblatt had asked at one point: 'A good many years ago, Mr Reese, you had a discussion about cheating, did you not, with a very well-known player now dead, S J Simon? Do you remember? If you do not remember, let me try and remind you.' I answered: 'You remind me, I do not know; in what connection?' Eventually I was reminded. Simon had written some amusing articles about 'all-in bridge' and it was one of his conceits that no-one could get the better of him by playing unfairly. There was some talk of a match in which the Sharples brothers were to have played. Goldblatt put it to me that a code was actually devised, but I certainly had no recollection of that. Anyway, it was an open discussion 20 years back, and nothing came of it. One might wonder what was the chain of events that led to such a matter being raised at this Inquiry, but otherwise it did not seem important. However, it rankled with Boris.

'This is not a criminal prosecution at the Old Bailey,' he said with passion. 'This is an impartial inquiry.'

Sir John Foster: 'The Inquiry is impartial, but one side has to be a prosecutor.'

Mr Schapiro: 'You yourself have referred to the "so-called prosecution". There is no "so-called prosecution" here, it is a prosecution, and I take strong exception to it. It is completely out of order in my view.'

'It is always very difficult in these inquiries,' remarked Sir John a little later. 'Like you have in the Budget Tribunal (the Lynskey affair), you must have a person putting the contradictory things.'

Boris consumed some vodka during the luncheon interval and the atmosphere afterwards was a little less tense. Asked how he normally held the cards, he repeated what he had said earlier, that he held them near the bottom of the fan, with one, two or possibly three fingers showing, depending on how an observer might interpret what he saw. Goldblatt suggested that someone looking down from above would underestimate rather than overestimate the number of fingers. The witness said he hadn't considered that. Then Goldblatt sprung a small trap:

'I want to ask you about the evidence of Kehela. You will remember that he was the first one to talk about finger patterns. Do you remember that he said that most of the coincidences between fingers and heart distribution were when three or four hearts were held by one or the other player?'

The defence had suggested that such coincidences as Kehela had observed were to be expected, occurring when the cards were held in the commonest way. Goldblatt was implying that this explanation did not agree with what the witness was saying about his own habits. I don't think Boris quite realised what it was all about, but when the point was put to him he stonewalled quite effectively.

'You are trying to trap me into something, and I do not see whether I should accept it. I do not see how it is relevant. I have told you that is how I hold my cards. You can construe it like that. Mr Kehela says this, Mr Swimer says that, and Mr Butler says the other. It is not for me to theorise on that.'

Goldblatt turned next to Swimer, meeting the first point head on:

'Swimer says that you were one of the people who encouraged him to take the captaincy once your team had agreed among themselves to ask him to act as captain. Did you do anything to encourage Swimer to take the captaincy?'

'I find that rather amusing. I did everything possible to stop him being appointed captain. I was the one who held out right to the end, even when I was overruled, when Konstam was about to write the letter to the effect that this was a majority decision.'

Sir John Foster: 'After he had been accepted by the team, did you encourage him to accept the captaincy?'

Mr Schapiro: 'No.'

Then Goldblatt came to the famous encounter outside the hotel: 'You went across to speak to him [Swimer]?'

'Yes, I did.'

'Was he then in company with his wife and Rose?'

'That I honestly cannot remember.'

'What was your frame of mind at the time? Were you in a blazing temper with him?'

'I certainly was.'

'If you were in that frame of mind you would not have wished, would you, to take Swimer on one side to talk to him?'

'I never said I took him on one side.'

Goldblatt was suggesting that if Boris's account of the incident were true he would have spoken out in the full hearing of anybody who happened to be there. The witness rejected this. Then Counsel put to him Swimer's version of the interview.

'Did Swimer at any stage in this conversation, either at the beginning or later on, say, "How could you do it, I am your friend"?'

'No.'

'I suppose you deny saying, "It was that evil man, he made me do it"?'

'Most emphatically. Had I made a confession – which I did not and which it is ludicrous to suggest – I would not have made it to Swimer. And had I made a confession to Swimer, the last thing I would have done would have been to blame Reese. One thing that all my friends – and not only my friends – know is that I have got a sense of loyalty. I would never take refuge and blame an old associate like that. It is completely out of character.'

After asking the witness how he accounted for Swimer's actions, Goldblatt passed on to the other British observer.

'Now help me a little as regards Butler. You say …'

'I can help you a lot about Butler.'

Boris and I had both remarked in our evidence that we had seen Butler making entries in his notebook, meaning that if we had been engaged in any cheating we would immediately have stopped. Goldblatt made a rather odd point about this.

'If one were cheating by means of the code that the prosecution alleges here, Mr Schapiro, it would follow, would it not, that every time one held cards some signal or another signal would be given?'

'I haven't thought about it. I suppose so.'

'It must follow, because one has got to hold cards somehow or other, and one could not hold them without giving a signal in the code. Suppose that when using this code during a session one wished to stop using it, can you think of a way in which it could be done?'

'I would ring a bell. That would be the clearest way, I suppose.'

After this gravity-removing interlude everyone had a go at the small problem of how to warn partner to stop if there were no pre-arranged signal. A glance, or a pressure of the foot, would do, I imagine. Counsel turned next to the American observers, Becker and Hayden. Hayden had said that she played badly in the fourth session because she was observing the signals for the first time and this had upset her concentration.

Mr Goldblatt: 'Mr Schapiro, going back to the fourth session against the United States, would you agree that during that session Hayden was playing particularly badly? This was a session when Britain scored 63 points to America's 2. Hayden said in her evidence that she played particularly badly.'

'That was the session where they had a row. Yes, she was playing badly. That is true.'

'Did anything appear to be upsetting Hayden during that session, or can you not remember?'

'Yes, her partner.'

After asking the witness about his previous relationships with the Americans, which Boris described as unfriendly from their side, Goldblatt approached the standard question of what the captain ought to have done. Boris said again that if he was not going to reject the charge out of hand Swimer should have reported the matter to the chief tournament director.

Mr Goldblatt: 'Tell me this, what would the arrival of the tournament director or his assistants at the table to watch the play herald or indicate? Would it be a normal incident of championship play?'

'Normal, most certainly.'

'Would it be normal for a tournament director or his assistants to spend a considerable period watching play at one table?'

'Normal, and anyway he can instruct his scorers to do that. He has plenty of minions he could instruct, unbiased ones.'

Of course, that was right. With only four tables to administer and few duties to perform, the tournament director might watch at any table for as long as he liked.

Passing to the technical evidence, Goldblatt began with some questions designed to suggest that many of the defensive points, as applied to Schapiro's bidding, were over-ingenious. First, he put it to the witness that the analysis by Flint and myself went far beyond the analysis performed by the player at the table. In some cases yes, in some cases no, Boris replied. He might have added that most of the points made by Flint and myself were perfectly simple when they began: we had to expand on them to meet a sometimes off-beat cross-examination.

Counsel then approached the same argument from another angle. Boris had said in his evidence that during the tournament he had thought we were doing quite well, but looking at the hands later he realised our results had been moderate. 'It follows, does it not,' said Goldblatt, 'that since coming away from Buenos Aires you have spotted a considerable number of points on various hands which had not struck you when the hands were being played?'

Mr Schapiro: 'No, not necessarily. When one thinks one is doing well, particularly me, I tend to overlook what the opponents in the other room may be doing. I am inclined to be very optimistic about how well I have done.'

Sir John Foster: 'Are not we all?'

Yes, no doubt the profession of barrister offers many such temptations.

The cross-examination on the hands dealt mainly with the witness's own reasons for his bidding. Goldblatt explained at one point: 'I am asking Mr Schapiro to give subjective evidence about the actual bids he made and it may be necessary, having regard to his answers, at the end of the day to relate that subjective evidence to the explanations that the assessors have given about the hands.'

As Boris said, it was not easy to recapture what he thought at the time, especially as he had heard a great deal of analysis since then. Still less could he remember whether, nine months ago, he had made a bid with or without long consideration.

The cross-examination was resumed two days later in the half hour that remained when Ortiz-Patino had finished his evidence. There was a flare-up when Goldblatt put a direct suggestion in the way that Counsel do.

Mr Goldblatt: 'You see, my suggestion to you on this hand [Italy 35] is that you were nudged into the 3NT bid by knowledge of four hearts in the South hand. You entirely disagree, don't you?'

Mr Schapiro: 'Well, need I bother to reply to a question like that? I refute it emphatically, and I resent it. I always resent being accused of cheating, and I resent it, I really do, I cannot help it.'

Caplan intervened in defence of his colleague and Sir John commented, 'That would mean you resented the Inquiry.'

Mr Schapiro: 'I do resent the Inquiry.'

And so he had from the first. He had always maintained that people on the British Bridge League Council who had played with and against us for 20 years should have thrown the accusation straight out. Their reply, of course, was that there was a serious charge to be met and that a summary rejection would look like a cover-up.

As the session finished, the General asked, 'Is this the end of Mr Schapiro?'

Goldblatt replied, 'I am afraid not. I have got more hands to deal with, another three-quarters of an hour at the present rate.' When Boris next gave evidence, the three-quarters of an hour stretched to two hours. Goldblatt continued his efforts to ascertain Schapiro's subjective attitude to various calls. He scored a minor success when for purposes of comparison he turned to a new hand altogether and the witness, without looking to see what had happened at the table, set off on a contemptuous tirade against opening 1NT – the bid he actually made. 'Are you quite sure you are doing yourself justice, Mr Schapiro?' Goldblatt interrupted mildly. The exchanges were often colourful, but of little evidential import.

We did not know it when the February sessions ended, but three months were to pass before the Inquiry could be resumed.

12 Anniversary

AFTER THE LAST HEARING in February we fixed three full days for March and spoke lightly of a possible end of the affair in April. A General Election was overhanging, however, and as soon as this was confirmed all plans were abandoned. Sir John was standing again at Northwich and Goldblatt at Twickenham. One further day was proposed, but this had to be cancelled as Goldblatt was engaged in another case. The next we heard, after the usual telephoning between the lawyers' clerks, was that nothing could be arranged before the end of June. This was extremely annoying for the defence, both because of the delay in reaching a conclusion and because we would lose the impetus of some excellent evidence. Boris and I were asked for our views by the press, and the *Sunday Times* reproduced some of our less temperate remarks in a piece headed 'Waiting for Goldblatt'. It was a clever title (echoes of *Waiting for Godot*) but a little unfair on Goldblatt, who was very seldom responsible for the changes in plan.

In April the 1966 World Championship was played in Italy. Britain, having finished fourth in the European Championship, had not qualified. The US finished second but was again well beaten by Italy. Dick Frey, the American journalist whose part in events at Buenos Aires may be recalled, observed quite wittily that he was tired of heading his article on the world championship each year, 'Why We Lost'. Next time, he said, it would either be 'Why We Won' or 'Why Don't We Get Somebody Else?'

In May there was an improvement in the time-table. One of Caplan's cases ended sooner than expected and hearings were arranged for three days in the second half of the month. The first of these was cancelled but we met on May 24. It was a year to the day since the ominous announcement at Buenos Aires. Boris's evidence had not been completed but we decided to interpose Konstam, who was due to go on a bridge cruise early in June.

Konstam's evidence-in-chief

The witness was described as a tournament player since 1933, six times winner of the European championship, a member of the team at Buenos Aires, and bridge correspondent of the *Sunday Times*. He had also captained several teams in Camrose Trophy matches (the home internationals). 'The captain,' he remarked, 'is always recruited from one of the elder statesmen, sort of thing, like myself.'

Mr Caplan: 'Have you – and this is almost an obvious question – on a number of occasions in the past 30 years played both with and against Mr Reese?'

'Yes.'

'And both with and against Mr Schapiro?'

'Yes.'

'Taking them separately, what do you say from your knowledge and experience of their reputation as bridge players in terms of conduct?'

'I have never found them anything but extremely ethical and extremely fair. I do not know anyone who has thought differently. They may have their enemies in other walks of life but at the bridge table I cannot think of anyone who has thought they were anything but a very fine partnership, very formidable opponents and extremely fair.'

The witness was asked about events leading up to the appointment of Swimer as captain, and his story confirmed what the court had heard several times already. Whenever the debate about the captaincy was mentioned, the General, perhaps relating it to the idea of a regiment choosing its colonel, always expressed amazement that the team should be consulted.

Lord Bourne: 'It must be the only sport on the face of the earth which has its captain picked this way. What is the British Bridge League for if it is not to appoint a captain?'

Mr Konstam: 'What are the selectors for if they do not select the team? They stage a lot of trials which are meaningless, and things like that.'

Yes, I have been saying the same for 20 years. Caplan's next question was a surprise to me:

'I would like to pass on, if I may, to deal with the question of personality, and I know it is rather unfortunate that I have to do so. You mentioned Mr Butler. He has given some evidence here about observations which he says he made one evening after dinner. Can you give us any assistance generally about Mr Butler's capacities after dinner?'

I didn't mention it before in this book, but during my evidence I used some phrase about Butler such as 'even in his pre-prandial state', and Boris had been rather more specific. These remarks were technically out of order, because the suggestion had not been put to the witness himself. There was an interjection now from Goldblatt and a comment by Sir John, 'We know what he means.'

Mr Konstam: 'Do you mean, does he have a lot to drink?'

Mr Goldblatt: 'You will remember that this was not a line which was adopted at all in cross-examination. It is an attack by a side door upon the habits and behaviour of Butler, who has not been given a chance to deal with it.'

Mr Caplan: 'If my learned friend wants it I shall ask to have Butler recalled. We are trying here to get at the truth. I personally hope that nothing will be allowed to stop the truth coming out.'

Sir John Foster: 'If you say somebody had been drinking and you have not asked him it is a bit hard on him.'

Mr Caplan: 'If you think it will really advance matters to get Mr Butler's views on his own sobriety, then I shall ask for him to be recalled. Here is a piece of evidence which in my considered opinion is of importance in this very serious case, as far as my clients are concerned.'

The General was not up with the play:

Lord Bourne: 'I do not quite see the connection. Surely Mr Butler gave evidence to us in the middle of the day. Why does this business of after dinner come in?'

Sir John Foster: 'The allegation is that when he took up his observations after dinner … There has been no real evidence about this.'

Mr Goldblatt: 'Mr Reese rather brushed it aside. Mr Schapiro made more of a point of it. As I say, obviously I did not take it up then. If my friend is going to make a considered thing of it, obviously it should have been put to Mr Butler at an earlier stage.'

Mr Caplan: 'It is a matter of some delicacy.'

Mr Goldblatt: 'It is a matter of much more indelicacy if a witness does not have a chance to answer.'

Sir John Foster: 'There it is, Mr Konstam. Perhaps without a question you can give your opinion.'

Mr Konstam: 'Quite frankly, this is something I would rather not answer. If I have to answer it I will answer it. In my own mind I am not terribly clear. In these tournaments I have very little to do with Butler after dinner. I know that he is not a teetotaller. I really do not want to go much further than that.'

Mr Caplan: 'Let me put it to you in this way: Would you yourself be prepared to place much reliance on any detailed observations said to have been made by him late in the day?'

Mr Konstam: 'Since you ask me the question, I would not be prepared to place too much reliance on Butler's observations at the bridge table either before or after dinner. That is nothing to do with the amount he had to drink.'

Caplan passed to a new subject and one had the impression that the matter would be allowed to rest. It was not part of our case that Butler had dined well before he came to watch that night; but there it is, when a person is normally convivial it can have a bearing on the exactness of his judgment. The witness was asked next about the scene that had taken place between Gerber, the American captain, and Schapiro on the first Saturday at Buenos Aires.

Mr Konstam: 'I was sitting in the lounge of the hotel, talking to Gerber. Mr Schapiro came up and Gerber was smoking a cigar. Schapiro made some remark which from a friend would be a joke but from someone who is not a friend might be considered as slightly less than a joke. Gerber snapped at him rather hard, rather embarrassingly.'

'What did he say?'

'According to my recollection Schapiro said something like "Take that cigar out of your mouth, you old Texan". Gerber snapped back: "Mr Schapiro, I do not wish you to address me; I do not want to address you; if at the end of the tournament you happen to beat us I will congratulate you, but apart from that I do not want anything to do with you." Mr Schapiro walked away in some surprise and I was rather embarrassed about the whole thing. I got up and walked away with Schapiro. He seemed to think that Gerber was joking but I said to him: "Don't think that he is joking; he just doesn't like you, Boris, and that is all there is to it."'

Caplan passed to the team meeting at which Boris and I had an altercation. Konstam confirmed the previous evidence about the bad relations that had existed between us at that time but was dubious about Caplan's suggestion that people not in harmony would be unlikely to engage in cheating together. 'I do not think they would cheat in those circumstance,' he said, 'but then I do not think they would cheat in any circumstances.'

Sir John, having seen most things in his time, was always resistant to peripheral arguments of the defence about the improbability of the whole affair. He commented now:

'When you get to this psychological thing there are all kinds of alternatives, are there not? You have the example of homosexuals, who sometimes act in the most imprudent way. You do find people doing very silly things and risking their whole career. There is no limit to human psychological quirks.'

Konstam repeated the point made by several previous witnesses that it would be easy to develop an undetectable method.

Mr Caplan: 'You say that there are any numbers of ways whereby important information can be given in a way which, in your view, could never be detected at all?'

'Yes.'

'Do you think such a system which prevents them being detected is beyond the capacity of a first-class bridge player like Mr Reese?'

'I do not think it is beyond anyone's capacity.'

The witness made much of a new point that spectators would surely notice if a player frequently looked across the table at his partner. Taking a pack of cards, he showed that it is by no means as easy as one might imagine to distinguish at a single glance between two fingers and three, still less between three fingers and four.

Commenting on previous occasions where there had been allegations of cheating, Konstam emphasised that the proof had always come from the internal evidence, Nobody had seen any signals passing. 'In order to establish that there was cheating there would have to be a pattern, there would have to be a regular pattern [of inspired decisions].' In Konstam's opinion we had played worse at Buenos Aires than for many years.

Several questions followed about the proper course to take if one considers that one's opponents have been cheating. The witness was very clear about this. Until you have proof, he said, you must do nothing. If you have proof, let your captain take it to the tournament committee. The committee will inform the captain of the accused players, and he in turn must consult with his whole team. Asked about Swimer's course of action, Konstam replied with the same hint of gentlemanly embarrassment as when he was asked about Butler:

'I am not here to sort of blackguard someone who is not present, that is not the way I do things. I can only say that had I been captain I would not have acted in the way that Swimer did. I would have had the thing settled there and then, immediately the accusations were made known, and I would have taken the rest of the team into my confidence.'

Suppose, Caplan went on, that further observations were thought necessary. Should this be done by independent people like the tournament director, or by the players?

Konstam answered: 'Rather an impartial journalist or something like that, someone who knew the game.'

The question did not arise in his mind, he added, for he had already said that in his opinion play should stop immediately the accusation was made.

Sir John Foster: 'You would exclude, then, impartial observation? You would be in a difficulty as captain. You would have given up the opportunity of having impartial observers?'

Mr Konstam: 'I put it this way. I find it extremely difficult to understand how these accusations came to light without the Americans already having sufficient evidence to put before a committee. I do not think anyone should bring these accusations until they are 100 per cent sure. Now, if they are 100 per cent sure, I see no reason why anyone should waste time with another two days' observation.'

The witness gave this important answer at the end of his examination:

Mr Caplan: 'Mr Swimer gave evidence to the effect that when Mr Schapiro played with you he always held the cards in the same way with four fingers on the back of the cards. What do you say about that from your knowledge of Mr Schapiro?'

Mr Konstam: 'I have played with Mr Schapiro a great number of years and my impression is that he holds his cards very low down, like that, with only one or two fingers on the cards.'

Konstam cross-examined

Counsel began on the subject of observation:

Mr Goldblatt: 'You made the point that the display of a finger pattern would appear to be crude because you regard it as a movement which could be noticed over two or three days. I would like you to explain that a little. What is it that you think was liable to be noticed from the display of changing finger patterns?'

'Supposing you are going to pick up your hand like this and then you do that, that is noticeable, is it not? It would not take a lot to notice that if I pick up my hand and when I have looked at my hand I adjust my fingers. That is apt to be noticeable, is it not?'

This was a new point for the defence and a very good one. In reply to further questions the witness said that holding the cards in different ways on different hands was also something that might catch the attention of people watching the game.

Mr Goldblatt: 'Can you pinpoint any player within your knowledge who does consistently hold his cards in a different way, or is this something you would not notice yourself?'

Mr Konstam: 'No, something I would not notice.'

Mr Goldblatt: 'At any rate you made the point that if a signal is going to be given it should be a clear signal which can be seen with a glance and not with a stare?'

The witness maintained that more than a glance would be needed, adding: 'If you are always signalling and I am always glancing at my partner, someone is going to say, "That fellow is always looking at his partner, what's behind it?"'

Konstam was emphatic that suspicions of cheating must always be confirmed by a 'pattern' in the bidding and play. Goldblatt put his standard question in this form:

'What I am postulating is that before a session begins somebody tells you that two players are using a code to signal to one another the number of hearts they hold. This is the code; it is explained to you. You sit down to observe the session and you find that on each occasion the number of fingers displayed by each person corresponds with the code about which you have been told. If we assume that this happens throughout an entire session, would you look for a pattern in the hands?'

'Very definitely, because supposing I am sitting here with my fingers like this [demonstrating], and you are told what to look for – you are told that you have got to look for how many fingers I am showing and that these are going to correspond with the number of hearts – and you are sitting over there behind Mr Caplan [facing the player], you are observing but can you with any certainty tell me how many fingers I am showing? It is not always that easy to count and see the way I am holding my hand.'

Sir John Foster: 'You have rather denied the premise, have you not? You have said, "Yes, theoretically, but I don't believe that."'

When questions were asked about the notes allegedly taken by Swimer, the witness again steered his bark cleverly through narrow waters. He said: 'I feel sure there must be a difference between concocting a case against someone and forming a wrong impression. There must be something that comes in between these two. I mean to say, that Swimer should enter a conspiracy in order to shop two of his team-mates is rather a strong way of putting it. To say that he may well have been mistaken or that the signal he thinks he saw bore no meaning to the players concerned, is rather a different thing, is it not? Do you follow what I mean?'

After the adjournment Goldblatt turned to the Americans: 'I was going to ask you what sort of evidence you envisaged the Americans as having before they made their accusation of cheating against Reese and Schapiro?'

'Presumably the sort of evidence that they tried – I do not say to manufacture, I do not mean this in any discourteous way – to produce later. They cannot have been very well satisfied with their evidence, otherwise they would have produced it immediately to the committee and not asked other people to help them in watching for evidence.'

The Americans had not done that, according to their story, but it was interesting that Konstam should have gained that impression. He repeated that they should have taken their proof, if they had any, to the tournament committee. But was not Butler a leading committee man, Goldblatt asked. Konstam replied: 'Butler is on the Appeals Committee, which deals with all protests and appeals or complaints. It has always been the practice in all my years of experience that when a complaint has been made against a member of a team, his country's representative on the Appeals Committee should immediately withdraw. I am certain that had Mr Butler been favourable to Reese and Schapiro the Americans would have asked him to withdraw. Of that there is no doubt at all.'

Mr Goldblatt: 'You mentioned the possibility of an impartial journalist being called in as an observer in relation to matters that were suspect but not proved?'

Mr Konstam: 'Yes. I mentioned an impartial journalist as being one of the people who might have been considered.'

'Do you place Truscott in that category?'

'As a journalist, yes. As an impartial one, no.

'Where do you suggest his partialities lie?'

'With Becker and Hayden, since you ask.'

Sir John Foster: 'Is that reasoning backwards or would you have said so at the moment he was asked?'

Mr Konstam: 'Oh yes, it was well known at the time, and at New York as well.'

Sir John Foster: 'It is not arguing backwards?'

'No, no.'

Konstam meant that Truscott's friendship with Becker and Hayden had been evident when we played in New York in 1964. These little digs were the more effective for being elicited in response to direct questions in cross-examination, I passed a note to Caplan, reminding him of Truscott's evidence. He had said: 'Mrs Hayden is a friend of mine in the sense that we live in the same area. We have family connections. We see each other's children play together.'

Konstam re-examined

The witness was given further opportunity to state his position on what had become perhaps the central issue in the case.

Mr Caplan: 'If you have a pattern in which there is not only no pattern of cheating but a pattern of no cheating, of bids quite inconsistent with the type of cheating alleged, to which do you pay more attention – the absence of a pattern of cheating and the pattern that belies cheating or, on the other hand, people saying that they have seen signals passing? To which do you pay more attention?'

Mr Konstam: 'I pay more attention to the pattern of the hands, because people are fallible, eyesights are bad, people get in the way of seeing things, people think they see things that in fact they do not.'

'These are all charitable assumptions. But would you in any event prefer what the cards showed to what people said?'

'Obviously. I cannot see any rhyme or reason why anyone should cheat and then not take advantage of it.'

Figgis's evidence-in-chief

At an early stage of the case Caplan discovered that over the week at Buenos Aires we did worse in heart contracts than in other denominations and also worse than other pairs playing in hearts. 'Did worse' is of course a vague term, requiring definition, for making a contract is not an absolute test of merit. I pointed out to Counsel that this sort of evidence had its limitations, but he considered that it would carry weight with the tribunal. Accordingly Eric Figgis, a member of the British Bridge League Council and a chartered accountant, was asked to prepare a statistical survey. This was the first set of figures he submitted in evidence:

(1)   Percentage of success in situations where the heart suit was involved

Team-mates at other table:	78.3%
Opponents at own table:	47.8%
Pair holding parallel cards:	47.1%
Reese and Schapiro:	44.4%

(2)   Percentage of success in situations where the heart suit was not involved

Team-mates at other table:	71.1%
Reese and Schapiro:	65.2%
Pair holding parallel cards:	62.5%
Opponents at own table:	60.0%

A combination of these tables, covering all hands played, showed our team-mates well on top with 72.6 per cent. We came second with 59.2 per cent, and the other pairs followed closely. Thus our performance in heart contracts came right at the bottom of a league table comprising twelve percentages.

Another set of figures introduced at this time was in my opinion entitled to carry more weight. In his opening address Goldblatt had instanced 29 hands from Britain's matches against Italy and the US as tending to prove that our bidding or play had been influenced by illicit knowledge. Analysis of the swings (i.e. the comparative results obtained at the two tables) on these 29 hands produced this result*:

Total match points gained by opponents:	66
Total match points gained by Britain:	43
Net result of diabolical machinations:	–23

Sir John Foster: 'In the room in which no cheating was alleged, they played better there?'

Mr Caplan: 'The pair holding the same cards as Reese and Schapiro did better. You have two players who are pre-eminent and said to be cheating, and yet in the hands where they are said to have cheated most the team of four loses 23 points on balance. This seems to be a remarkable result of cheating.'

Figgis cross-examined

For the remainder of the present session Goldblatt confined himself to questions about the method of analysis. When the witness was asked on what basis he had entered a contract as a success or a failure, it turned out that he had used more subjective judgment than most of us had realised. A partscore made was entered as a failure if game was missed, and a contract that failed was reckoned a success if it appeared, by comparing the result at the other table, to be a worthwhile sacrifice. These adjustments clearly increased the value of the statistics, but for the

*see Appendix (d)

tribunal a simple division into contract made or contract not made would have been at any rate more easily comprehensible.

Lord Bourne: 'Could you not have got the same general conclusions without going into these matters of judgment?'

Mr Figgis: 'Not always. Sometimes the cross-sections become complex.'

Mr Caplan: 'I see what the General has in mind. It is something I have in mind, too. Suppose you take a perfectly simple proposition, that a contract is regarded as a success if it is made and a failure if it is not made. You assume that over 198 hands all other factors will tend to cancel each other out. If you do it in that way, could you compile a league table of the sort you have already given us?'

Figgis undertook to do this, adding that he would not expect to find the situation much different. While Caplan and the tribunal were considering some of the effects of this method, the witness suddenly exclaimed: 'On second thoughts this is abhorrent, not simple. I think it will lead to wrong results.'

'It may do,' said Caplan tightly, 'but, on the other hand, it would be valuable if you could do it, Mr Figgis.'

The witness explained that he had introduced subjective tests only where it was necessary to obtain any equitable result.

Sir John asked: 'Have you ever done this before? It might be useful for judging who played best in a trial for the international team.'

Mr Figgis: 'Yes, I have made that very point. I think I have discovered a way where you can statistically analyse the results at a table in the most consistent and meaningful way.

Mr Goldblatt: 'We will see, Mr Figgis.'

Mr Figgis: 'I do not say that segregating the heart suit is wanted for this, but the principle ...'

Lord Bourne: 'If you are not careful you will prove that the wrong people won the match.'

The session ended soon after. Caplan was still of the opinion that a simple record of contracts won and lost would have made a greater impact and confided to Leigh Howard, 'This is what comes of having a stubborn client.'

When Figgis resumed his evidence a fortnight later, Goldblatt took him through some of the hands where Schapiro and I had been allotted a debit or credit in hearts. Having established that one or two of the markings were open to argument, Counsel went on to suggest that exchanging information about hearts would not necessarily manifest itself in hands played in hearts.

Mr Goldblatt: 'Why do you say that one would expect pairs cheating in hearts to be more successful in hearts? What is the foundation of that conclusion?'

Mr Figgis: 'Logic.'

It was reasonable to expect, the witness went on, that any mechanical help would raise the percentage of success above normal. He might have added an explanation in bridge terms. All pairs sometimes play in bad contracts with a trump combination like 4-2 or 5-1. A pair knowing the combined length in hearts would easily avoid such errors and choose that suit only on the right occasions.

Goldblatt asked more questions on the same lines, seeking to minimise the connection between cheating in hearts and success in heart contracts. 'If there is no advantage at all, what are we all here for?' exclaimed the witness, causing much amusement.

Counsel shot one more arrow into the sky. In Figgis's list the greatest discrepancy was between the 78.3 per cent success of our team-mates in heart contracts and the 47.8 per cent of our immediate opponents, playing the same cards. If one was going to draw inferences from statistics, Goldblatt suggested, might it not be said that this poor performance of our opponents was one of the consequences of our illicit manoeuvres?

The effect of the witness's reply was that so unlikely a proposition would need concrete instances to support it. There might, theoretically, have been hands where with a shortage in hearts we had made unnatural pre-emptive bids and so stopped our opponents from getting together. In fact, there were none of that sort. Leigh Howard intervened to protest that Goldblatt was shifting his argument, since in his opening address he had dealt almost exclusively with hands where one of us had a suit of hearts. 'He is perfectly entitled to change his line of attack if he wants to,' Eric murmured to me, 'but I wanted to make sure the tribunal realised it.'

In the few minutes left for re-examination Caplan asked the witness how many 'complex' hands there had been – hands where he made subjective judgments before entering the result in one column or another. About 20, the witness answered. He had prepared a document setting out the plain record of contracts made or not made, but it was not put in at this stage. By this test our performance in hearts occupied eleventh place out of twelve in the league table; not very significant in itself, but one recalled Truscott's comment, 'an almost perfect record in heart contracts'.

Franklin's evidence-in-chief

Our last witness was Harold Franklin, of Leeds. Harold has a rubicund, oval face, a bristly grey moustache, and a rocking gait. As the leading figure in provincial bridge and a most able organiser, he sits on many committees, including the British Bridge League Council. He and I have been associated in many professional enterprises and share a juvenile interest in sport, but it was soon clear that he intended to appear before this Inquiry as an independent official. He had in mind, I think, that as a member of a body to which the tribunal would eventually report its findings he must be seen to be uncommitted.

We met on this occasion in one of the interview rooms at the House of Commons, reaching it by devious underground passages which must surely have been trodden by Guy Fawkes. From time to time throughout the day the division bell sounded and Sir John left us for ten minutes to record his opposing thumb-print.

Early questions established the witness as a bridge journalist, an international player, and a leading tournament director. 'Have you on three occasions had the felicity of captaining the British ladies' team?' Caplan asked.

'Somewhat more than three,' Harold replied, with a faraway look.

Mr Caplan: 'I want to go to the early part of last year. You were, were you not, a member of the British Bridge League selection committee which selected the British team for Buenos Aires?'

'Yes.'

Mr Caplan: 'In that connection did you see and have certain communications which put you in the picture so far as Reese's position was concerned in regard to playing with Schapiro in that event?'

Mr Franklin: 'I did, yes.'

Mr Caplan: 'Would you be good enough to tell us about that in some detail?'

Mr Franklin: 'We did have before us in the selection committee a request from Reese that he be not considered with Schapiro as a partnership in the world championship.'

Harold knew all about this but was evidently not going to volunteer any comment. Caplan tried something else: 'Were you a member of the British Bridge League Council which considered the Report which we have seen from the World Bridge Federation in relation to the events in Buenos Aires?'

Mr Franklin: 'I was.'

Mr Caplan: 'Was a statement later issued by the British Bridge League giving reasons why the League felt it could not act on that Report?'

Mr Franklin: 'Such a statement was published, and issued to the press.'

Mr Caplan: 'What were the reasons why the British Bridge League felt it could not act on that Report?'

Mr Franklin: 'I have to speak largely from memory. Somebody else may possibly have the document on file.'

Somebody had, so eventually we got the reasons. They were reported as follows in the English Bridge Union's quarterly review (edited by Franklin himself):

(1) The World Bridge Federation did not see fit to publish its findings or take any action on them, but referred the Report to the British Bridge League.

(2) Two persons who gave evidence about the matter sat as members of both the Appeals and Executive Committee and adjudicated on it and one of them prepared the Report.

(3) Some of the evidence related to hands played at the Championship. No details of these hands appeared in the Report, making it impossible to assess the value of the evidence.

(4) It appeared that the players had been given inadequate opportunities to defend themselves.

Caplan asked next about the ability of anyone sitting in the captain's seat, slightly behind a player, to give any reliable evidence about finger positions. This was a cue for the witness to describe a series of events which had happened at roughly the same time as our own affair. It concerned two northern players and seemed a good story – the atmosphere of suspicion lasting over many months, the conflicting reports of the official observers, the impossibility of observing from behind a player, the final vindication; but Harold narrated it without emphasis on the points that might have been useful to us.

Asked about his experience of tournaments where Boris and I had played together, the witness said he had never had to consider any sort of complaint against us in 16 years.

Mr Caplan: 'What kind of a reputation do Reese and Schapiro hold in regard to the ethics of their conduct?'

Mr Franklin: 'I would have thought a very high reputation, especially in international competitions than at home, where Schapiro tends to be somewhat frivolous at the table and tends to talk a little too much, which may be considered from various points of view exceptionable.'

Caplan turned to the likely effects of cheating: 'I am trying to evaluate the worth of what one might call the internal evidence. If a pair is cheating, is it to be expected that they will reach advantageous contracts from time to time which otherwise they would not have reached?'

'If they are an intelligent pair, certainly.'

'Secondly, is it to be expected that they will avoid some bad contracts which without cheating they might not have avoided?'

'If they are an intelligent pair and are cheating intelligently, certainly.'

'In consequence of that, what do you say as to what a close analysis of the bidding and play of a cheating pair would reveal?' Caplan meant, Would it not be reflected in the results?

Franklin misunderstood the question and set off on a dissertation about what he would expect the contents of a cheating code to be. Caplan approached the point again by referring to a previous witness:

Mr Heredia has said that where there is cheating between players then a close analysis of the hands will show that the cheating is written in the cards.'
'One would expect it from intelligent players.'
As Caplan went on to a new point, Sir John asked: 'Is it agreed that cheating could be detected from an analysis of the cards?'
Mr Franklin: 'The analysis of the cards would create a suspicion or a presumption, yes.'
Asked for his conclusion about the hands, the witness said: 'My general conclusion is that there is nothing in the hands which supports per se any suggestion of illicit understanding. In other words, I do not think I can recall a hand – and certainly no number of hands – for which there is not a perfectly normal explanation in bridge terms.'
Caplan took the witness through some hands played during the so-called observed sessions. Then he turned to the affair at San Francisco, where Becker and Hayden had been accused. They had since played for the US in the World Pairs Olympiad, so the accusation must have been rejected. However, an article by Alvin Landy in the March Bulletin of the ACBL contained some interesting passages. It was headed 'No Room for Rumours' and was ostensibly a denunciation of people who started them. A pair in the National Trials had been the victims of such an attack, the article said, and the League had arranged for an inquiry at which 'the hands were made the subject of an exhaustive analysis. Needless to say, no evidence of wrongdoing was found'. It was also said that a player who had suspicions should convey them to the tournament director and not 'voice them in the wrong quarters'.
The article was produced and the discussion went like this:
Mr Caplan: 'There had been some accusation of cheating in San Francisco earlier this year, is that right?'
Mr Franklin: 'That is so, yes.'
'Of some Ieading players?'
'From a leading pair, yes.'
'From or against?'
'Against a leading pair and from several leading players. Apparently in America, one gathers from this article, this goes on all the time, these accusations of cheating, because there is a sentence ...'
Sir John Foster: 'I do not think it is relevant.'
Mr Caplan: 'If I may say so, I think it is. We have had this question of the proneness of the Americans to do this. "No tournament goes by without its load of sour-grape whispers being fed into the grapevine." This is what the article says. It seems to be a sort of invariable thing.'
Sir John Foster: 'In Mr Landy's opinion. It does not logically affect anything. What is the question to Mr Franklin?'
Mr Caplan: 'What I want to know is, Have you seen in this article any reference to what is the proper course to be taken in regard to an

allegation, and does it accord with your own view as an experienced tournament director?'

Mr Franklin: 'The proper course to be taken if there is any allegation is quite clearly to report it in the first instance to the tournament director.'

Caplan left the subject soon after, without referring to the way in which the accusation was tested, and with no names mentioned.

Franklin cross-examined

Harold had played Humpty Dumpty sitting on the wall during most of his evidence-in-chief, but after a few prods from Goldblatt's stick he began to open up a little.

Mr Goldblatt: 'I am sure you would be prepared to accept that, sitting beside a player, and looking across at the hand opposite, you would have a perfectly good view of the backs of the opposite player's cards and of the face of the cards of the player beside whom you were sitting?'

Mr Franklin: 'I think that is what I said – one has a perfect view opposite and no view at all of the backs of the card one is looking at.'

'Therefore any view one formed as to the finger displays on the back of the cards of the player beside whom you were sitting would be formed by inference from what you saw on the face of the cards?'

'I should like to believe that I would not form any view by inference. In other words, I either could see how he held his hand or could not see how he held his hand.'

Goldblatt suggested that the two opponents would each have a good view of the backs of the cards.

The witness answered: 'They should not have if they are observing the proprieties and procedure of high-class bridge. It is stated in the proprieties which form part of the Laws of Bridge that a player should look at his own hand and specifically avoid looking at his opponents' cards – that is to say, the places from which they draw their cards or where they hold their cards.'

Sir John Foster: 'It does not stop them having a good view if they want one?'

Mr Franklin: 'It would be noticed if that were done because it is regarded as highly unethical. They would be in a position to see, yes.'

In recent sessions Goldblatt had been developing certain lines of argument to counter the case we were building on the internal evidence. He sought now to obtain some support from the witness. Franklin agreed that information about hearts, though not the most valuable information that could be exchanged, would certainly be of some value. In what direction would he expect a first-class player to use that information? Goldblatt asked. One way, said the witness, would be to concentrate on other aspects of the hand, so as not to duplicate information. Goldblatt enumerated some obvious ways in which the advantage might appear and the witness replied:

'I should have thought that the outstanding feature there would have been in the play of the cards. The particular bids or steps one might take I would not know. I would expect to see some benefit from it. For example, if I knew how many spades my partner held on every hand, or how many points he held, I would expect to see evidence of courses of action which appeared to be predicated on that knowledge.'

'It is very difficult to say what those courses would be: is that right?'

'Certainly I would expect to avoid accidents,' Franklin replied, mentioning two hands from his earlier evidence where with pre-knowledge we could have avoided obviously bad contracts.

Mr Goldblatt: 'Your difficulty, and the difficulty of other experts dealing with these matters, is that, while they have a vast experience of bridge played normally, nobody has experience of how bridge comes out if played according to a particular cheating system. Would you agree with that?'

None of the witnesses had considered this lack of experience a handicap in forming judgments. Harold answered: 'That is true in part; but one has a rather precise knowledge of the bidding methods of a particular partnership, derived from study of thousands of hands played by them in international matches. I think I would detect variations from those methods.'

Goldblatt's next two questions were an attempt to find an explanation for our moderate performance at Buenos Aires: 'There are difficulties in using your illegitimate knowledge of suit distribution in the bidding that may well unbalance a finely attuned bidding system?'

Mr Franklin: 'I should have thought that two highly intelligent partners with a knowledge of each other's holding in a particular suit could have so adjusted their bidding as to show other features and take that factor into account.'

Mr Goldblatt: 'Would you agree that there was the possibility of distortion rather than improvement in the bidding?'

Mr Franklin: 'Not in the hands of experts, no.'

Goldblatt turned to the witness's overall conclusions. Harold stressed that our bidding seemed to him quite normal. If he were doing a report in depth, he remarked, there were not more than one or two hands where he would want to ask either player why he had made a particular call.

Mr Goldblatt: 'It comes to this. You do not draw any positive inference from a study of the hands, but you see no departure from normal as against your experience of Reese and Schapiro.'

Mr Franklin: 'I do not think it is entirely that.'

Mr Caplan: '"It comes to this" does not purport to be a question. It purports to be a resumé of what has been said.'

Mr Goldblatt: 'My friend is constantly objecting to questions in that form. It may not be his style of questioning, but it is as much a matter of style as bridge partnerships are a matter of style.'

Mr Caplan: '"It comes to this" is a positive statement.'

Mr Goldblatt: 'Not when there is a question mark at the end.'

In the staging of mock battles learned counsel have nothing to learn from all-in wrestlers.

Mr Franklin: 'I would not go all the way with you on that, because I would not disregard the hands on which the results argue against pre-knowledge.'

Mr Goldblatt: 'How strongly do you put that aspect of the matter?'

'I think that is very important; I put that very high. I have said that I see nothing which I would question and that I regard their performance as normal. There is none the less a variety of hands where one might have expected other things to have happened had they been favoured by pre-knowledge.'

'Do you come to a general conclusion having regard to the existence of a variety of hands, or do you merely note the existence of that variety of hands?'

This question was obscure to me. Harold replied: 'I come to the firm conclusion that the internal evidence – I have no knowledge of any other sort of evidence and I do not close my mind to other possibilities – I should have thought argued strongly against any pre-knowledge. That is my firm conclusion.'

Goldblatt's next question was in line with his theory about 'pattern'. He said in effect: Irrespective of whether there may be a normal bridge explanation for the bid made, do you agree that pre-knowledge of the heart suit would have pointed to the same call?

Mr Franklin: 'That is not the way I approach the matter. I have considered each hand and tried impartially to consider the bids which I would have expected Reese or Schapiro to make in that situation. I have found virtually none or very few hands where I could not have judged their bids in advance.'

Mr Goldblatt: 'In that appraisal you have entirely disregarded any effect which knowledge of the heart suit may have had on those bids?'

Mr Franklin: 'For the heart suit to have effect, they would have had to do something abnormal. If a player has made a perfectly normal opening bid, the opening bid I would have expected him to make, I fail to see how I should be expected to introduce some other aspect into my consideration.'

Yes, that fitted exactly with what Flint and I had repeatedly said: that where a call is in accordance with the player's known methods, no argument can be founded on it whatsoever. These good points that Franklin was making were all the stronger when considered in relation to the stiffness of his earlier evidence.

In re-examination the witness agreed that a simple sign to show whether one was good or bad for the bid just made would be more valuable information than the length of the heart suit. It was all over by lunchtime, leaving the afternoon free for Goldblatt to begin his closing speech.

13 At the End of the Day

'AT THE END OF THE DAY' was a phrase used by both Counsel when anticipating the end of the evidence. After so long and diffuse a hearing, with 30 sessions spread over a year, closing speeches of two or three days by each side would have been normal, but there was a general understanding that Counsel would take not much more than a day each. Goldblatt, starting after lunch on June 27, was expected to continue on July 1. Caplan proposed to make a written submission and to speak only for an hour or two.

Closing speech for the British Bridge League

Goldblatt began with some comments on his own position: 'To enable this tribunal the more easily to come to a decision,' he said, 'I have adopted throughout the case the role of prosecutor, in order that the two sides of the argument should be fairly presented to you. Standing apart from the role of prosecutor for one moment, let me say that if at the stage we have now reached, the evidence having been concluded, I were able to take the view that the only fair assessment of that evidence was that the allegations of cheating had not been established, then it would be at this stage my pleasant task to invite you to come to the firm conclusion that the allegations had not been established.

'However, there being evidence upon which, in my submission, it is perfectly proper to invite you to come to the conclusion that those allegations have been established, and established to the requisite standard which I invited you to apply, I shall continue in my closing summary of the case to adopt the same role as throughout its conduct and put before you the reasons for saying that the case has been proved.

'For the purposes of my opening address I divided the case into two headings – observation and inference. It is my submission that the crucial decision which you have to make is on the direct evidence of what was observed; and if that direct evidence leads you to the conclusion that cheating took place, then that conclusion could be dispelled only if you were able to say that, on the whole of what you have heard in relation to inference, you cannot accept the direct evidence of observation.

'It may be suggested by my learned friend that in putting the matter thus I am running counter to my opening remarks as to onus of proof. The reason why I am not is this. For all the expertise that we have had from those commenting on the hands, none of these players, ex hypothesi, has any substantial experience of this form of cheating with which we are concerned or any known yardstick by which to judge it.'

When he came to individual hands, he said, he would argue that the type of analysis made by the various witnesses did not rule out the possibility that the bid or play had in the first instance been affected by knowledge of partner's holding. Not rule out the possibility? It sounded like the old circular argument: 'My case is that they had illicit knowledge of the hearts; here are some hands which players possessing illicit knowledge would have bid the same way; therefore they may well have been applying illicit knowledge.'

'Observation is crucial,' Goldblatt went on, 'for this reason, that, as my learned friend accepts, if Reese and Schapiro did not cheat, Becker, Hayden, Truscott and Swimer conspired. It is one or the other.'

Mr Caplan: 'I do not accept that. My learned friend makes his statement. If you find that Reese and Schapiro are innocent, this is a possible result. There are other possible theories as to why the observations were not accurate. I do not have to prove conspiracy. I do not accept that conspiracy is the only answer.'

Mr Goldblatt: 'There might have been other ways of presenting the defence. My friend expressly disclaimed them. That is why I put the matter as I did.'

The defence had not disputed that if the notes of the observation were entirely accurate the degree of correspondence would be far beyond the bounds of possible coincidence. That was not the same as saying that the whole story was an invention. In my own evidence I had not alleged a conspiracy in the sense of three, four or five people forming a deliberate plot in advance. On the other hand, the defence did not concede, and obviously could not concede, that the notes were an objectively true record of what had occurred.

Goldblatt was determined to develop the argument, 'See how unlikely it is that there was any sort of conspiracy.' He began by saying, not very convincingly, that the people concerned were by no means four people with an identity of interest. 'It is perfectly true that Becker and Hayden are a playing partnership. It is perfectly true that Truscott has nowadays a friendly and commercial association with one of those two in the world of bridge journalism.' But Truscott and Swimer, he implied, were the least likely people in the world to wish to sustain an unjust accusation against two of their countrymen.

Butler and Kehela, as observation witnesses, were considered on a slightly different basis from the others. 'The position with those two witnesses is this. Each of them saw things which corresponded with the code that had been promulgated by that time. Butler kept a note of what he saw; Kehela did not. Butler's judgment and accuracy have been attacked on various grounds, but at the end of the day you have Butler's notes and you are in a position to compare them with the hand records. Although there are question marks against some of his noted items, there is no observation by Butler which is frankly inconsistent with the code as promulgated.'

Counsel maintained that the evidence of Kehela was too imprecise to be of any value to the defence. 'We do not get beyond the proposition,' he said, 'that there were several hands where Kehela observed no correspondence between the signals and the heart holdings, the amount of the "several" not being firmly established. Is that evidence from a witness who is accurate, careful, reliable, or is it too casual to be of great assistance one way or the other? I am not placing reliance on Kehela. I am only pointing out that, in so far as one throws Kehela's evidence into the balance, it tends to support the cheating allegations and tends to go against the contention that they were not cheating.'

Speaking with more rhetorical force than at any time before, Goldblatt ended this session as follows: 'What distinguishes this case from the ordinary run of cheating cases of which we have heard is that an interpretation was made of these finger signals. That interpretation might not have been of enormous value if it had only emerged after the conclusion of the championship. But in my submission it is of the greatest possible assistance to you in deciding the honesty or otherwise of the prosecution witnesses that the basis of the allegations, the code and its meaning, was put about before the conclusion of the championship and before Reese and Schapiro had ceased to play with one another. Other people knew about this code. In my submission that fact is fatal to the existence of a conspiracy. It points so strongly to the honesty of these four that it compels you to the conclusion that they are honest.'

Resuming a week later, Goldblatt began with an assessment of the technical evidence. He referred to a number of hands individually and sought to develop two general theories: that the prosecution points were easy to see on a quick assessment, whereas the defence arguments involved much deeper analysis; and that it was difficult to know at this stage what the players had really been thinking about when they made their bids.

Some brief remarks followed about the defence witnesses. The court might think that Flint had been a little vehement in support of Reese and Schapiro. On the first day of his evidence, especially, there had been a distinct atmosphere of resentment against the line of questioning. In this respect his evidence ran parallel to that of Reese. Each witness dissolved into a more objective attitude later. This might affect the weight of their overall conclusions.

Goldblatt's comment on Heredia was that he had set a noticeably high standard for his assessment of cheating. He meant by this that Heredia looked for a pattern in the hands and, not finding the sort of examples he expected, had been prepared to reject the allegations out of hand. Franklin's evidence amounted to much the same, and really, Counsel maintained, this did not run very much counter to the way in which he had presented the case on inference in his opening, when he conceded that there was probably no hand, taken on its own, for which an explanation could not be found.

Ortiz-Patino had been impressed by the fact that in ten examples of heart leads at the first or second trick there had been only one false card. 'You may feel,' said Goldblatt, 'that this evidence is not worth a great deal. It may be that there is not much to be gained from regular false-carding and that players possessing illicit knowledge would use it to achieve an occasional break-through.'

Goldblatt spent rather more time dissecting the statistical evidence. He had noted that in the session where Britain beat America 63-2 the Figgis analysis did not indicate any marked difference between the performance of the two sides. He also commented that no explanation had been given of the different performance in hearts between the opponents of Reese and Schapiro and the pair holding the corresponding cards at the other table.

Counsel turned next to some more general defence arguments. The evidence did not support the idea that the method of signalling was crude, he said. Patino's remarks had been directed against players making changes in the course of a hand. No-one had said it was crude to alter the finger positions as between one hand and another. (My recollection was that several witnesses on both sides had made this point directly or indirectly.) As for the claim that the information about heart length was of middling value, it was not his duty to point to motives or explain the advantage. The heart signal had the merit of precision and simplicity. 'It was an easy additional prop for Mr Schapiro, who doesn't like commands.'

'The fact that there were strained relations between Reese and Schapiro,' he went on, 'is neither here nor there. Granted that Reese and Flint preferred to play together, how does that affect whether Reese and Schapiro cheated?' That seemed fairly easy to answer: if two players are so keen to win that they evolve a cheating system, the presumption is that they will want to exploit it.

Goldblatt then tried a little psychology, reviving his odd theory that the alleged cheating was some sort of substitute for the Little Major.

'The Italians are playing a complicated system. Reese invents an even more complex system as an answer, then falls in love with the artistry of his own creation.' ('Pygmalion,' interjected Caplan.) 'Then he is told he must play with Schapiro, who won't play these fancy frills. Is this cheating code introduced for reasons not so much of advantage as of disdain? For the intellectual satisfaction of playing against the obscure Italians something obscure of his own?'

Counsel reminded the court of the discussion between S J Simon and myself 20 years ago, when there was some talk of a match in which one team would play 'all-in'. 'It is evidence of interest on Reese's part in injecting an amoral element into bridge.' Really, where had we got to in this independent inquiry into events at Buenos Aires in 1965? If Goldblatt had asked, I could have told him that the initiative came entirely from 'Skid', who was excited by the success of his two articles, 'All-In Bridge' and 'More All-In Bridge'.

After the adjournment Goldblatt reverted to the direct evidence of observation. This, he said, could hardly be stronger. There was no doubt that observation had taken place during the Friday afternoon session against Italy, no doubt that on the Saturday morning MacNab, Gerber and von Zedtwitz all knew of the allegations and the code.

Passing to the observations of Swimer and Butler, Goldblatt stressed that the hand records had not been available till the afternoon of the following day. He referred to the comparison between the notes and the hand records at the Sunday meeting. 'You may remember Reese's typically scathing description of this as a "pantomime".'

'Did the notes of Becker and Hayden exist?' he asked. 'If not, how could Becker and Hayden work out and promulgate the code, as we know they did? The acid test of this is that Butler was told the code before he watched.'

Wasn't that a little illogical? If the Americans told Butler about a code, all it proved was that they had a theory.

Further verisimilitude, Goldblatt continued, was contained in the notes themselves. They were not complete, not watertight. With their annotations and other probing entries, they represented what one would expect to see in notes honestly compiled. 'Swimer,' said Goldblatt, 'was an obviously uncomfortable witness. He might have given the impression that he was holding something back. Was the evidence that he was reluctant to give true or untrue? In my submission, it is obvious that if it were untrue he would have come out with it earlier.' Some people might put it the other way round, I thought.

Recalling the famous meeting with Schapiro outside the hotel at Buenos Aires, Counsel read extracts from Swimer's version, to demonstrate its plausibility. There was a catch in his voice when he came to the memorable words attributed to Schapiro, 'It was that evil man, he made me do it. I wouldn't play the Little Major and he made me do it.'

Goldblatt spoke next of the previous relations between the two parties. He quoted my remark that I had a cordial professional relationship with Becker and no particular feelings about Hayden. As for Swimer's supposed resentment towards Schapiro, Flint and Konstam had both given some account of this. Konstam had been less emphatic and it might be thought that he was the more objective witness.

Turning to my part in the affair, Goldblatt asked, 'Despite what he told you about his temperament, wouldn't you expect Reese to let rip with Swimer?' Then he referred to a passage in my evidence when I was describing events on Sunday afternoon. Konstam had asked me what was going on and I had answered, 'Do your best, it will be cleared up.' I added, in my evidence, 'Not that I thought so.' Goldblatt saw something significant in these last words.

Schapiro's evidence, he went on, had been in purple passages. There was his rip-roaring account of the walk with Swimer. Describing what happened after the meeting at which the charge was first made, Schapiro had said: 'I thought Reese must be mad. He said to me, "You've done nothing, keep calm, go for a walk."' This might be taken either way, Counsel suggested. He meant that it might have been warning advice, as from one conspirator to another.

'As for the photographs,' Goldblatt concluded, 'each is capable of bearing out the allegations. We have had any number of tests to prove the truth or falsity of the allegations of cheating. Wherever one tries to test, as a matter of known fact, the order of events, the notes taken, the photos that exist, all falls into line, and the assertion that the direct evidence cannot be controverted has been borne out in the last hour and a quarter. It hangs together and is overwhelmingly persuasive. If that is not so, all are lying, Butler too, in my submission. I invite you to say that their honesty is conclusively demonstrated and that the only one conclusion is that the allegations are made out.'

There had been two central themes in this speech: that a verdict of not guilty would mean that at least four witnesses had fabricated evidence; and that the promulgation of the code before the championship had ended was proof that the Americans were both sincere and confident of the truth of what they were saying. For the rest, my own view was that we had little or nothing to answer. Much of the speech had necessarily been defensive – to mitigate the effect of the arguments we would be using. This applied especially to the comments on the technical evidence.

I had already seen Caplan's written submission, and this, as will appear later, contained his answer to the conspiracy theme. In his comparatively short speech, made a week after Goldblatt's, he dealt mostly with other matters.

Closing speech for the defence

Caplan began by handing in copies of his written submission, about 25,000 words in length. This, he said, contained the essential points of his case. His present speech would be of a general character.

The written and spoken addresses naturally overlapped in some respects. For the most part I follow here the lines of the written submission.

The first section was headed 'The General Approach'. 'One starts with what is undeniable,' Caplan wrote. 'Reese and Schapiro are famous players, each has won many triumphs, whether playing as a pair or with other partners. Their reputation for ethical conduct has always been extremely high. It was Mr Butler who said "there was never a breath of suspicion against them." And this reputation is all the more remarkable in the context not only of the jealousy which seems to abound in the realm of bridge, and of their long pre-eminence, but of the undoubted fact that each has a tongue which has given offence to many and neither is embarrassed by modesty or given to suffering gladly those whom they believe to be fools.'

Not suffer fools gladly? Not embarrassed by modesty? Surely he was thinking of two other people!

After referring to the obvious gravity of the charge, Caplan made some comments on the burden of proof, which had a special importance in this case. 'Guilt of Mr Reese and Mr Schapiro would necessarily involve that they had been guilty of conspiring together; but their innocence does not involve proving affirmatively anything whatsoever against their accusers, either individually or jointly; it does not involve proving that any of the witnesses against them have conspired together or that their alleged observations were careless or were influenced by prior unfounded suspicion or by thinking they saw what they had been led to believe they would see.'

Turning to the technical evidence, which had occupied so much of the Inquiry's time, Caplan observed: 'No independent expert has been called to say that the bidding or the play of either Mr Reese or Mr Schapiro lends any support to the case that they were cheating in the manner alleged. That there is such a solid body of technical evidence and that it is all on one side is itself significant.'

Counsel examined the question of whether the evidence had shown any pattern of right decisions over the whole 198 hands. The next paragraph is from the speech before the tribunal: 'You do not find any such pattern. All the expert witnesses have said that if there were cheating close analysis would reveal signs of it. The argument advanced as to why those signs are not manifest is that the players exercised such skill, judgment and self-control that they were able to conceal the signs. That explanation simply will not wash. There are so many instances of imperfect judgement at the table that it is not in this world that they could be 100 per cent perfect in this other respect. Remember, too, that Britain was doing badly in this championship; the temptation to "press" would be overwhelming; it is inconceivable that on no occasion should anything be done to betray the illicit knowledge.'

Still more significant, Caplan suggested, were the numerous hands where the bidding or play was wholly inconsistent with knowledge of the heart distribution. 'By what means is it sought to rebut this evidence? The first and rather pathetic suggestion was that Reese and Schapiro were so tired at some stages during an arduous tournament that they could not appreciate even the most elementary use to which their illicit information could be put. Contrast this with the argument that their supposed unflagging alertness throughout the tournament prevented even the slightest trace of their illicit knowledge from appearing in their bidding or play.

'The other attempted explanation was that there might be some "level of analysis" below some other "level or levels of analysis" (doubtless to be arrived at by a process akin to stripping an onion!) at which the disastrous bid or pass might be found to be consistent with cheating. This kind of argument is simply desperate casuistry. No "level of analysis" but only temporary insanity could explain some of the calls made or not made if the players knew how many hearts they both held.'

The next part of the written submission was headed 'The Direct Evidence'. 'One curious aspect of this,' Caplan began, 'is that, despite its impressive facade at first view, closer examination reveals so many dubious features. This would be consistent with concoction having played a part in its formulation; but for reasons already given it is not necessary to unravel and determine how much might be due to this, either at the outset or at one or more stages thereafter. Before considering the disharmony between various parts of the story as it is now told, it may be useful to glance at some matters of which sight can easily be lost.'

Under this heading Caplan mentioned (a) that a player must display some number of fingers, and three or four are the commonest numbers; (b) he must hold some number of hearts, and three or four are the commonest numbers; (c) how many fingers a player is showing must often be doubtful and open to different interpretations; (d) an observer seeing the number of hearts held may well interpret doubtful finger positions in a way that would accord with that number; (e) there is nothing unusual in a player holding his cards in different ways at different moments; photographs of Reese taken over many years supported this; and (f) there had been first-class evidence that an observer sitting behind a player could form no reliable view as to how many fingers he was showing to his partner.

All these limitations, Caplan continued, would apply to contemporary notes made in all honesty and with every attempt at accuracy. He now had to consider, in the light of certain dubious features, to what extent that assumption was justified.

'There have been produced some notes allegedly made at the time of observation by Becker and Hayden. Such contemporary notes would have been most cogent evidence to present against Reese and Schapiro at Buenos Aires. But so far as independent testimony goes, including that of Mr Butler, the existence of these notes was unknown at that time!' This last remark should perhaps have been qualified. According to his evidence, Swimer had received a general impression of notes having been taken by several people, including Truscott; but he did not ask to see them.

'In the records of the two committee meetings,' Caplan continued, 'there is no trace of such notes being even heard of by anybody, let alone seen. When Truscott broached the allegations to Butler on the Saturday there was no reference, so far as Butler could remember, to any notes of observation by Becker and Hayden. Instead, Truscott's weapon of persuasion was a small group of hands. The assessors have expressed their view regarding what kind of evidence of cheating those hands were. It passes belief that Truscott would have sought to rely on that sort of stuff if there had then been in existence notes of observation made the day before.'

So far, Caplan emphasised, it was completely unnecessary to predicate that Becker, Hayden and Truscott had formed a conspiracy either among themselves or with Swimer. Then he began to trace the way in which events might have developed: 'Let it be granted that Becker, on the first Monday, did observe that Reese and Schapiro were not always holding their cards in the same way. Except to anyone almost pathologically suspicious, this would not immediately arouse thoughts about cheating. But Becker straightaway draws the worst conclusion. He communicates his suspicions to Hayden, and after the Thursday session she concludes that he is right. They call in Truscott, who is a friend and neighbour of Hayden and with whom they are both closely acquainted. It is suggested that he should observe a session against Italy and take notes. Becker and Hayden also come along, but as the note-taking is left to the quasi-independent Truscott, who has positioned himself for this purpose, they both stand high up among the gallery of spectators. "I climbed to the top of the grandstand" (Hayden), and "I was looking down at quite a severe angle" (Becker).'

'Unhappily it transpires that Truscott has forgotten to bring his pencil with him! Whether or not this was the only reason, Hayden discovers to her annoyance that he has taken no notes.'

At this stage they have not associated the alleged signals with the heart suit and Truscott, with the hand records and such material as he possesses in the way of notes or recollection, is unable to discover any code. Later, Becker and Hayden join him. On that imperfect basis of their joint recollections, possibly aided by incomplete notes, they arrive at the theory that the finger positions are associated with the heart suit. They tell Gerber of what they believe to be their discovery, making him promise not to pass it on without consulting them. But Gerber does so, and shortly after we have Truscott seeking to persuade Butler with the aid of a group of hands.

Caplan advanced three further arguments in support of the version he had outlined:

(1) In the notes produced at the Inquiry there were explicit examples of the spreading of fingers to distinguish a holding of five hearts from two hearts; but Swimer and Butler, after their briefing by Truscott, knew nothing of this refinement.

(2) According to the story told by the other side, Truscott, possessing notations of several hands together with the hand records, tried vainly for two hours to find some correlation. How could he fail to apply the simple method of comparing hands where the same signal was given? Their common feature could not remain hidden for long. If in fact Truscott did not possess full notes, then this problem ceased to exist.

(3) Further support was lent by the character of the notes themselves, which contained much evidence of doubtful observation – the 'probing entries' to which Goldblatt had referred. Thus Caplan's main answer to Goldblatt's 'conspiracy' theme was to suggest that the notes could have been 'improved' to give additional verisimilitude 'after the events of Saturday night and the Sunday meetings had produced a sensational situation riveting worldwide attention'. He also mentioned as a possibility that the limited number of boards covered, the uncertainties in the markings, and the poor observing situations taken up by Becker and Hayden, might have resulted in notes which by a measure of coincidence showed some correlation between the hearts held and the fingers seen. This last assumption, he pointed out, would involve no reflection at all on the American trio, except perhaps their willingness to be suspicious.

From Becker, Hayden and Truscott, Caplan passed to Swimer. 'The part played by Swimer is on any view a remarkable one; and there are features of his evidence and of his personality which are equally remarkable.' The first aspect to which Caplan drew attention was the entire absence of dubiety or qualification in Swimer's testimony. When he watched Schapiro play with Konstam, he insisted that during each of 14 hands Schapiro held his cards with four fingers showing. When be observed from the captain's chair he put down 20 figures in his notes without a single expression of uncertainty, despite the fact that he was watching from an unfavourable position; not only that, but the correlation with hearts was unvaryingly 'correct'. Even when he observed from high up in the grandstand he never made a mistake or a doubtful notation.

'This unique certainty of observation puts Swimer's evidence in a class of its own,' Caplan declared. 'Also in a class of its own was the "bombshell" which he detonated during his re-examination when claiming that Schapiro had actually made a confession to him at Buenos Aires.'

After some further comments about this, Caplan reviewed the testimony that had been given about Swimer's attitude and actions from the time of the trials for Baden Baden onwards. 'Jealousy, resentment, failure and knowledge of ineffectiveness are powerful ingredients in a psychological brew,' he observed. This was 'evidence' of a kind that the tribunal might take or leave, I thought, but there could be no doubt of the force of the final point made in this section. This concerned the manner in which Swimer had recorded the two occasions where I held a void in hearts. In the column where on all other hands the finger display was recorded there was now no figure at all. In one place there was an asterisk, in the other a note which looked like 'right hand down'. This suggested that Swimer looked first, not at the fingers I was showing, but at the number of hearts in my hand.

'There is no need,' said Caplan in conclusion, 'to postulate that Swimer joined any "conspiracy", if there was one, either then or thereafter; but I must invite you to reject certain parts of his testimony.'

Turning to Butler, Caplan observed that the defence did not make any imputations against his good faith. No doubt he believed himself to be fairly and accurately observing the last nine boards of the Saturday session against Argentina. 'Whether his belief was wholly correct is another matter; and it is also another matter what inference can properly be drawn from the observations he made. None of this is intended to be critical of Butler. It is true that, as more than one person has indicated, he is not the most clear-headed of persons.' Counsel quoted some plain-spoken comments made by Truscott when shown a passage of the Report which did not agree with the evidence he was giving ('there are many other things here which will show him muddled in other ways'). Caplan's summary of Butler's evidence was that the expressed uncertainties in his notes and the possibilities of error were too considerable for his observation to be anything but inconclusive; this apart from the fact that much of his testimony was contradicted by that of Kehela.

Both in the written and spoken addresses Caplan spent much time analysing Kehela's evidence. 'What matters in Kehela's observation,' he said, 'is the high proportion of hands where there was no co-incidence'. (Caplan wrote this last word with a hyphen and throughout the case gave it a sinister sound by pronouncing the second 'i' long, as in the verb.) 'Kehela's final words in evidence were: "I am satisfied that Reese and Schapiro were not using signals throughout the session I watched." Even this perfectly plain statement has been the subject of a smoke-screen of confusion by the suggestion that cheating was taking place during some part of the session but not the whole of it.'

Kehela's evidence, Caplan observed, represented a menace to those who had committed themselves to the allegation that Reese and Schapiro were cheating. 'Almost predictably, therefore, a desperate attempt has been made by a member of the American team to discredit its deputy captain who gave that evidence. A story is put forward, casting Kehela not only in the role of a deliberate liar but also as one who, after making up his mind at Buenos Aires that he will tell lies thereafter, then while still at Buenos Aires proceeds to let it be known that this is what he is going to do! A tall story indeed, but "desperate situations need desperate remedies".'

'Hayden gives an account in which implausibility is to be masked by circumstantiality.

'The scene is outside the bridgerama room. The time is Saturday night while the third and last session of the day is in progress between Italy and America. Hayden is not playing and is "pacing the floor outside bridgerama". The account goes on: "After about three or four boards Sammy came out of bridgerama." There is a short conversation about how badly the match is going and how the Italians have been doubled in a contract of Three Clubs which they are going to make with an overtrick. "Then he asked me if I wanted to go for a walk and I said yes. It was dark now. We went for a walk, ten or 15 minutes ..." During the walk Kehela says, "I went and watched and I sat behind Reese and I saw it. I never would have believed it otherwise ... If anybody asks me about this I will deny it, I will deny that there is sufficient evidence."'

The 'Three Clubs doubled' hand was board 127 of the Italy–US match, the third board of the session. The time would have been about 10pm. But Kehela did not watch Britain–Argentina until at least an hour later, for it will be remembered that he observed during the second half of that session; and the two matches began officially at the same hour. Thus there was a serious error in the chronology.

Becker had also added his piece on this subject of Kehela's deceitfulness. He described how Kehela accosted him just before he entered the bridgerama room and said, 'I know they cheated, but must you make a great scandal of it?' This story, said Caplan, could be true, for at that time Kehela believed what he had been told about the cheating. Becker's story was intended to supplement that of Hayden, 'but you may think,' Caplan said to the tribunal, 'that it was the inspiration for Hayden's falsehood. It is reminiscent of the thirteenth note of a cuckoo clock, which is not only demonstrably false in itself but casts a doubt on all that has gone before.'

The third part of Caplan's written submission was entitled 'The Defence: Generally'. Here he dealt with what he described as the inherent improbability of the charge, developing the argument as follows: 'Everything that is known about Reese and Schapiro, both at and before Buenos Aires, contradicts the charge made against them.

'To begin with, any thought that they had long since been operating this alleged cheating system can be rejected out of hand. Watched by a multitude of eyes over the years, how could it have escaped detection until Buenos Aires that at every deal each picked up his cards and rearranged his fingers to conform with the code? There has also been evidence that they never raise their eyes during the bidding. To see any signals in these circumstances would require furtive glances to be made by each while pretending not to look; and nothing is more obvious than furtiveness.

'Any cheating at Buenos Aires must therefore have been of recent origin. But again this does not accord with the known facts. There was the bad feeling between them both before and during the championship, and the evidence that Reese throughout wanted to play with Flint.

'The very system they are supposed to have used makes nonsense of the accusation. Nobody could sensibly suggest that Reese, if he had turned his mind to it, would not have known what was the most valuable information to impart or would have been unable to devise a undetectable method of imparting it. In addition, the very cast of his mind argues against the accusation. For such a person it would be the negation of intellectual satisfaction to triumph by means of childish cheating rather than by the use of his intelligence and powers of analysis.'

In the fourth section of his written document Caplan reverted to the technical evidence. He quoted several passages where witnesses had summarised their conclusions and had commented on the power of the internal evidence to overthrow the evidence of observation. A list was attached of the hands on which the defence relied; this was simply a reminder; we assumed that the tribunal and the assessors remembered, or had access to, the arguments relating to each deal.

Caplan summed up as follows: 'The "direct evidence", including as it does that of Kehela, is contradictory; and to the extent that it is not contradictory and is relied upon to make a case against Reese and Schapiro, it is too fraught with alternative possibilities and unsatisfactory features whether in the way of observations which are not wholly reliable, or in the way of malice, or of prior suspicion, or of the necessity to maintain and even "improve" a position taken up from which no retreat was possible, or even in the way of some compound of such elements with a minor degree of coincidence thrown in to bedevil the truth. In this connection one calls to mind the words of de Heredia: "I must tell you, this type of affair is full of emotion. One finds that the people concerned in it have a strong interest. The need for scandal surpasses the need for justice."

'On the other hand, the technical evidence is unanimous, free from doubt, and overwhelming. It admits of no other conclusion than that players of the calibre of Reese and Schapiro could not have played as they did if aided by illicit knowledge of the heart suit.

'The evidence given, taken in its entirety, therefore goes far beyond producing a reasonable doubt concerning the allegations made:

affirmatively and conclusively it proves the charge to be untrue and entitles Reese and Schapiro to be unequivocally exonerated so that the slur is removed from their reputation.'

The great skill of Caplan's written submission was that it presented a continuous and consistent theory of events, where previously the defence had been somewhat vague and disunited. At the same time Counsel kept in the foreground that it was not our duty to supply the explanations that would reconcile the story of observation with the internal proof that there had been no illicit knowledge.

At the end of the speeches Sir John intimated that he proposed to make his report to the British Bridge League. Caplan said he assumed a copy would be sent simultaneously to his clients. Sir John thought it was a question of what the BBL wanted, and Priday intervened to say that there need be no dispute about this: he assumed that the Council would invite Mr Reese and Mr Schapiro to be in attendance when the report was received, so that its contents could be communicated to them within a few minutes. Sir John let fall that he did not expect to present his report until about the second week of August, four to five weeks ahead. This was the first sure indication we had that the judgement would consist of more than a two-line verdict.

While Leigh Howard and Boris and I were talking with Caplan after the final hearing, congratulating him on his speech, Boris said: 'Reese gets annoyed when I ask this question, but never mind about that, I am going to ask it. What do you think the tribunal will say?'

Caplan fenced with him, as professional men do. 'I am in no better position to give an opinion about that than anyone else who has listened to the evidence. When one is as close to it all as I have been, it can be difficult to see things in perspective.'

Sir John and the General had their first meeting a few days later. They had available a report from the assessors, who submitted detailed comments on all the hands raised by either side during the closing speeches. The assessors gave each hand a grading such as 'strong', 'fair', 'slight value', 'no value'. They kept their own counsel at this stage, but we were fairly confident that the weight of their opinion would be on our side.

While at Deauville for the annual tournament I heard that the BBL had called a meeting for Tuesday, August 9. Later I had a letter from the acting secretary, saying that the meeting would be at the Russell Hotel and adding bleakly, 'If you wish to attend you should be present about 4.00pm.' We gathered that Priday, Franklin and Figgis, determined not to repeat the error of officials at Buenos Aires who had arbitrated on their own evidence, would not attend the meeting; nor, of course, would Butler.

On Tuesday Eric, Boris, Tim Holland and I assembled at Crockford's and drove to the hotel in Tim's Rolls-Royce, arriving at about 3.50pm. The

Council had been sitting since 2.30. With all the reporters and cameramen we sat for an hour in the lounge, discussing bridge hands, the afternoon's racing, the possible form of the judgement, the significance of the delay. The London correspondent of the *New York Times* described us sipping tea and wrote, 'The sang-froid of great card players served them well. An outsider could not have guessed that this was possibly the most important moment of their lives.'

Soon after 5.00pm Reg Corwen, one of the English delegates, came into the lounge and said, 'They're ready for you now.' According to plan, I said that we wanted our solicitor to go in first and speak to the Council. Reg seemed taken aback but after further parley he went off with Eric. The message Eric delivered was that, before we met the BBL, we wanted an opportunity to study the report in private.

After about three minutes he rejoined us and said: 'They won't divulge the report, and that's flat. It is what I expected. Depending on the verdict, it may be that they want to protect you or there may be criticisms of witnesses on the other side which they do not want to broadcast. In either case, publication by the BBL would not necessarily be privileged. Now where do we go from there?'

'It seems to me,' said Tim, drawing on his cigar, 'that there's nothing for it but to go in and hear what they have to say.'

Eric led Boris and myself to the room where the Council, about ten of them, was assembled. We took chairs at the end of the table, facing Louie Shenkin, the Scottish delegate who had taken the chair for this Inquiry. He said he would read the statement he would be giving to the press:

> The joint report by Sir John Foster and Lord Bourne into certain allegations of cheating at the world championships in 1965 made against Messrs Reese and Schapiro was received by the Counsel today. After full discussion of the arguments and recommendations by Sir John Foster and Lord Bourne the finding in the report that Messrs Reese and Schapiro were not guilty of cheating was accepted. A copy of the report will be sent to the World Bridge Federation.
>
> The Council wishes to express its sincere thanks to Sir John Foster and Lord Bourne for having conducted the Inquiry as a public duty and without fee, and to the assessors and all witnesses who voluntarily attended to give evidence at the Inquiry.

I said: 'As you know, during the past year we have suffered a great deal of damaging publicity. Surely we are now entitled to know the contents of the report? There might be some observations in it that would be of value to us.'

I meant, for immediate publicity or for possible legal proceedings. Shenkin answered: 'We have considered that aspect of the matter, but we have decided not to publish the report.'

I thanked the Council for their conduct of the whole affair from the beginning. It was true, they had been placed in a hideous predicament and had never taken the easy way.

Meanwhile, Boris had tottered out to break the news to Tim. Then Shenkin read the statement to the reporters. Boris and I gave interviews for about half an hour before leaving for Crockford's. The news was already on the tape and a reception committee headed by Kenneth Konstam was waiting for us. We had a bottle of champagne and sent telegrams to Leonard Caplan, holidaying in Spain, to Rixi Markus at Bad Gastein, and other great supporters.

Television, radio and press all gave us excellent publicity. Next day there was news of the first American reaction. Charles Solomon, the president of the WBF, announced that it was doubtful whether the World Bridge Federation would accept the British decision. Becker, Hayden and Truscott issued a joint statement which began: 'After lengthy deliberation the British have seen fit to exonerate two of their representatives in world championship play, despite the testimony of leading bridge personalities including the captain of their own team and the chairman of the British Bridge League.' Well, I said early on that Truscott was gauche. Rixi put it well in a letter to me: Why did they come to give evidence if they did not respect the status of the Inquiry?

Our solicitor at once wrote to the BBL, saying that in view of these developments it was all the more important that we should have access to the report. The chairman replied shortly that it would not be published for the time being. When asked why, members of the council said monotonously, 'No comment.'

As at Buenos Aires, all the reporters wanted to know, Would I be playing again? I said on the BBC news: 'I haven't made up my mind about that. There are a few people in the tournament game who have taken an ambiguous attitude about this affair, and it wouldn't be pleasant to play with them.'

But I thought to myself: I'll play in the Gold Cup. Boris has won that ten times and I have only won it eight times. I must put an end to that.

Appendix 1
The Technical Evidence

A list follows of all the hands to which reference was made by one side or the other. Usually the whole deal is given but sometimes it is sufficient to give just the hand that was the subject of the allegation. The first group, referred to during the Inquiry as 'Truscott's octet', consists of the eight hands produced before the Buenos Aires committee in my presence as tending to show that Schapiro and I knew how many hearts each other held. These hands were also used to arouse the suspicions of Butler and Swimer.

The eight 'committee' hands

Italy 22

East/West Game; Dealer East

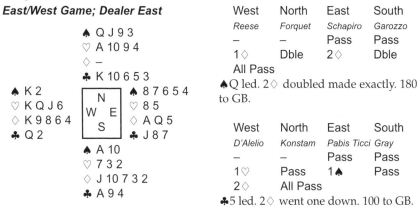

♠ Q J 9 3
♡ A 10 9 4
◇ –
♣ K 10 6 5 3

♠ K 2
♡ K Q J 6
◇ K 9 8 6 4
♣ Q 2

♠ 8 7 6 5 4
♡ 8 5
◇ A Q 5
♣ J 8 7

♠ A 10
♡ 7 3 2
◇ J 10 7 3 2
♣ A 9 4

West	North	East	South
Reese	*Forquet*	*Schapiro*	*Garozzo*
–	–	Pass	Pass
1◇	Dble	2◇	Dble
All Pass			

♠Q led. 2◇ doubled made exactly. 180 to GB.

West	North	East	South
D'Alelio	*Konstam*	*Pabis Ticci*	*Gray*
–	–	Pass	Pass
1♡	Pass	1♠	Pass
2◇	All Pass		

♣5 led. 2◇ went one down. 100 to GB.

Criticism: That the normal opening bid for West is a 'prepared' One Heart and that One Diamond was preferred because partner was known to hold only two hearts. *Answer*: In first or second position West must open One Heart, so that he can rebid Two Diamonds over a response of Two Clubs. (To open One Diamond and follow with Two Hearts, a 'reverse', would be unsound.) The situation is different when partner has passed originally. When he opens One Diamond, West intends to rebid 1NT over a response of One Spade, and to pass a response of Two Clubs. There is no need to make the prepared opening. One Diamond is definitely a safer opening than One Heart on this aceless hand.

A further point is that the presence of a doubleton heart in partner's hand, if known, is no bar to opening One Heart. A bad result is more to be feared when partner has three hearts and may raise the suit in a competitive sequence.

Italy 23

Game All; Dealer South

♠ A J 10 9
♡ A Q 8 6
◇ 9 4 2
♣ 5 3

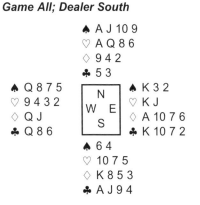

♠ Q 8 7 5
♡ 9 4 3 2
◇ Q J
♣ Q 8 6

♠ K 3 2
♡ K J
◇ A 10 7 6
♣ K 10 7 2

♠ 6 4
♡ 10 7 5
◇ K 8 5 3
♣ A J 9 4

West	North	East	South
Reese	*Forquet*	*Schapiro*	*Garozzo*
–	–	–	Pass
Pass	Pass	1◇	Pass
1♠	Pass	2♠	All Pass

♣5 led. 2♠ went two down. 200 to Italy.

West	North	East	South
D'Alelio	*Konstam*	*Pabis Ticci*	*Gray*
–	–	–	Pass
Pass	1♡	Dble	1NT
All Pass			

♠5 led. 1NT went one down. 100 to Italy.

Criticism: That West should respond One Heart, the lower of touching suits on a weak hand, and that One Spade was preferred because partner was known to hold a doubleton heart.

Answer: On a hand so weak for play in a suit contract it is folly, and certainly not my style, to choose a very bad suit. One Spade, 1NT, and pass are all, in my view, preferable to responding One Heart. One danger of that bid is that partner, who has opened fourth in hand, may pass on a doubleton, as happened on US 74.

This example was not included by Counsel in the list of 35 mentioned in his opening address.

Italy 25

East/West Game; Dealer North

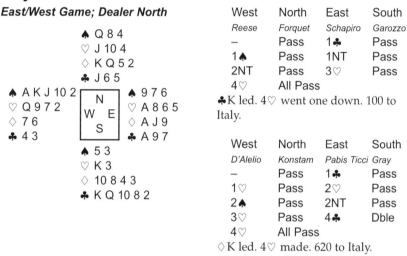

♠ Q 8 4
♡ J 10 4
◇ K Q 5 2
♣ J 6 5

♠ A K J 10 2   ♠ 9 7 6
♡ Q 9 7 2   N   ♡ A 8 6 5
◇ 7 6   W   E   ◇ A J 9
♣ 4 3   S   ♣ A 9 7

♠ 5 3
♡ K 3
◇ 10 8 4 3
♣ K Q 10 8 2

West	North	East	South
Reese	*Forquet*	*Schapiro*	*Garozzo*
–	Pass	1♣	Pass
1♠	Pass	1NT	Pass
2NT	Pass	3♡	Pass
4♡	All Pass		

♣K led. 4♡ went one down. 100 to Italy.

West	North	East	South
D'Alelio	*Konstam*	*Pabis Ticci*	*Gray*
–	Pass	1♣	Pass
1♡	Pass	2♡	Pass
2♠	Pass	2NT	Pass
3♡	Pass	4♣	Dble
4♡	All Pass		

◇K led. 4♡ made. 620 to Italy.

Criticism: That East's Three Hearts was unnatural and was influenced by knowledge of four hearts in his partner's hand.

Answer: At rubber bridge East might pass 2NT, but in the present form of scoring it is necessary to press for close games. Missing a vulnerable game which is made at the other table costs 11 IMPs, whereas a partscore swing (2NT made, as against a penalty of 100) is worth only 6 IMPs. Once East decides to bid on, Three Hearts is clearly best. The general texture (three aces and lack of intermediates) favours a suit contract and Three Hearts may well elicit a rebid of Three Spades. Players who respond One Spade to One Club usually have five and there will probably be a weakness in one of the minors. It will be especially important to play in spades if partner has a suit that needs to be developed, like K-J-10-x-x.

There are two defensive arguments. One Club is technically correct on the East hand, but it would occasion no comment if Schapiro were to open One Heart, as he might be tempted to do if he knew there were four hearts opposite. Much stronger, West has a difficult choice of calls over 1NT and would surely favour Two Hearts if he knew that his partner held four.

Italy 26

Game All; Dealer East

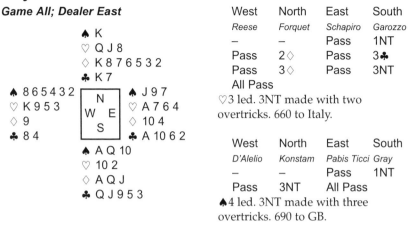

♠ K			
♡ Q J 8			
◇ K 8 7 6 5 3 2			
♣ K 7			

West	North	East	South
Reese	*Forquet*	*Schapiro*	*Garozzo*
–	–	Pass	1NT
Pass	2◇	Pass	3♣
Pass	3◇	Pass	3NT
All Pass			

♡3 led. 3NT made with two overtricks. 660 to Italy.

West	North	East	South
D'Alelio	*Konstam*	*Pabis Ticci*	*Gray*
–	–	Pass	1NT
Pass	3NT	All Pass	

♠4 led. 3NT made with three overtricks. 690 to GB.

Criticism: That West's lead of a heart in preference to a spade was influenced by the knowledge of four hearts in East's hand.

Answer: It is important to understand the Italian bidding. Two Diamonds was conventional and Three Clubs showed the range of the no-trump opening. It was clear that the opponents had reserves of strength and it was likely that there was a long suit out. West must hope that his partner has a trick in the long suit and must seek to establish tricks quickly. The best chance is to find partner with something like Q-10-x-x-x in hearts and a side trick, or possible with A-J-10-x-x. A spade lead is much too slow. Also, the suit will surely be blocked unless partner has at least three cards, including the seven. After such bidding West cannot rely on the king of hearts being a quick entry card.

Italy 54

East/West Game; Dealer East

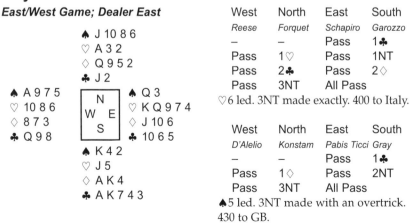

West	North	East	South
Reese	*Forquet*	*Schapiro*	*Garozzo*
–	–	Pass	1♣
Pass	1♡	Pass	1NT
Pass	2♣	Pass	2◇
Pass	3NT	All Pass	

♡6 led. 3NT made exactly. 400 to Italy.

West	North	East	South
D'Alelio	*Konstam*	*Pabis Ticci*	*Gray*
–	–	Pass	1♣
Pass	1◇	Pass	2NT
Pass	3NT	All Pass	

♠5 led. 3NT made with an overtrick. 430 to GB.

Criticism: That West's choice of a heart lead was influenced by knowledge of five hearts in his partner's hand.

Answer: Again the bidding is important. South's One Club was conventional and strong, the response of One Heart was conventional and showed some values, the rebid of 1NT was natural. North's Two Clubs enquired for major suits and South's Two Diamonds denied length in either major.

West infers (1) that the opponents have reserves of strength, so that an aggressive lead is called for, (2) that North has length in at least one major, and (3) that South's length is in the minors. Clearly West will lead a major suit through the dummy rather than a minor up to South. If North has four spades a spade lead will be disastrous, but if North has four hearts a heart lead will not necessarily cost a trick. In addition, it is desirable to keep the ace of spades over a likely honour in the South hand.

Italy 117

North/South Game; Dealer North

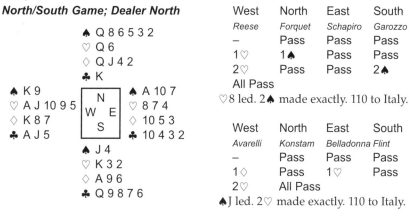

♠ Q 8 6 5 3 2
♡ Q 6
◇ Q J 4 2
♣ K

♠ K 9
♡ A J 10 9 5
◇ K 8 7
♣ A J 5

♠ A 10 7
♡ 8 7 4
◇ 10 5 3
♣ 10 4 3 2

♠ J 4
♡ K 3 2
◇ A 9 6
♣ Q 9 8 7 6

West	North	East	South
Reese	*Forquet*	*Schapiro*	*Garozzo*
–	Pass	Pass	Pass
1♡	1♠	Pass	Pass
2♡	Pass	Pass	2♠
All Pass			

♡8 led. 2♠ made exactly. 110 to Italy.

West	North	East	South
Avarelli	*Konstam*	*Belladonna*	*Flint*
–	Pass	Pass	Pass
1◇	Pass	1♡	Pass
2♡	All Pass		

♠J led. 2♡ made exactly. 110 to Italy.

Criticism: That West reopened with Two Hearts in preference to double or 1NT because he knew that his partner held three hearts.

Answer: The hand is obviously going to be played in a partscore contract and it is meaningless to say that West should reopen with a double just because he has 16 points (apparent reduced in value by the spade call on his left). A double may result in partner playing Two of a minor with a 4-3 combination and the lead coming through the king of spades. 1NT is better than double, but Two Hearts is both safe and tactically superior. West will be able to manage the play quite well even if partner has only a doubleton; he will accept ruffs, not draw trumps. The strong intermediates are of course very important. Two Hearts also prevents the opponents from contesting with Two of a minor suit. As the bidding went, South was lucky to find his partner with six spades.

US 30

Love All; Dealer East

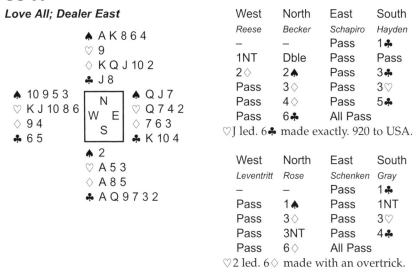

♠ A K 8 6 4
♡ 9
◇ K Q J 10 2
♣ J 8

♠ 10 9 5 3
♡ K J 10 8 6
◇ 9 4
♣ 6 5

♠ Q J 7
♡ Q 7 4 2
◇ 7 6 3
♣ K 10 4

♠ 2
♡ A 5 3
◇ A 8 5
♣ A Q 9 7 3 2

West	North	East	South
Reese	*Becker*	*Schapiro*	*Hayden*
–	–	Pass	1♣
1NT	Dble	Pass	Pass
2◇	2♠	Pass	3♣
Pass	3◇	Pass	3♡
Pass	4◇	Pass	5♣
Pass	6♣	All Pass	

♡J led. 6♣ made exactly. 920 to USA.

West	North	East	South
Leventritt	*Rose*	*Schenken*	*Gray*
–	–	Pass	1♣
Pass	1♠	Pass	1NT
Pass	3◇	Pass	3♡
Pass	3NT	Pass	4♣
Pass	6◇	All Pass	

♡2 led. 6◇ made with an overtrick. 940 to GB.

Criticism: That West's 1NT, though admittedly part of a convention, was dangerous on a five-card suit and was based on the knowledge that partner held four hearts.

Answer: We were playing, and had announced, the Gardener 1NT overcall, whereby an overcall of 1NT may be genuine or may be a 'nonsense' of an unspecified type. If partner wants to know the type he bids Two Clubs; the overcaller will then show an escape suit or, if genuine, bid 2NT. The convention enables the defending side to make nuisance bids without misleading partner.

Of course a slight risk attaches to the overcall, as to any defensive or pre-emptive bid. This was the second board we played against Becker/Hayden and it was natural that I should attempt a diversion, especially as we were not vulnerable and my partner had passed. West's Two Diamonds was just a further attempt at confusion; once he takes out 1NT doubled he is 'in charge'.

US 36

Game All; Dealer West

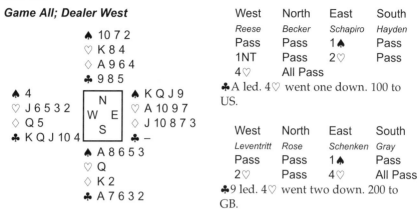

♠ 10 7 2
♡ K 8 4
◇ A 9 6 4
♣ 9 8 5

♠ 4
♡ J 6 5 3 2
◇ Q 5
♣ K Q J 10 4

♠ K Q J 9
♡ A 10 9 7
◇ J 10 8 7 3
♣ —

♠ A 8 6 5 3
♡ Q
◇ K 2
♣ A 7 6 3 2

West	North	East	South
Reese	*Becker*	*Schapiro*	*Hayden*
Pass	Pass	1♠	Pass
1NT	Pass	2♡	Pass
4♡	All Pass		

♣A led. 4♡ went one down. 100 to US.

West	North	East	South
Leventritt	*Rose*	*Schenken*	*Gray*
Pass	Pass	1♠	Pass
2♡	Pass	4♡	All Pass

♣9 led. 4♡ went two down. 200 to GB.

Criticism: That it is more natural for East to rebid Two Diamonds and that he bid Two Hearts because he knew his partner held five hearts.

Answer: The usual way to bid a limited three-suiter is to open the middle suit and follow with the lowest. If the highest suit is bid first, because it is strong, then it is perfectly correct to continue in descending order. If East bids diamonds on the second round, the heart suit, such as it is, will be lost altogether in most sequences.

The hand presents two strong counter-arguments. If East knows that his partner holds five hearts he will surely open One Heart, which is quite normal, though not in my view sensible with such holdings in the two suits. An even stronger point is that if West knows that his partner holds four hearts he will surely respond Two Hearts instead of the rather strained 1NT. Note that the American West bid Two Hearts at the other table. It is quite wrong to say, 'Oh, but West knows they will get into hearts eventually.' Partner may have a hand on which he cannot possibly introduce the hearts over 1NT.

Further hands quoted by Counsel for the British Bridge League

Counsel for the British Bridge League put forward altogether 35 hands in support of the 'case on inference'. One was later withdrawn as the vulnerability situation had been misread. Seven were among Truscott's octet, already described. The remaining 27 are analysed below. Counsel put forward first the hands that he described as most suspicious in the context, so we begin at the apex of his case.

Italy 18
North/South Game; Dealer East

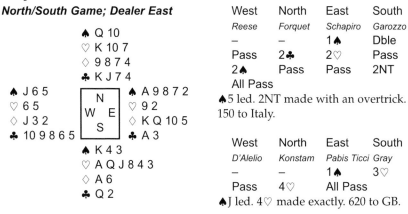

♠ Q 10
♡ K 10 7
◇ 9 8 7 4
♣ K J 7 4

♠ J 6 5   ♠ A 9 8 7 2
♡ 6 5   ♡ 9 2
◇ J 3 2   ◇ K Q 10 5
♣ 10 9 8 6 5   ♣ A 3

♠ K 4 3
♡ A Q J 8 4 3
◇ A 6
♣ Q 2

West	North	East	South
Reese	Forquet	Schapiro	Garozzo
–	–	1♠	Dble
Pass	2♣	2♡	Pass
2♠	Pass	Pass	2NT
All Pass			

♠5 led. 2NT made with an overtrick. 150 to Italy.

West	North	East	South
D'Alelio	Konstam	Pabis Ticci	Gray
–	–	1♠	3♡
Pass	4♡	All Pass	

♠J led. 4♡ made exactly. 620 to GB.

Criticism: That East bid Two Hearts because he knew his partner held only two hearts and so would not give an inconvenient raise.

Answer: The Italians were playing 'Herbert' responses to take-out doubles, so that North's Two Clubs (as attested by his subsequent inactivity) showed fair values. Thus East knew his partner must be very weak. It was likely that the vulnerable opponents had the values for game and also likely, on the surface, that their best suit would be hearts. So East may well try to keep them out of a heart contract. As to the alleged risk, if I, as West, had held a singleton spade and four or five hearts, I would certainly have been alive to the possibility that partner's heart bid might not be genuine.

The hand actually contains a negative point for the defence. If the illicit knowledge is presumed, then West has a very obvious Two Hearts available on the way round. It is a set-up situation for a psychic of that type.

Italy 127
North/South Game; Dealer South

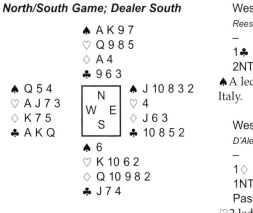

♠ A K 9 7
♡ Q 9 8 5
◇ A 4
♣ 9 6 3

♠ Q 5 4   ♠ J 10 8 3 2
♡ A J 7 3   ♡ 4
◇ K 7 5   ◇ J 6 3
♣ A K Q   ♣ 10 8 5 2

♠ 6
♡ K 10 6 2
◇ Q 10 9 8 2
♣ J 7 4

West	North	East	South
Reese	Forquet	Schapiro	Garozzo
–	–	–	Pass
1♣	Dble	1♡	2◇
2NT	Pass	3♣	All Pass

♠A led. 3♣ went two down. 100 to Italy.

West	North	East	South
D'Alelio	Rose	Pabis Ticci	Gray
–	–	–	Pass
1◇	Dble	Pass	1♡
1NT	Pass	2♣	2◇
Pass	2♡	2♠	All Pass

♡2 led. 2♠ made exactly. 110 to Italy.

Criticism: That East judged it safe to bid One Heart because his partner would know he held only a singleton, and that West refrained from supporting the hearts because of this same knowledge.

Answer: The psychic bid after the take-out double is an extremely well-known manoeuvre, on which it is unnecessary to comment. West, with 19 points, having heard a double on his left and a free response on his right, was bound to suspect the heart bid. He tested the situation with 2NT and his suspicions were confirmed when partner reverted to the original suit, clubs.

It will be noted that if West possesses the illicit knowledge he can take advantage of it very effectively by doubling Two Diamonds and leading the ace of hearts, or king of clubs followed by the ace of hearts. As the cards lie, this produces a penalty of 800.

In one way this hand cancels out the previous example, Italy 18. There it was alleged that East made a psychic bid in hearts because he knew his partner was short and would not raise. Here the partner of the psychic bidder holds four hearts.

Argentina 68

Game All; Dealer West

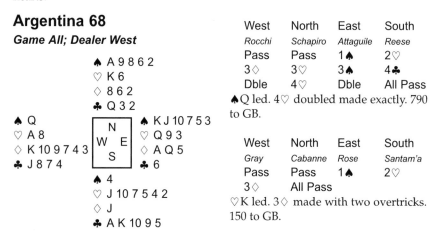

West	North	East	South
Rocchi	*Schapiro*	*Attaguile*	*Reese*
Pass	Pass	1♠	2♡
3♢	3♡	3♠	4♣
Dble	4♡	Dble	All Pass

♠Q led. 4♡ doubled made exactly. 790 to GB.

West	North	East	South
Gray	*Cabanne*	*Rose*	*Santam'a*
Pass	Pass	1♠	2♡
3♢	All Pass		

♡K led. 3♢ made with two overtricks. 150 to GB.

Criticism: That North's raise to Three Hearts and, still more, his bid of Four Hearts over the double of Four Clubs were influenced by knowledge that partner held six hearts.

Answer: As to Three Hearts, the raise on K-x of a vulnerable overcall at the two level is perfectly normal and requires no comment. The criticism of the Four Heart bid rests on a misunderstanding of South's Four Clubs. The second suit, after the hearts have been raised, need not be a long suit at all; Four Clubs could be bid on a holding like A-J-10-x simply to tell partner where the side strength lay. It would be quite wrong for North to pass Four Clubs with less than four good trumps. I quoted an exactly parallel example from my book, *Develop Your Bidding Judgment* (page 82).

Italy 35

East/West Game; Dealer South

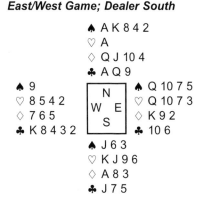

♠ A K 8 4 2
♡ A
◇ Q J 10 4
♣ A Q 9

♠ 9
♡ 8 5 4 2
◇ 7 6 5
♣ K 8 4 3 2

♠ Q 10 7 5
♡ Q 10 7 3
◇ K 9 2
♣ 10 6

♠ J 6 3
♡ K J 9 6
◇ A 8 3
♣ J 7 5

West	North	East	South
Forquet	*Schapiro*	*Garozzo*	*Reese*
–	–	–	Pass
Pass	1♠	Pass	1NT
Pass	3NT	All Pass	

♣2 led. 3NT made with two overtricks. 460 to GB.

West	North	East	South
Gray	*Belladonna*	*Flint*	*Avarelli*
–	–	–	Pass
Pass	1◇	Pass	1NT
Pass	2♠	Pass	3♠
Pass	4◇	Pass	5♣
Pass	6♠	All Pass	

♡3 led. 6♠ went one down. 50 to GB.

Criticism: That North's 3NT was not a natural choice and was influenced by knowledge that his partner held four hearts.

Answer: Defence witnesses did not dispute that Three Diamonds would have been a better rebid. Schapiro tends to take short cuts when an eventual 3NT seems the likely contract, and his own explanation here was that he bid too quickly.

The defence argued that if the cheating system existed, North would have more, not less, reason to prefer Three Diamonds to 3NT. His is exactly the sort of hand where knowledge of the heart situation could be exploited. North would bid Three Diamonds and South, knowing of the singleton opposite, would be well placed to judge whether to show his hearts, or bid 3NT, or support one of North's suits. The other side contended that this reasoning was over-subtle and that Schapiro bid 3NT because knowledge of four hearts opposite made this contract appear safe. As though a player in a world championship were unable to work out a simple situation…

Italy 49

North was the dealer and neither side was vulnerable. As West I held:

♠ J 9
♡ K 10 9 5 3 2
◇ K 9
♣ J 10 4

South, Garozzo, opened One Club and I overcalled with Two Hearts. Criticism of this bid was withdrawn when it was explained that we were playing pre-emptive jump overcalls of the conventional One Club.

Italy 125

Game All; Dealer North

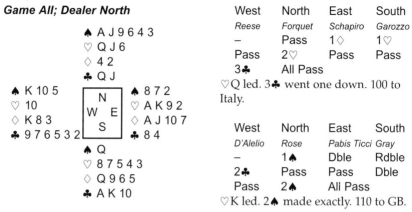

West	North	East	South
Reese	*Forquet*	*Schapiro*	*Garozzo*
–	Pass	1◊	1♡
Pass	2♡	Pass	Pass
3♣	All Pass		

♡Q led. 3♣ went one down. 100 to Italy.

West	North	East	South
D'Alelio	*Rose*	*Pabis Ticci*	*Gray*
–	1♠	Dble	Rdble
2♣	Pass	Pass	Dble
Pass	2♠	All Pass	

♡K led. 2♠ made exactly. 110 to GB.

Criticism: That the normal opening on East's hand is One Heart and that East opened One Diamond because he knew his partner held a singleton heart.

Answer: Whether he opens One Heart or One Diamond, East intends to pass a response of 1NT and to raise One Spade to Two Spades. If he opens One Heart he can rebid Two Diamonds over Two Clubs, but this mildly encouraging change of suit is unsatisfactory on a minimum hand containing only four-card suits. Having opened One Diamond, East intends to rebid Two Diamonds over a response of Two Clubs. Though unorthodox, this involves no more risk than bidding a poor hand as a two-suiter. There is no ideal way to bid the East hand – One Heart, One Diamond and pass all have their disadvantages. Schapiro added that knowledge of a singleton heart in partner's hand would not deter him from opening One Heart. Compare Italy 22; the disadvantage of opening a four-card major on a minimum hand arises when partner has three cards, not two or one.

A defensive point was made in connection with West's Three Clubs. Partner has opened One Diamond and is likely to have some spades, as they have not been mentioned by anyone. If he is known to hold four hearts he must be short in clubs, probably a singleton, so that Three Clubs, dubious in any event, becomes most unattractive.

Italy 131

East/West Game; Dealer South

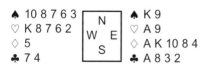

East opened fourth in hand with One Diamond, West bid One Spade and East 2NT, which was passed out.

Criticism: That if West was going to respond at all he should have bid One Heart; and that over 2NT he would have proceeded to Three Hearts had he not known that his partner held only two cards in the suit.

Answer: There are no grounds, academic or otherwise, for responding in the lower five-card suit. About the pass of 2NT I said in my evidence: 'If I had bid again over

2NT and put down this rubbish as dummy the tournament would have come to a sudden and tempestuous ending.' The result was the same at both tables, 2NT one down. This example was among those shown by Truscott to Swimer as evidence that we were signalling in the heart suit.

Argentina 42 and 45, Italy 46 and US 76

Counsel for the British Bridge League joined these four hands together in evidence that with five hearts and 5-3-3-2 distribution I opened 1NT when partner was short in hearts, One Heart when he held three cards or more. Argentina 45 was later withdrawn as the vulnerability had been misread. These were the others:

On Argentina 42 I was vulnerable and held in second position:

♠ K 8
♡ A Q 8 7 3
♢ Q 7 6
♣ A J 4

I opened 1NT, as would anyone playing a 15–17 1NT.

The two hands on Italy 46 were:

Schapiro
♠ Q 5 4 3
♡ K 5 3
♢ 7 2
♣ A 10 8 3

```
    N
  W   E
    S
```

Reese
♠ A K 7
♡ A J 10 7 4
♢ 10 9 8
♣ J 2

Neither side was vulnerable. Who opens 1NT on the South hand? Our bidding went: 1♡ – 1♠ – 2♠ – pass. Four Hearts could have been made. What may reasonably be said about the bidding is that, if both players knew how many hearts are held opposite, (1) North will prefer a raise to Two Hearts on the first round, (2) South may rebid Two Diamonds instead of raising spades, and (3) North may well try Three Hearts over Two Spades.

The hands on US 76 were:

Reese
♠ K Q 7
♡ A J 8 5 2
♢ Q 9 3
♣ 8 2

```
    N
  W   E
    S
```

Schapiro
♠ 9 8 4
♡ 6 4
♢ J 7 6 2
♣ Q 5 4 3

Not vulnerable against vulnerable opponents, I opened 1NT. This is unorthodox and in general I would not recommend it, but we made varied use of the non-vulnerable 1NT against the Americans.

Defence witnesses made the point that, if West knows his partner is short in hearts, it is safer on this moderate hand to open One Heart than 1NT. An opening 1NT is always more exposed to a penalty double.

The defence was able to make much of the sequel. North doubled 1NT and the next two players passed. Now I rescued myself into Two Hearts, was doubled again and went five down, losing 900 – a strange result for a pair supposed to be cheating in the heart suit!

If West knows that East has a doubleton heart his best course, when 1NT is doubled, is to redouble. East is sure to hold four cards in either spades or diamonds, for with a poor hand distributed 3-2-3-5 he would have taken out into Two Clubs when 1NT was doubled. It should be possible to slide out of trouble in one or other of these suits. To lose 700, as against a vulnerable game, is not serious.

Argentina 131

East/West Game; Dealer South

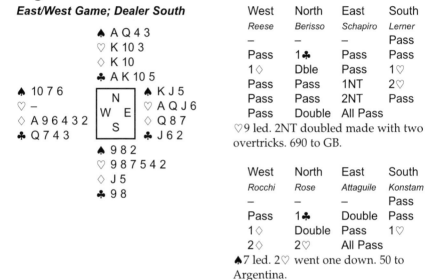

♠ A Q 4 3
♡ K 10 3
◇ K 10
♣ A K 10 5

♠ 10 7 6
♡ –
◇ A 9 6 4 3 2
♣ Q 7 4 3

♠ K J 5
♡ A Q J 6
◇ Q 8 7
♣ J 6 2

♠ 9 8 2
♡ 9 8 7 5 4 2
◇ J 5
♣ 9 8

West	North	East	South
Reese	*Berisso*	*Schapiro*	*Lerner*
–	–	–	Pass
Pass	1♣	Pass	Pass
1◇	Dble	Pass	1♡
Pass	Pass	1NT	2♡
Pass	Pass	2NT	Pass
Pass	Double	All Pass	

♡9 led. 2NT doubled made with two overtricks. 690 to GB.

West	North	East	South
Rocchi	*Rose*	*Attaguile*	*Konstam*
–	–	–	Pass
Pass	1♣	Double	Pass
1◇	Double	Pass	1♡
2◇	2♡	All Pass	

♠7 led. 2♡ went one down. 50 to Argentina.

Criticism: That East's pass on the first round, in preference to double or One Heart, was influenced by knowledge of a void heart in his partner's hand; and that West risked reopening with One Diamond because he knew his partner held four hearts. *Answer*: the East hand is too balanced for a suit overcall and it is seldom right to double with a 4-3-3-3 distribution. The hand is well suited for waiting tactics. West's reopening is natural enough, especially near the end of a match we were winning by about 200 IMPs.

US 64

East/West Game; Dealer West

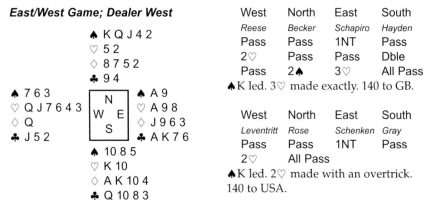

West	North	East	South
Reese	*Becker*	*Schapiro*	*Hayden*
Pass	Pass	1NT	Pass
2♡	Pass	Pass	Dble
Pass	2♠	3♡	All Pass

♠ K led. 3♡ made exactly. 140 to GB.

West	North	East	South
Leventritt	*Rose*	*Schenken*	*Gray*
Pass	Pass	1NT	Pass
2♡	All Pass		

♠ K led. 2♡ made with an overtrick. 140 to USA.

Criticism: that East's Three Hearts was dangerous and was influenced by the knowledge that West held a six-card suit.

Answer: This unlikely charge was supported by reference to a different hand where the responder to 1NT took out into Two of a suit on a bad hand as a desperation measure. Of course, in a competitive situation one does not assume that partner has a complete minimum for his bid.

Italy 1

On the first board of the tournament, with neither side vulnerable we held these hands:

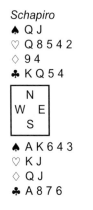

Schapiro
♠ Q J
♡ Q 8 5 4 2
◇ 9 4
♣ K Q 5 4

♠ A K 6 4 3
♡ K J
◇ Q J
♣ A 8 7 6

North dealt and passed, and the bidding proceeded: 1♠ – 2♡; 3♡ – 3♠; 4♠.

Criticism: That North's bid of Three Spades was influenced by the knowledge that his partner held only two hearts.

Answer: A response of Two Hearts normally shows at least a five-card suit and may therefore be raised on a doubleton. As his hearts could scarcely be worse it is natural and correct for North to suggest spades as possibly an alternative contract. The same contract was reached at the other table.

Italy 14

With neither side vulnerable I held as South:

♠ 9 8
♡ A Q 5 4 3
◇ Q 9 3
♣ A 9 8

After a pass by the dealer I passed in second position.

Criticism: That the decision to pass instead of opening One Heart was influenced by knowledge that partner held a doubleton heart.
Answer: Second in hand especially I avoid weak openings on hands with no 'body' when there is no tactical advantage in bidding. Two other examples were quoted from this tournament where I passed hands that were opened at the other table.

Italy 48

East/West Game; Dealer West

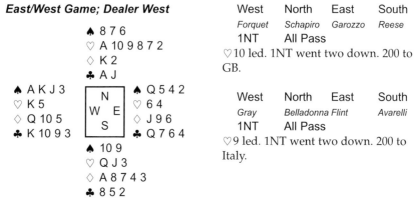

West	North	East	South
Forquet	*Schapiro*	*Garozzo*	*Reese*
1NT	All Pass		

♡10 led. 1NT went two down. 200 to GB.

West	North	East	South
Gray	*Belladonna*	*Flint*	*Avarelli*
1NT	All Pass		

♡9 led. 1NT went two down. 200 to Italy.

Criticism: South played the jack of hearts on the first trick and West won with the king. He took four rounds of spades, on which South discarded the seven of diamonds and the three of diamonds and North discarded the jack of clubs. A club was led to the king and ace. North then laid down the ace of hearts, South unblocking, and the defence made the rest of the tricks. It was said that North's play of the ace of hearts, instead of a diamond in response to his partner's signal, was made because he knew the declare held only one more heart.
Answer: West has already shown 14 points in the play and must hold the queen of diamonds, as with A-Q-x-x-x South would not discard twice from that suit. The maximum for West's 1NT is 17 points, so he cannot hold the queen of hearts as well, which would make 18. That is the analytical answer. It was also plain to Schapiro, from declarer's demeanour and general line of play, that he was taking what tricks he could. If he had started with K-Q-x he would have played in a more devious manner.

The deal provided a strong defensive point. North has a perfectly reasonable Two Heart overcall of 1NT and would surely have made this if he had known that South held three hearts. It was also contended by the defence that if illicit knowledge had existed there would have been many examples of inspired defensive play. This was the only hand put forward in that sense.

Argentina 44

East/West Game; Dealer West

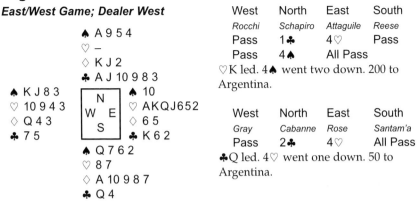

♠ A 9 5 4
♡ –
◇ K J 2
♣ A J 10 9 8 3

♠ K J 8 3   ♠ 10
♡ 10 9 4 3   ♡ A K Q J 6 5 2
◇ Q 4 3   ◇ 6 5
♣ 7 5   ♣ K 6 2

♠ Q 7 6 2
♡ 8 7
◇ A 10 9 8 7
♣ Q 4

West	North	East	South
Rocchi	*Schapiro*	*Attaguile*	*Reese*
Pass	1♣	4♡	Pass
Pass	4♠	All Pass	

♡K led. 4♠ went two down. 200 to Argentina.

West	North	East	South
Gray	*Cabanne*	*Rose*	*Santam'a*
Pass	2♣	4♡	All Pass

♣Q led. 4♡ went one down. 50 to Argentina.

Criticism: That North hazarded Four Spades because he knew his partner held only two hearts and so was likely to hold more cards in the black suits.

Answer: An aggressive player like Schapiro would never lie down to East's Four Hearts. Apart from this, the argument bringing in the heart suit is very strained. The position was slightly different at the other table because there North had already told his partner that he had a strong club suit; thus he had less in reserve after his opening bid.

Argentina 136

Love All; Dealer West

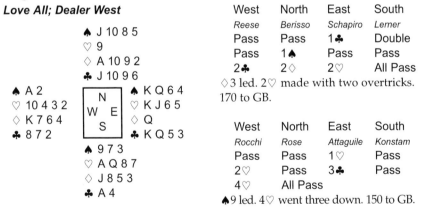

♠ J 10 8 5
♡ 9
◇ A 10 9 2
♣ J 10 9 6

♠ A 2   ♠ K Q 6 4
♡ 10 4 3 2   ♡ K J 6 5
◇ K 7 6 4   ◇ Q
♣ 8 7 2   ♣ K Q 5 3

♠ 9 7 3
♡ A Q 8 7
◇ J 8 5 3
♣ A 4

West	North	East	South
Reese	*Berisso*	*Schapiro*	*Lerner*
Pass	Pass	1♣	Double
Pass	1♠	Pass	Pass
2♣	2◇	2♡	All Pass

◇3 led. 2♡ made with two overtricks. 170 to GB.

West	North	East	South
Rocchi	*Rose*	*Attaguile*	*Konstam*
Pass	Pass	1♡	Pass
2♡	Pass	3♣	Pass
4♡	All Pass		

♠9 led. 4♡ went three down. 150 to GB.

Criticism: That East's bid of Two Hearts was influenced by knowledge that his partner held four hearts.

Answer: It was perfectly natural for East, over Two Diamonds, to contest in the cheapest suit available, especially as there were grounds for placing West with length in hearts – not that such analysis was necessary before making the bid.

More significant is that East did not open One Heart, as is quite normal with this distribution. If North had not bid over Two Clubs East would have passed and the hand would have been played in clubs instead of hearts.

US 37

North/South Game; Dealer North

Reese	Schapiro
♠ K Q 6	♠ A 8
♡ K 10 9 7 4	♡ Q 3
◇ 6 5	◇ Q J 10 7 3 2
♣ J 9 6	♣ K 10 4

After a pass by North, East opened 1NT – a common manoeuvre when not vulnerable. This was passed out.

Criticism: That West's failure to take out into Two Hearts was influenced by the knowledge that his partner held only two hearts.

Answer: With the comparatively balanced 5-3-3-2 distribution one rescues 1NT only on weak hands unsuitable for play in no-trumps. We were one down in 1NT; at the other table East/West played in Two Diamonds and made Three.

US 39

Game All; Dealer South

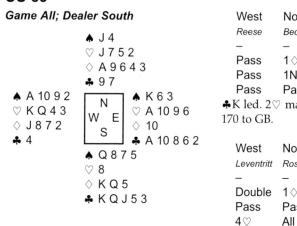

```
                    ♠ J 4
                    ♡ J 7 5 2
                    ◇ A 9 6 4 3
                    ♣ 9 7
   ♠ A 10 9 2    ┌─────────┐    ♠ K 6 3
   ♡ K Q 4 3     │    N    │    ♡ A 10 9 6
   ◇ J 8 7 2     │ W     E │    ◇ 10
   ♣ 4           │    S    │    ♣ A 10 8 6 2
                 └─────────┘
                    ♠ Q 8 7 5
                    ♡ 8
                    ◇ K Q 5
                    ♣ K Q J 5 3
```

West	North	East	South
Reese	*Becker*	*Schapiro*	*Hayden*
–	–	–	1♣
Pass	1◇	Pass	1♠
Pass	1NT	Pass	2◇
Pass	Pass	2♡	All Pass

♣K led. 2♡ made with two overtricks. 170 to GB.

West	North	East	South
Leventritt	*Rose*	*Schenken*	*Gray*
–	–	–	1♣
Double	1◇	2◇	3◇
Pass	Pass	3♡	Pass
4♡	All Pass		

♣9 led. 4♡ made exactly. 620 to USA.

Criticism: That East's reopening bid of Two Hearts was influenced by knowledge of four hearts in his partner's hand.

Answer: Four Hearts is on for us, but to escape suspicion we have to let the opponents play in Two Diamonds!

East was stronger than he might have been and that is what led to my failure to raise. Note that (1) West, if he knows partner has four hearts, may well double on the first round, as at the other table, and (2) if East knows that his partner has four hearts he can bid One Heart on the way round without causing any comment.

US 46

Love All; Dealer East

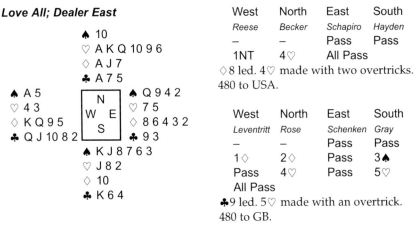

	♠ 10	
	♡ A K Q 10 9 6	
	♢ A J 7	
	♣ A 7 5	
♠ A 5		♠ Q 9 4 2
♡ 4 3	N	♡ 7 5
♢ K Q 9 5	W E	♢ 8 6 4 3 2
♣ Q J 10 8 2	S	♣ 9 3
	♠ K J 8 7 6 3	
	♡ J 8 2	
	♢ 10	
	♣ K 6 4	

West	North	East	South
Reese	*Becker*	*Schapiro*	*Hayden*
–	–	Pass	Pass
1NT	4♡	All Pass	

♢8 led. 4♡ made with two overtricks. 480 to USA.

West	North	East	South
Leventritt	*Rose*	*Schenken*	*Gray*
–	–	Pass	Pass
1♢	2♢	Pass	3♠
Pass	4♡	Pass	5♡
All Pass			

♣9 led. 5♡ made with an overtrick. 480 to GB.

Criticism: That West's 1NT was 'rendered more attractive' by knowledge of the doubleton heart opposite.

Answer: We made many such 1NT bids, often with good effect, as here. As to the heart situation, compare the hand before last, US 37, where the partner of the irregular opener held five hearts.

US 50

North/South Game; Dealer East

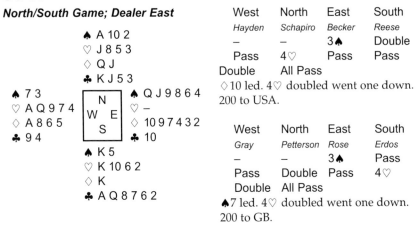

	♠ A 10 2	
	♡ J 8 5 3	
	♢ Q J	
	♣ K J 5 3	
♠ 7 3		♠ Q J 9 8 6 4
♡ A Q 9 7 4	N	♡ –
♢ A 8 6 5	W E	♢ 10 9 7 4 3 2
♣ 9 4	S	♣ 10
	♠ K 5	
	♡ K 10 6 2	
	♢ K	
	♣ A Q 8 7 6 2	

West	North	East	South
Hayden	*Schapiro*	*Becker*	*Reese*
–	–	3♠	Double
Pass	4♡	Pass	Pass
Double	All Pass		

♢10 led. 4♡ doubled went one down. 200 to USA.

West	North	East	South
Gray	*Petterson*	*Rose*	*Erdos*
–	–	3♠	Pass
Pass	Double	Pass	4♡
Double	All Pass		

♠7 led. 4♡ doubled went one down. 200 to GB.

Criticism: That South's double was influenced by knowledge that his partner held four hearts.

Answer: We were playing optional doubles over Three bids, with the understanding, as in the Roman system, that such doubles promise support in two, not necessarily three, suits. The double is more flexible than Four Clubs. It has these advantages: (1) it leaves room for 3NT (which North might well have bid here); (2) it will suit South if North can pass the double; (3) the double is more likely than Four Clubs to lead to a game contract in hearts. Of course, there is a certain risk in that a response of Four Diamonds will be unwelcome, but South has further resources, and anyway one has to take risks against pre-emptive openings.

The North/South bidding at the other table is worth noting. North's double is far more risky than anything we did; if his partner bids Four Diamonds and that is doubled, all he can so is leave the building. As to South, I said in my evidence: 'I can understand why, with four hearts and six clubs, he chose to bid Four Hearts, but imagine the howls if we had followed that sequence.'

US 56

Love All; Dealer West

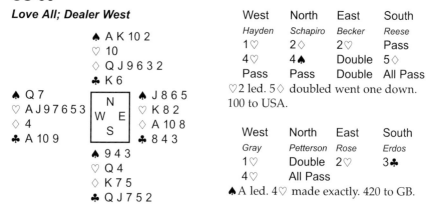

West	North	East	South
Hayden	*Schapiro*	*Becker*	*Reese*
1♡	2♢	2♡	Pass
4♡	4♠	Double	5♢
Pass	Pass	Double	All Pass

♡2 led. 5♢ doubled went one down. 100 to USA.

West	North	East	South
Gray	*Petterson*	*Rose*	*Erdos*
1♡	Double	2♡	3♣
4♡	All Pass		

♠A led. 4♡ made exactly. 420 to GB.

Criticism: That North bid Four Spades because he knew his partner held only two hearts and so was more likely to have support for one of North's suits.
Answer: Once North has overcalled with Two Diamonds instead of doubling, he is more or less committed to showing the spades later. As on Argentina 44, the connection with hearts is very remote.

Italy 20

The opponents were in 3NT and Schapiro had to lead from:

♠ 5 4 2
♡ J 10 7 6 5
♢ A
♣ 10 7 5 3

He chose the ♡5 and it was suggested that he departed from the conventional fourth best because both players already knew the heart distribution.

The opponents had used the Stayman convention and the declarer had denied a holding of four hearts. In such circumstances it is common for the defenders to false-card, as they expect partner to be able to read the distribution.

In view of the criticism on this hand, the defence put in an analysis of all occasions when a defender played a card denoting length in the heart suit on either of the first two tricks. Out of ten opportunities this was the only time when a non-conventional card was led or played.

Italy 39

With both sides vulnerable I held as South:

♠ K Q 4 2
♡ Q 6 5 4
◇ J 9 8 4
♣ 6

Against 3NT, with the choice between the majors, I led the four of hearts. Partner held four hearts and also four spades. Nobody likes to lead from K-Q-4-2. A spade lead would in fact have saved two tricks.

Italy 134

No suit having been mentioned, Schapiro had to lead against 3NT from:

♠ J 5 4
♡ K 7 4 3
◇ 9 7 5 4 2
♣ 2

He led the ◇ 4. Partner held two hearts.

Criticism: That whereas on Italy 26 West preferred a heart from K-x-x-x to a spade from x-x-x-x-x, here East preferred a diamond because he knew his partner held only two hearts.

Answer: The situation had now been reached at which we had to defend ourselves for making entirely normal leads. None of the special circumstances attaching to Italy 26 existed here; the only resemblance was that the opening leader held K-x-x-x of hearts on both occasions.

Italy 137

East/West Game; Dealer North

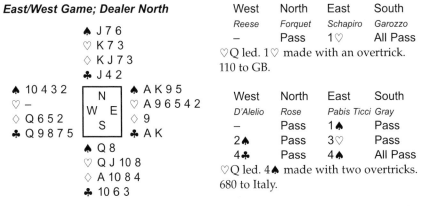

	♠ J 7 6
	♡ K 7 3
	◇ K J 7 3
	♣ J 4 2

♠ 10 4 3 2   ♠ A K 9 5
♡ —   ♡ A 9 6 5 4 2
◇ Q 6 5 2   ◇ 9
♣ Q 9 8 7 5   ♣ A K

♠ Q 8
♡ Q J 10 8
◇ A 10 8 4
♣ 10 6 3

West	North	East	South
Reese	*Forquet*	*Schapiro*	*Garozzo*
–	Pass	1♡	All Pass

♡Q led. 1♡ made with an overtrick. 110 to GB.

West	North	East	South
D'Alelio	*Rose*	*Pabis Ticci*	*Gray*
–	Pass	1♠	Pass
2♠	Pass	3♡	Pass
4♣	Pass	4♠	All Pass

♡Q led. 4♠ made with two overtricks. 680 to Italy.

Criticism: That West's pass of the opening One Heart was influenced by the knowledge that his partner held six hearts and was therefore less likely to hold length in the other suits.

Answer: For West to do anything but pass One Heart would be completely anti-system, and nothing more need be said about that.

The hand obviously refuted the contention that we always found the best fit when hearts were involved, and arising from this there was much discussion about East's opening bid. Playing Acol he has a choice between One Heart, Two Hearts (forcing for one round) and Two Clubs. How would it affect him to know that partner was void in hearts? No doubt it can be argued either way – that he would go quietly for fear of a misfit, or that he would open with a forcing bid to be sure of not missing a fit in another suit. The Italians always explore such hands to the full, and if East thinks of that he must open Two Hearts so as not to risk a possible game swing.

Argentina 30

Love All; Dealer East

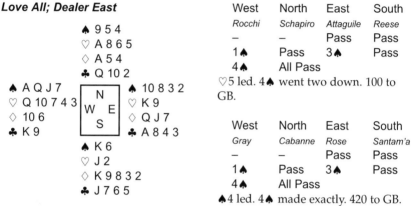

♠ 9 5 4
♡ A 8 6 5
◇ A 5 4
♣ Q 10 2

♠ A Q J 7   ♠ 10 8 3 2
♡ Q 10 7 4 3   ♡ K 9
◇ 10 6   ◇ Q J 7
♣ K 9   ♣ A 8 4 3

♠ K 6
♡ J 2
◇ K 9 8 3 2
♣ J 7 6 5

	West	North	East	South
	Rocchi	*Schapiro*	*Attaguile*	*Reese*
	–	–	Pass	Pass
	1♠	Pass	3♠	Pass
	4♠	All Pass		

♡5 led. 4♠ went two down. 100 to GB.

	West	North	East	South
	Gray	*Cabanne*	*Rose*	*Santam'a*
	–	–	Pass	Pass
	1♠	Pass	3♠	Pass
	4♠	All Pass		

♠4 led. 4♠ made exactly. 420 to GB.

Criticism: That North's lead of a low heart was 'unusual' and 'unattractive' and was influenced by the knowledge that his partner held a doubleton heart.
Answer: The choice is basically between a trump and one of the plain suits. Schapiro dislikes leading a trump simply because other leads are hazardous. Because of his even distribution, North may judge that he must 'try something' with the opening lead. An underlead of the ace of hearts is at least as good as anything else. We would probably have heard nothing about this hand if the declarer had entered dummy and picked up the trumps; instead, he returned a heart at trick two and sustained two overruffs.

Hands introduced by the defence

The defence extracted many arguments from hands brought forward by the other side (see, for example, Italy 46 and 48, US 36, 39 and 76). These additional defensive hands are given in straight sequence from the three matches.

Italy 7

Game All; Dealer South

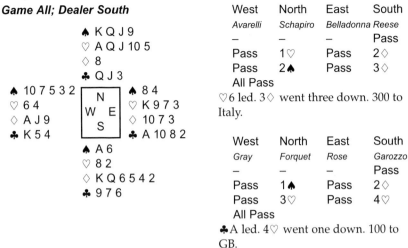

♠ K Q J 9
♡ A Q J 10 5
♢ 8
♣ Q J 3

♠ 10 7 5 3 2
♡ 6 4
♢ A J 9
♣ K 5 4

N W E S

♠ 8 4
♡ K 9 7 3
♢ 10 7 3
♣ A 10 8 2

♠ A 6
♡ 8 2
♢ K Q 6 5 4 2
♣ 9 7 6

West	North	East	South
Avarelli	*Schapiro*	*Belladonna*	*Reese*
–	–	–	Pass
Pass	1♡	Pass	2♢
Pass	2♠	Pass	3♢
All Pass			

♡6 led. 3♢ went three down. 300 to Italy.

West	North	East	South
Gray	*Forquet*	*Rose*	*Garozzo*
–	–	–	Pass
Pass	1♠	Pass	2♢
Pass	3♡	Pass	4♡
All Pass			

♣A led. 4♡ went one down. 100 to GB.

Whether North should pass Three Diamonds or go to Three Hearts is close. I personally think that with a hand likely to be worth six or seven tricks in hearts it is more sensible in any event to rebid Three Hearts. Certainly if North knows that his partner has a doubleton heart he must prefer Three Hearts to leaving partner to play in diamonds. Whether partner has one or two hearts will make a big difference to the prospects of retaining control in the play. The hand went badly in Three Diamonds when East ruffed the third round of spades with the ten of trumps. In the endgame dummy was squeezed in hearts and clubs.

Italy 27

Love All; Dealer South

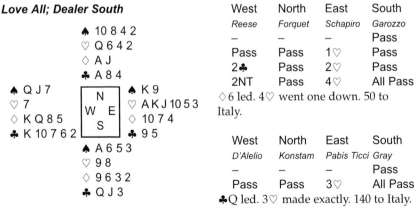

♠ 10 8 4 2
♡ Q 6 4 2
♢ A J
♣ A 8 4

♠ Q J 7
♡ 7
♢ K Q 8 5
♣ K 10 7 6 2

N W E S

♠ K 9
♡ A K J 10 5 3
♢ 10 7 4
♣ 9 5

♠ A 6 5 3
♡ 9 8
♢ 9 6 3 2
♣ Q J 3

West	North	East	South
Reese	*Forquet*	*Schapiro*	*Garozzo*
–	–	–	Pass
Pass	Pass	1♡	Pass
2♣	Pass	2♡	Pass
2NT	Pass	4♡	All Pass

♢6 led. 4♡ went one down. 50 to Italy.

West	North	East	South
D'Alelio	*Konstam*	*Pabis Ticci*	*Gray*
–	–	–	Pass
Pass	Pass	3♡	All Pass

♣Q led. 3♡ made exactly. 140 to Italy.

Over 2NT East has four possible sources of action – pass, Three Hearts, 3NT, Four Hearts. If he wants to try for game, 3NT seems the best chance. But if he knows that partner has a singleton heart, then a sign-off of Three Hearts looks obvious.

Italy 36

Game All; Dealer West

Schapiro
♠ Q 9 6
♡ 9 8 7
◇ K Q 8 3
♣ Q J 10

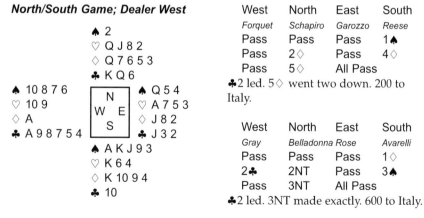

Reese
♠ A K 5
♡ K Q J 5
◇ 10 5
♣ K 6 5 3

I opened fourth in hand with One Heart, North responded 1NT, and there we rested, missing an easy game which was bid at the other table.

There is a technical reason why an opening bid on a four-card major with 16 points should generally be avoided: if the opener has a difficult choice whether or not to try for game. If he passes, and partner has a maximum, as here, game may be missed. I ignored this principle when I opened One Heart on this occasion.

If I know that partner has only three hearts I do not mind suppressing my good suit. An opening One Club or 1NT must appear more attractive. A response of 1NT to One Club is stronger than 1NT over a major, so after 1♣ – 1NT the dilemma mentioned above no longer exists; South can raise to 2NT.

Italy 44

North/South Game; Dealer West

♠ 2
♡ Q J 8 2
◇ Q 7 6 5 3
♣ K Q 6

♠ 10 8 7 6   ♠ Q 5 4
♡ 10 9   ♡ A 7 5 3
◇ A   ◇ J 8 2
♣ A 9 8 7 5 4   ♣ J 3 2

♠ A K J 9 3
♡ K 6 4
◇ K 10 9 4
♣ 10

West	North	East	South
Forquet	*Schapiro*	*Garozzo*	*Reese*
Pass	Pass	Pass	1♠
Pass	2◇	Pass	4◇
Pass	5◇	All Pass	

♣2 led. 5◇ went two down. 200 to Italy.

West	North	East	South
Gray	*Belladonna*	*Rose*	*Avarelli*
Pass	Pass	Pass	1◇
2♣	2NT	Pass	3♠
Pass	3NT	All Pass	

♣2 led. 3NT made exactly. 600 to Italy.

Neither Flint nor I included this hand in our evidence, but Heredia extracted two points from it.

South's Four Diamonds is very questionable and indeed was criticised at the time as an overbid. If he knows that North has four hearts South will surely bid only Three Diamonds, leaving North room to introduce the hearts as a genuine suit. It is the sort of hand that may well be playable with seven trumps. Another way of looking at it is that four hearts in the opposite hand doesn't look like a good fit to South, so he should incline to the sounder call of Three Diamonds.

Secondly, North's Five Diamonds was highly doubtful, and if he knows that South has three hearts it becomes all the more unattractive. As South has bid spades and raised diamonds, it must appear that he has a singleton club. This will mean duplication of values in North's only good feature, and he will quickly pass Four Diamonds.

Italy 55

Game All; Dealer South

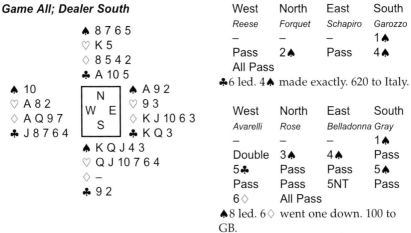

	♠ 8 7 6 5
	♡ K 5
	♢ 8 5 4 2
	♣ A 10 5

♠ 10	♠ A 9 2
♡ A 8 2	♡ 9 3
♢ A Q 9 7	♢ K J 10 6 3
♣ J 8 7 6 4	♣ K Q 3

	♠ K Q J 4 3
	♡ Q J 10 7 6 4
	♢ –
	♣ 9 2

West	North	East	South
Reese	*Forquet*	*Schapiro*	*Garozzo*
–	–	–	1♠
Pass	2♠	Pass	4♠
All Pass			

♣6 led. 4♠ made exactly. 620 to Italy.

West	North	East	South
Avarelli	*Rose*	*Belladonna*	*Gray*
–	–	–	1♠
Double	3♠	4♠	Pass
5♣	Pass	Pass	5♠
Pass	Pass	5NT	Pass
6♢	All Pass		

♠8 led. 6♢ went one down. 100 to GB.

This was a disastrous hand for our team. We were lucky to beat Six Diamonds at the other table, but still lost 11 IMPs because Schapiro and I allowed ourselves to be shut out of the bidding.

By our standards, West is slightly under strength for a vulnerable double. The danger of a double is that partner, in a competitive auction, may bid hearts on a moderate suit and be disappointed in the support. If West knows that his partner has only two hearts, that objection disappears. The double becomes safe and tactically desirable.

East also had a chance to enter the auction. The opening bid of One Spade in the Italian system, and the response of Two Spades, are both limited. At this point East can expect his partner to be short of spades, and if he also knows that West has only three hearts he can safely, and quite plausibly, enter with 2NT, the 'unusual no-trump' denoting strength in the minors. Once we come into the bidding we can bid up to the five level at least and so gain on the board.

Italy 56

Love All; Dealer West

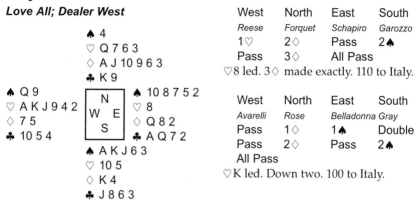

West	North	East	South
Reese	*Forquet*	*Schapiro*	*Garozzo*
1♡	2♢	Pass	2♠
Pass	3♢	All Pass	

♡8 led. 3♢ made exactly. 110 to Italy.

West	North	East	South
Avarelli	*Rose*	*Belladonna*	*Gray*
Pass	1♢	1♠	Double
Pass	2♢	Pass	2♠
All Pass			

♡K led. Down two. 100 to Italy.

This was primarily a 'play' hand, but we remarked in passing on the opening bid of One Heart. If I know my partner has a singleton heart it must be better tactics to pass originally, as did the Italian West. At the least, this example refutes the criticism made on Italy 14, where it was said that I passed a moderate hand because partner was short in hearts.

When East led the eight of hearts against Three Diamonds, I won with the king and returned a club. Obviously we could beat the contract only if partner had two tricks in clubs. I had visions of him making two clubs, then putting me back with the ace of hearts. Now a third heart will establish a trump trick for the defence as the cards lie, for East's eight of diamonds will force dummy's king.

If I know that partner has a singleton heart I must cash the second heart at once and hope that the defence will come to two clubs, two hearts and a trump. As the play went, North had ample discards for his three remaining hearts, for after two rounds of clubs the remaining clubs in dummy were high. We took four tricks but never made a second heart.

Italy 126

Love All; Dealer East

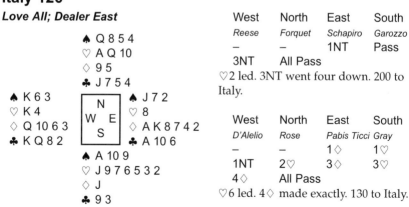

West	North	East	South
Reese	*Forquet*	*Schapiro*	*Garozzo*
–	–	1NT	Pass
3NT	All Pass		

♡2 led. 3NT went four down. 200 to Italy.

West	North	East	South
D'Alelio	*Rose*	*Pabis Ticci*	*Gray*
–	–	1♢	1♡
1NT	2♡	3♢	3♡
4♢	All Pass		

♡6 led. 4♢ made exactly. 130 to Italy.

East's opening 1NT does not belong to any recognised psychic type, but we had sometimes bid 1NT with little defensive strength and here, at the beginning of the final session, Schapiro tried a variation. It was a peculiar bid by any reckoning and becomes more so if he knows there are only three hearts in the combined hands. Flint put it this way in his evidence: if his partner is strong, East by opening 1NT will at best place the declaration in the wrong hand; if partner is weak, the bid of 1NT will not shut out opponents who have ten hearts between them.

Italy 128

East/West Game; Dealer West

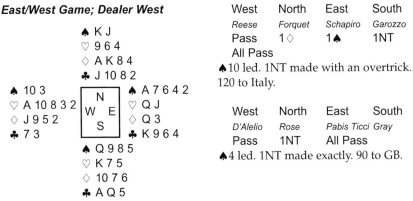

West	North	East	South
Reese	*Forquet*	*Schapiro*	*Garozzo*
Pass	1◇	1♠	1NT
All Pass			

♠10 led. 1NT made with an overtrick. 120 to Italy.

West	North	East	South
D'Alelio	*Rose*	*Pabis Ticci*	*Gray*
Pass	1NT	All Pass	

♠4 led. 1NT made exactly. 90 to GB.

This was another 'play' hand. Schapiro allowed dummy to hold the first spade. A club was led to the queen, a second spade to the jack, and Schapiro ducked again. No doubt he ought to win and try the hearts, even without illicit knowledge. If he knows for a fact that partner has five hearts, then it is obvious that he must take the first spade and switch at once to hearts, hoping to find partner with something like K-x-x-x-x and an entry in clubs. At the other table East tried the jack of hearts at an early stage. The declarer ducked, then covered the queen on the next round, so the defence took five heart tricks.

US 31

North/South Game; Dealer South

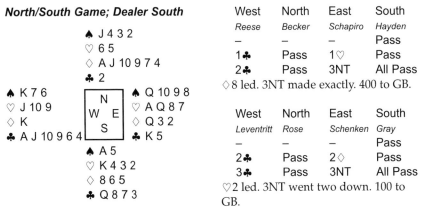

West	North	East	South
Reese	*Becker*	*Schapiro*	*Hayden*
–	–	–	Pass
1♣	Pass	1♡	Pass
2♣	Pass	3NT	All Pass

◇8 led. 3NT made exactly. 400 to GB.

West	North	East	South
Leventritt	*Rose*	*Schenken*	*Gray*
–	–	–	Pass
2♣	Pass	2◇	Pass
3♣	Pass	3NT	All Pass

♡2 led. 3NT went two down. 100 to GB.

Flint made a delicate but not unpersuasive point about the bidding. If East knows that his partner has no more than three hearts he has an admirable opportunity for a lead-inhibiting semi-psychic One Diamond response. This is a tactical move we often adopt. Note that East did precisely this at the other table, where Two Clubs was a natural, but limited, opening.

US 35

With both sides vulnerable I held as West:

♠ Q 10 7
♡ Q J 7 6 4
◇ A 9 3
♣ K 9

South opened a natural One Club in front of me. Because the heart suit was weak I did not overcall. Partner held five hearts. With that knowledge obviously I would have overcalled, for if I pass we may be shut out of the bidding. For example, North may be able to respond One Spade and South raise to Two Spades. As it turned out, North was weak and passed the opening bid, so East was able to reopen with a double and we got to Four Hearts.

At the other table the American West doubled the opening bid on my cards. This hand, very strong for us, was mentioned in Caplan's opening speech.

US 55

Game All; Dealer South

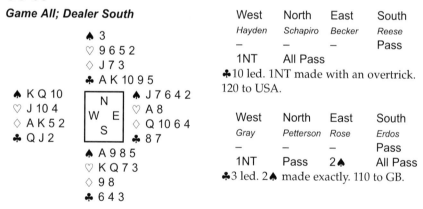

West	North	East	South
Hayden	*Schapiro*	*Becker*	*Reese*
–	–	–	Pass
1NT	All Pass		

♣10 led. 1NT made with an overtrick. 120 to USA.

West	North	East	South
Gray	*Petterson*	*Rose*	*Erdos*
–	–	–	Pass
1NT	Pass	2♠	All Pass

♣3 led. 2♠ made exactly. 110 to GB.

This hand, together with Argentina 34 and 130, formed a strong group of 'lead' hands. Defending against 3NT, North must lead a club, hoping to take four tricks in the suit even if he gives one away. Defending 1NT, North can expect his partner to have some entry cards and neither the king of clubs, which may be bad from the entry point of view, nor the ten of clubs particularly commends itself. Knowing that partner has four hearts, North will be very happy to adopt that alternative. Note that a heart lead can make three tricks difference to the result in 1NT.

US 65

Love All; Dealer North

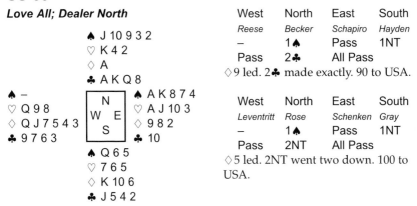

♠ J 10 9 3 2
♡ K 4 2
♢ A
♣ A K Q 8

♠ —
♡ Q 9 8
♢ Q J 7 5 4 3
♣ 9 7 6 3

N
W E
S

♠ A K 8 7 4
♡ A J 10 3
♢ 9 8 2
♣ 10

♠ Q 6 5
♡ 7 6 5
♢ K 10 6
♣ J 5 4 2

West	North	East	South
Reese	Becker	Schapiro	Hayden
–	1♠	Pass	1NT
Pass	2♣	All Pass	

◇9 led. 2♣ made exactly. 90 to USA.

West	North	East	South
Leventritt	Rose	Schenken	Gray
–	1♠	Pass	1NT
Pass	2NT	All Pass	

◇5 led. 2NT went two down. 100 to USA.

The first point we made was that if he has illicit knowledge East can well bid Two Hearts on the second round. The opponents have surely found a fit in clubs and there must be defensive prospects in hearts, on the basis that West has three hearts together with presumably a shortage in spades.

In Two Clubs the diamond lead ran up to the ace, declarer cashed two top trumps, then led the jack of spades, losing to East's king. East now made the mistake of leading a second diamond, allowing North to dispose of a heart loser and eventually make the contract.

If East knows that West has three hearts, together with a void in spades, he cannot fall into this error, for obviously West's remaining cards will be six diamonds and four clubs. The game must be to give partner a spade ruff and then hope to pick up three tricks in hearts.

US 68

Game All; Dealer West

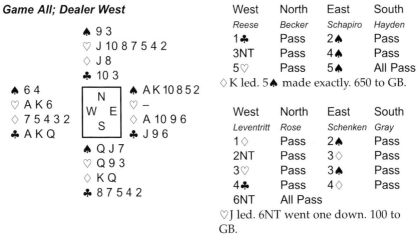

♠ 9 3
♡ J 10 8 7 5 4 2
♢ J 8
♣ 10 3

♠ 6 4
♡ A K 6
♢ 7 5 4 3 2
♣ A K Q

N
W E
S

♠ A K 10 8 5 2
♡ —
♢ A 10 9 6
♣ J 9 6

♠ Q J 7
♡ Q 9 3
♢ K Q
♣ 8 7 5 4 2

West	North	East	South
Reese	Becker	Schapiro	Hayden
1♣	Pass	2♠	Pass
3NT	Pass	4♠	Pass
5♡	Pass	5♠	All Pass

◇K led. 5♠ made exactly. 650 to GB.

West	North	East	South
Leventritt	Rose	Schenken	Gray
1◇	Pass	2♠	Pass
2NT	Pass	3◇	Pass
3♡	Pass	3♠	Pass
4♣	Pass	4◇	Pass
6NT	All Pass		

♡J led. 6NT went one down. 100 to GB.

The disadvantage of opening with a suit like 7-5-4-3-2 on quite a good hand is that partner, throughout the bidding, will assume that a holding such as K-x-x constitutes a good fit. So I conceived the idea of opening One Club on A-K-Q instead. It was an experiment I shall not repeat.

The first point we made was that if West knows his partner has a void in hearts, and so a distributional hand, he will make the normal opening of One Diamond. The consequence of my foolish manoeuvre was that we never mentioned our longest combined suit.

The second and much stronger point was that, if West knows his partner is void in hearts, he will not choose Five Hearts as a slam try. He will know that this will fail to excite, so the only result will be to play in Five Spades instead of Four Spades.

The opposition contested this hand vigorously. Their point was that if West knows that East knows that West knows that East knows that West knows that East is void in hearts, then Five Hearts becomes just the job on A-K-x. One can make a theoretical case along those lines, but the simple point remains valid: at the table West would surely choose Five Spades as his slam try, not Five Hearts.

US 74

Game All; Dealer East

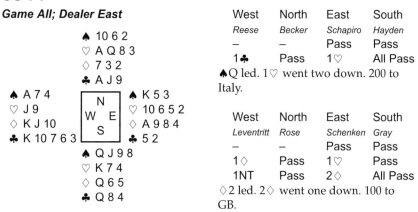

♠ 10 6 2
♡ A Q 8 3
◇ 7 3 2
♣ A J 9

♠ A 7 4
♡ J 9
◇ K J 10
♣ K 10 7 6 3

♠ K 5 3
♡ 10 6 5 2
◇ A 9 8 4
♣ 5 2

♠ Q J 9 8
♡ K 7 4
◇ Q 6 5
♣ Q 8 4

West	North	East	South
Reese	*Becker*	*Schapiro*	*Hayden*
–	–	Pass	Pass
1♣	Pass	1♡	All Pass

♠Q led. 1♡ went two down. 200 to Italy.

West	North	East	South
Leventritt	*Rose*	*Schenken*	*Gray*
–	–	Pass	Pass
1◇	Pass	1♡	Pass
1NT	Pass	2◇	All Pass

◇2 led. 2◇ went one down. 100 to GB.

Most players would respond One Diamond on the East hand. Schapiro explained his choice of One Heart as follows. When a passed hand responds on a four-card suit he is always conscious of the possibility that he may be left to play at the one level with a poor fit. If partner has a holding like Q-x-x in hearts, then the combined holding will make a trick or two if the hand is played in One Heart, but if the contract is One Diamond then Q-x-x opposite 10-x-x-x in a side suit will be worth nothing. Putting it another way, it is preferable to have the ace in a side suit. Of course, if East knows partner has a doubleton heart he will respond One Diamond, hoping for a better fit.

Another strong point was that West could have rebid 1NT (or even One Spade) without showing extra values and would surely have done so had he known that partner held only four hearts.

Heredia attached great significance to this hand, describing it as sufficient by itself to dispose of the allegation of illicit knowledge in the heart suit.

Argentina 33

Love All; Dealer North

```
           Schapiro
           ♠ 10 5
           ♡ Q 7
           ◇ A 9
           ♣ K Q J 7 5 4 2
          ┌───────┐
          │   N   │
          │ W   E │
          │   S   │
          └───────┘
           Reese
           ♠ K 6 2
           ♡ K 5 3 2
           ◇ Q 7 2
           ♣ 9 6 3
```

Schapiro opened One Club and I responded One Heart. We eventually played in 3NT, down one. South's distribution and point-count are well suited to a response of 1NT, and that would seem to be the natural choice if he knows that his partner holds two hearts. Not a striking hand, but it refuted prosecution hands where it was alleged that we refrained from mentioning hearts because partner was short in the suit. Italy 26, US 31 and US 74 were other examples.

Argentina 34

North/South Game; Dealer East

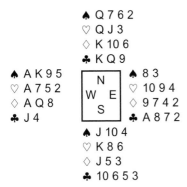

```
                ♠ Q 7 6 2
                ♡ Q J 3
                ◇ K 10 6
                ♣ K Q 9
  ♠ A K 9 5   ┌───────┐   ♠ 8 3
  ♡ A 7 5 2   │   N   │   ♡ 10 9 4
  ◇ A Q 8     │ W   E │   ◇ 9 7 4 2
  ♣ J 4       │   S   │   ♣ A 8 7 2
              └───────┘
                ♠ J 10 4
                ♡ K 8 6
                ◇ J 5 3
                ♣ 10 6 5 3
```

West	North	East	South
Rocchi	*Schapiro*	*Attaguile*	*Reese*
–	–	Pass	Pass
1♣	Pass	1◇	Pass
1NT	All Pass		

♡J led. 1NT went one down. 50 to GB.

West	North	East	South
Gray	*Cabanne*	*Rose*	*Santam'a*
–	–	Pass	Pass
1♡	All Pass		

♣K led. 1♡ made exactly. 80 to GB.

The bids of One Club and One Diamond were conventional. North's lead of the jack from Q-J-x was standard for us. A lead from this combination is always apt to give a trick away, and it seems an impossible choice if the leader knows that the opponents have the long heart. Either the ♠2 or a high club must appear more attractive. Flint also commented on my play of the eight of hearts at trick one, the normal play if I place partner with four or more hearts. Here the eight enabled the declarer to put on the ace and return the suit, as the ten, nine and seven were equals. This hand was mentioned in Caplan's opening speech.

Argentina 39

Game All; Dealer South

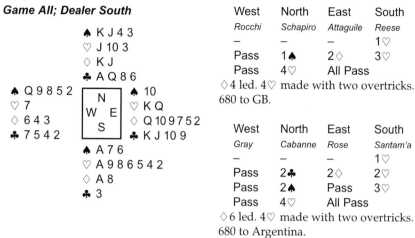

	♠ K J 4 3	
	♡ J 10 3	
	◇ K J	
	♣ A Q 8 6	
♠ Q 9 8 5 2	N	♠ 10
♡ 7	W E	♡ K Q
◇ 6 4 3	S	◇ Q 10 9 7 5 2
♣ 7 5 4 2		♣ K J 10 9
	♠ A 7 6	
	♡ A 9 8 6 5 4 2	
	◇ A 8	
	♣ 3	

West	North	East	South
Rocchi	Schapiro	Attaguile	Reese
–	–	–	1♡
Pass	1♠	2◇	3♡
Pass	4♡	All Pass	

◇4 led. 4♡ made with two overtricks. 680 to GB.

West	North	East	South
Gray	Cabanne	Rose	Santam'a
–	–	–	1♡
Pass	2♣	2◇	2♡
Pass	2♠	Pass	3♡
Pass	4♡	All Pass	

◇6 led. 4♡ made with two overtricks. 680 to Argentina.

Flint and I did not mention this hand, but Heredia made a good case for different action by North if he possesses the illegal knowledge. If he knows his partner has seven hearts he can almost count twelve tricks at his second turn. He can test his partner with Four Clubs or even launch into 4NT (Roman Blackwood). When South shows three aces, North can bid 6NT with confidence.

Argentina 63

North/South Game; Dealer South

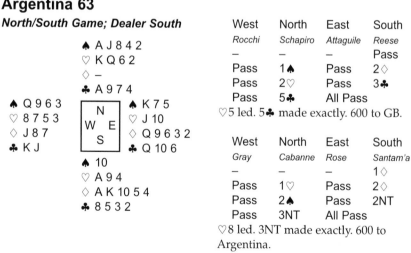

	♠ A J 8 4 2	
	♡ K Q 6 2	
	◇ –	
	♣ A 9 7 4	
♠ Q 9 6 3	N	♠ K 7 5
♡ 8 7 5 3	W E	♡ J 10
◇ J 8 7	S	◇ Q 9 6 3 2
♣ K J		♣ Q 10 6
	♠ 10	
	♡ A 9 4	
	◇ A K 10 5 4	
	♣ 8 5 3 2	

West	North	East	South
Rocchi	Schapiro	Attaguile	Reese
–	–	–	Pass
Pass	1♠	Pass	2◇
Pass	2♡	Pass	3♣
Pass	5♣	All Pass	

♡5 led. 5♣ made exactly. 600 to GB.

West	North	East	South
Gray	Cabanne	Rose	Santam'a
–	–	–	1◇
Pass	1♡	Pass	2◇
Pass	2♠	Pass	2NT
Pass	3NT	All Pass	

♡8 led. 3NT made exactly. 600 to Argentina.

After North's Two Hearts South has a difficult bid. He has passed originally on a maximum and Three Hearts would be an underbid, while Four Hearts might be the wrong contract. Three Clubs was intended to be 'fourth suit' – not necessarily a biddable suit at all but a request to partner to describe his hand further. If he understands the bid in that light North can bid 3NT or Three Spades or Four Clubs. Schapiro had some idea that, as South had passed originally, the clubs would be a genuine suit. If North knows that South has three hearts he will surely raise to Four Clubs only, giving partner a chance to show delayed heart support. Four Hearts plays much more easily than Five Clubs.

Argentina 75

Love All; Dealer South

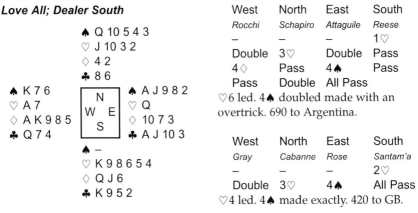

♠ Q 10 5 4 3
♡ J 10 3 2
♢ 4 2
♣ 8 6

♠ K 7 6
♡ A 7
♢ A K 9 8 5
♣ Q 7 4

N
W   E
S

♠ A J 9 8 2
♡ Q
♢ 10 7 3
♣ A J 10 3

♠ —
♡ K 9 8 6 5 4
♢ Q J 6
♣ K 9 5 2

West	North	East	South
Rocchi	Schapiro	Attaguile	Reese
–	–	–	1♡
Double	3♡	Double	Pass
4♢	Pass	4♠	Pass
Pass	Double	All Pass	

♡6 led. 4♠ doubled made with an overtrick. 690 to Argentina.

West	North	East	South
Gray	Cabanne	Rose	Santam'a
–	–	–	2♡
Double	3♡	4♠	All Pass

♡4 led. 4♠ made exactly. 420 to GB.

North's double of Four Spades, admittedly poor in any event, becomes even more improbable if he knows that South has six hearts. This reduces the chance of winning a heart trick in defence and must also suggest that South may have opened on distribution and holds few defensive tricks. The example was not strong (because the double was bad anyway), but it gave us an opportunity to draw passing attention to two other hands where Schapiro, generally an excellent judge of these situations, made unsuccessful doubles of game contracts. In each case knowledge of partner's heart holding (once a void and once an eight-card suit) would have made the double seem less attractive.

Argentina 130

Schapiro, sitting East, had to lead against 3NT from:

♠ J 9 3
♡ J 10 7 6
♢ 7 5 3
♣ A Q 8

South, on his left, had opened One Heart, North had responded One Spade, and South had supported to Two Spades. Against 3NT Schapiro led the seven of hearts, of which I held 5-2 doubleton. This can be a fair lead if I have four hearts or even three, but if I have a doubleton it is likely to lose both a trick and a tempo.

The opposition sought to make something of the fact that the lead was a false card. When a defender leads through dummy's suit he seldom leads a true card, for he expects partner to be able to read the situation better than declarer.

Argentina 141

North/South Game; Dealer North

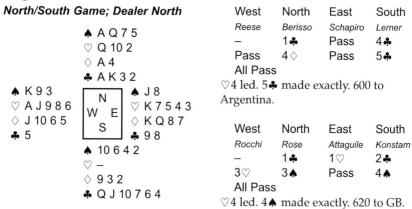

♠ A Q 7 5
♡ Q 10 2
◇ A 4
♣ A K 3 2

♠ K 9 3
♡ A J 9 8 6
◇ J 10 6 5
♣ 5

N
W E
S

♠ J 8
♡ K 7 5 4 3
◇ K Q 8 7
♣ 9 8

♠ 10 6 4 2
♡ —
◇ 9 3 2
♣ Q J 10 7 6 4

West	North	East	South
Reese	*Berisso*	*Schapiro*	*Lerner*
–	1♣	Pass	4♣
Pass	4◇	Pass	5♣
All Pass			

♡4 led. 5♣ made exactly. 600 to Argentina.

West	North	East	South
Rocchi	*Rose*	*Attaguile*	*Konstam*
–	1♣	1♡	2♣
3♡	3♠	Pass	4♠
All Pass			

♡4 led. 4♠ made exactly. 620 to GB.

Here East has a borderline overcall at the score. Obviously he would be inclined to make the overcall if he knew his partner held five hearts. Once again, the opponent at the other table did overcall. Although both spades and hearts lie badly, East/West can save advantageously in Five Hearts.

This was one of a group of hands on which the defence laid particular stress. The paths of constructive bidding are well laid out; on most hands there is an obvious 'system' bid. Overcalls are much more a matter of individual judgement, and here one would expect a pair using signals to make continually good decisions. In this respect we cited Italy 48 and 55, US 35 and 39 (twice), and the present hand. In every case an overcall would have been permissible and, with the illicit knowledge, clearly desirable, and except on Italy 48 the overcall was always made by the player at the other table.

Argentina 142

Love All; Dealer East

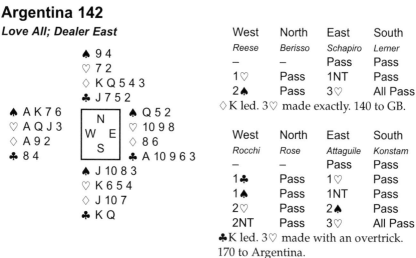

♠ 9 4
♡ 7 2
◇ K Q 5 4 3
♣ J 7 5 2

♠ A K 7 6
♡ A Q J 3
◇ A 9 2
♣ 8 4

N
W E
S

♠ Q 5 2
♡ 10 9 8
◇ 8 6
♣ A 10 9 6 3

♠ J 10 8 3
♡ K 6 5 4
◇ J 10 7
♣ K Q

West	North	East	South
Reese	*Berisso*	*Schapiro*	*Lerner*
–	–	Pass	Pass
1♡	Pass	1NT	Pass
2♠	Pass	3♡	All Pass

◇K led. 3♡ made exactly. 140 to GB.

West	North	East	South
Rocchi	*Rose*	*Attaguile*	*Konstam*
–	–	Pass	Pass
1♣	Pass	1♡	Pass
1♠	Pass	1NT	Pass
2♡	Pass	2♠	Pass
2NT	Pass	3♡	All Pass

♣K led. 3♡ made with an overtrick. 170 to Argentina.

We made two points about this hand. The opening One Heart was, at the least, contrary to the 'pattern' alleged by the other side. If West knows that his partner has three hearts he is much more likely to open One Spade. Then if partner responds 1NT he will raise to 2NT, concealing the heart strength, and similarly if partner responds Two Clubs he will rebid 3NT.

The second point concerned East's Three Hearts over 2NT. West's sequence of One Heart followed by Two Spades usually, though not necessarily, denotes five hearts, and that is why East supported the hearts over 2NT. If East knows his partner has only three hearts he can bid Three Clubs at this point – a perfectly natural bid allowing partner to rebid the hearts or bid 3NT or possibly Three Diamonds. In practice, Three Clubs would have led to 3NT, which is the best contract on the two hands.

Analysis of swings of hands quoted by Counsel for the British Bridge League

Counsel quoted 29 hands from Britain's matches against Italy and the USA where it was said that our action was influenced by illicit knowledge of the heart suit. The following table shows the IMPs won or lost by Britain on those 29 hands.

Hand No	Points gained	Points lost	Hand No	Points gained	Points lost
Italy 1	–	3	Italy 127	–	5
Italy 14	–	–	Italy 131	–	–
Italy 18	10	–	Italy 134	–	–
Italy 20	–	–	Italy 137	–	11
Italy 22	7	–	US 30	1	–
Italy 23	–	7	US 36	3	–
Italy 25	–	12	US 37	–	4
Italy 26	1	–	US 39	–	10
Italy 35	11	–	US 46	–	–
Italy 39	–	2	US 50	–	–
Italy 46	1	–	US 56	8	–
Italy 48	–	–	US 64	–	–
Italy 49	–	–	US 76	–	6
Italy 54	1	–			
Italy 117	–	6	Total	43	66
Italy 125	–	–	Net result		23

Appendix 2
The Foster Report

We were asked by the British Bridge League to enquire into allegations that Mr Reese and Mr Schapiro had cheated by giving finger signals at the World Bridge Championship in Buenos Aires in May 1965.

We agreed to conduct this inquiry in an honorary capacity and have held some thirty sittings which have been spread over approximately some ten months during which 14 witnesses have been called. The reason for this length of time is very largely (except for the period of the General Election) due to the fact that Counsel for the two persons accused was unable to agree to more frequent hearings owing to pressure of other cases in which he was engaged. We were assisted most expertly and most patiently by the two assessors, Messrs Priday and Hiron, who commented on and explained the analysis of over 50 hands put forward by both sides.

The reference to us arose out of a report by the World Bridge Federation drawn up at the end of the World Bridge Championship, in which the Federation announced its findings on the allegations of cheating brought by certain members of the American team and Mr Truscott, *The New York Times* bridge correspondent. The report recorded the fact that the Federation had found the allegations proved. The allegations were that Messrs Reese and Schapiro had signalled with their fingers the number of hearts in their hands. One finger on the outside of the cards when they were held in the right or left hand denoted one heart, two fingers two hearts, and so on to four fingers. Two fingers splayed indicated five hearts, and three fingers splayed represented six hearts.

The report was referred to the British Bridge League who decided that an independent inquiry should be held. It was agreed with the legal representatives of the two players accused (they were represented by Counsel and solicitors) and with the British Bridge League who were similarly represented, that the case against Messrs Reese and Schapiro should be presented by the British Bridge League. Accordingly this report is being communicated privately by us to the League, to whom we leave the decision of whether to publish all, or some, or none of the report.

The evidence before us can be divided into two classes; the evidence of witnesses who say they saw finger signals exchanged and the technical evidence as to the bidding and sometimes (but much less often) as to the play of the hands.

The conduct of the proceedings by the World Bridge Federation was most unsatisfactory. The allegations were first investigated before the Appeals Committee, then by the Executive Committee. Mr Butler, who is Chairman of the British Bridge League, was Chairman of the Appeals Committee at which Mr Swimer, the non-playing captain of the English team, also attended.

The evidence before the Appeals Committee was mainly concerned with the direct evidence of signals being exchanged. Mr Swimer and Mr Butler read from their notes as to the number of fingers shown by Mr Reese and Mr Schapiro in front of their cards. Mr Swimer gave evidence that he had watched the pair and that there was an exact correspondence between the number of fingers shown and the holding of hearts in 19 hands, while Mr Butler's evidence, confined to watching nine of the hands which Mr Swimer had observed, was that there was correspondence in some five or six hands. Similar evidence was given by these gentlemen to us.

Mr Truscott was reported by Mr Butler (to the Appeals Committee) as having observed signals and came to the conclusion that they represented heart holdings. Mr Truscott had told Mr Butler that in a number of cases the bidding had suggested that the pair knew the distribution of the heart suit. Mr Truscott had shown Mr Butler and Mr Swimer a number of hands which, according to Mr Truscott, 'indicated that this pair had never played a heart contract if it was unsuitable.' Mr Butler and Mr Swimer had agreed that in some cases the bidding looked suspicious. Mr Truscott also gave evidence to us on the same lines but was on this occasion much less positive about his 'indirect' evidence, i.e. his analysis of the bidding.

Mr Becker of the American team told the Appeals Committee that he had noticed finger signals during the play and that his partner, Mrs Hayden, had also noticed signals. Both these players gave evidence at the hearings before us in great detail to the same effect.

Mr Reese was called in before the Appeals Committee and denied the charge. He asked to see the evidence and Mr Truscott was called in with his analysis of the hands which he had previously shown to Mr Butler and Mr Swimer. Mr Reese did not agree that the bidding had been unnatural or had suggested knowledge of the heart suit.

Mr Schapiro when summoned before the Committee denied the charge and said it was absurd.

In the afternoon of the same day, Sunday May 25, 1965, there was a meeting of the World Bridge Federation Executive Committee at which Mr Butler and Mr Swimer repeated the evidence they had given before the Appeals Committee. Mr Reese and Mr Schapiro were called in and told of the detailed check of the hands observed, both by Mr Butler and Mr Swimer. After they withdrew, the charges were held proved.

We say that the proceedings at the Appeals Committee, and at the review by the Executive Committee, were unsatisfactory for the following reasons:

Mr Butler was Chairman of the Appeals Committee yet his evidence was of the greatest importance. Mr Swimer, who was also a witness, was nevertheless present throughout the sitting of the Appeals Committee.

The Appeals Committee did not seek all the available evidence, some of which was disclosed in Mr Butler's testimony. Neither Mrs Hayden or Mr Kehela, the American deputy-Captain, were called in to give evidence. Mrs Hayden's evidence in particular was of great importance as she had taken notes and had played against Messrs. Reese and Schapiro, both in the sessions where observations had taken place and before.

The two players were not, in our opinion, given sufficient opportunity of defending themselves. The main defence against the direct evidence was a denial but it was very important that this direct evidence should be tested as soon as possible to examine whether any errors or self-persuasion had occurred and the opportunities and positions for observations should have been closely examined as near the time for observation occurred as possible. This was not done. Nor was the technical evidence examined, except very perfunctorily.

The evidence at our hearings of the experts who came from various countries, was that if there is any cheating it is always revealed in the bidding and play. Mr de Hérédia (a professional tournament director), Mr Ortiz-Patino, Mr Flint and Mr Konstam were quite categorical that if a pair cheated, then this could be detected in the record of their bidding and playing the cards.

The evidence about the bidding and play did not support the allegations of cheating. There were hands where Messrs Reese and Schapiro had cards which, using conventional methods, would have justified a bid in hearts yet they either failed to find the suit at all or failed to bid high enough.

In US 74, Mr Reese left his partner in a One Heart contract when Mr Schapiro had four hearts to the ten and Mr Reese had jack and another, instead of calling One No Trump, which would have been a better contract in any case, and certainly better with the knowledge of the heart holding.

In Italy 56, Mr Reese, playing against Three Diamonds, failed to make the ace of hearts after winning with the king when his partner had a singleton in hearts.

In Argentina 141, they had ten hearts between them yet never found the suit.

Obviously categorical evidence from several prominent players in International Bridge to the effect that they saw Mr Reese and Mr Schapiro signal by changing fingers on the back of their cards raises a strong suspicion that the allegations were well founded. Against that must be set a number of considerations: the crudity of the signals, especially when one finger was shown, or when the fingers were splayed, with two or three fingers to show five or six hearts; the concoction of a code to communicate information which is not as valuable as other information which could have been communicated less crudely and more economically in the number of signals. Six different positions of the hands were required for the code. At some of the sessions in which they were alleged to be cheating, there was no point in their doing so since Great Britain could not win the tournament and in the last session at which observation took place, Great Britain was defeating the Argentinians anyway.

There is the further fact that Mr Reese and Mr Schapiro were on bad terms before the tournament at Buenos Aires; that Mr Reese had written a letter to the British Bridge League asking not to play with Mr Schapiro and that the two players had a row at Buenos Aires.

As indicated above, the play and bidding of the hands did not disclose any cheating. It was argued that players of the calibre of Mr Reese and Mr Schapiro would be so skillful as not to use the information so as to excite suspicion, but this would not account for the negative part of this matter, namely that Mr Reese and Mr Schapiro played worse than their usual form in Buenos Aires and often failed to achieve a contract which they should have established if they had been playing non-cheating conventional methods and which they could not have failed to have reached if they had foreknowledge of the hearts. In other words, when there was a legitimate choice, if these two had been cheating, they would have called a contract which they would have been justified in calling on their style of play and which a knowledge of hearts holding in partner's hand indicated clearly?

It is with reference to the 'direct' evidence of observation that we have most reason to regret the procedure adopted at Buenos Aires and by the British Captain. What should have happened, in our view, when the Captain was informed of the suspicions, is that the players should have been watched either by the Tournament Director or by neutral persons (in this case neither United States, British, Italian or Argentine nationals) appointed by the Federation for this task, which would probably have been delegated to the Tournament Director or his subordinates. Obviously the object should have been to obtain independent corroboration of the accusation. Allegations of cheating are made fairly frequently and, as we were told, without real basis, in International Bridge. The corroboration sought and obtained was that of Mr Butler and the English Captain. Mr Butler's evidence is, we think, not clear corroboration and Mr Swimer was a witness whose powers of observation and recollection were marred by difficult relations with the two players. At the end of his evidence he gave entirely fresh evidence that Mr Schapiro had confessed to him and that he, Mr Swimer, had told Mr Schapiro to deny the allegations. Mr Schapiro had, according to Mr Swimer, said that 'that evil man Reese' had forced him to cheat because Mr Schapiro would not play the Little Major. We do not believe that Mr Schapiro would consent to cheat because he was unwilling to play the Little Major or that Mr Schapiro would have chosen the English Captain to whom to confess as their relationship was distant and to an extent antagonistic. We cannot understand why, if this confession took place, Mr Swimer never reported it at Buenos Aires or told solicitor or Counsel for the British Bridge League, who called him as a witness.

As we said, the direct evidence is bound to raise suspicion. If accepted the odds against the observed fingers corresponding in so many cases to the number of hearts held were so astronomical (running into million-to-one) that the only conclusion would have been that the two players were cheating.

Mrs Hayden gave evidence before us, as did Mr Becker and Mr Truscott, that she had observed the players and noticed that Mr Reese and Mr Schapiro were making finger signals simultaneously. Later she, Mr Becker and Mr Truscott had 'discovered', on checking with the hand records available, that the fingers corresponded with the heart holding. The notes which she produced to us were not before the Appeals Committee, since Mrs Hayden was not called by them.

Mr Truscott, who went to watch after being told of their suspicions by Mr Becker and Mrs Hayden, also gave evidence to the same effect. In his case he told us he took no notes because he thought it might excite suspicion.

Mr Kehela, the Vice-Captain and Coach of the United States team, states that he had come to the conclusion that the two players accused were not cheating. Mr Kehela told us that he had watched some nine or ten hands; that while he was watching he was convinced that the pair were cheating; that this conviction was not due to what he saw but because he believed what he was told. Later, after looking at a record of the hands, he had come to the conclusion that Mr Reese and Mr Schapiro had not been cheating since the hands showed no evidence of such cheating. He decided that the correspondence in fingers and hearts holdings which he had observed was coincidental, i.e. not due to cheating. The other hands which he watched, the number of fingers shown and the number of hearts held did not tally. At the time he had watched the play he was not concerned to see if the pair were cheating since he had believed what he had been told, namely, that Mr

Reese and Mr Schapiro were exchanging signals and he was at that time only interested in seeing how they were cheating, a fact about which he was already convinced. It was only afterwards, he told us, that he realised from the bidding and play that there had been no cheating.

The effect of a finding of cheating is just as serious for those accused as a finding of guilt of a crime. The standard of proof required in a criminal court to return a verdict is that the jury or court should be satisfied beyond a reasonable doubt. We think that the same standard should be applied here and that the indirect or technical evidence raises such a doubt. There was no sign of cheating in the bidding or play of the cards. In fact the bidding and play were in instances such that it would appear that the pair could not be cheating. They failed to find contracts or failed to make bids which a foreknowledge of the heart holding would have enabled them to achieve without raising suspicion. Mr Reese and Mr Schapiro played badly in Buenos Aires, below their form and certainly no better than the other British pair against whom there were no accusations of cheating.

The indirect evidence is of importance in considering the findings of guilt before the Appeals Committee and the Executive Committee. When Reese 'asked to see the evidence ... Mr Truscott was called in with his analysis which he had previously shown to Mr Butler and Mr Swimer.'

Clearly the Appeals Committee attached importance to this 'indirect' evidence, but unfortunately the 'analysis' of Mr Truscott was superficial having regard to all the hands played by Mr Reese and Mr Schapiro. Mr Butler had reported that Mr Truscott had told him that 'a number of hands' had 'indicated that this pair had never played a heart contract without a fit and had avoided a heart contract if the fit was unsuitable.' This is not true. The eight hands produced to Mr Butler by Mr Truscott were Italy 22, 23, 25, 26, 34 and 117 and USA 30 and 36. Mr Truscott told us 'I did not find at that time any hands which the players had failed to locate a good fit in the heart suit or in which they had arrived at an unsatisfactory contract in the heart suit.' Later he said, 'It seemed to me they were locating the heart suit with great consistency.' It was wrong of the Appeals Committee to rely on the small sample of eight hands produced by Mr Truscott without considering the overall picture. We had a very full analysis, lasting over twenty-two days, of all the hands that might have a bearing on these allegations and we had clear evidence that neither the bidding nor the play of the hands revealed any foreknowledge of the hearts. If evidence of this sort had been before the Appeals Committee they might well have come to a different conclusion.

The other matter which raises a reasonable doubt in our minds is the evidence of Mr Kehela referred to in detail above. Mr Kehela both observed the play and after studying the bidding he came to the conclusion that the pair were not cheating. We therefore think that the direct evidence as to the exchange of finger signals, strong as it is, cannot be accepted because of the reasonable doubt which we feel on these two grounds.

We find that Messrs Reese and Schapiro were not guilty of cheating at the tournament in question.

JOHN FOSTER
BOURNE
4 August 1966